Roger Crowley read English at Cambridge before going to live in Istanbul. He now works in publishing and lives in Gloucestershire. His second book, *Empires of the Sea*, was *Sunday Times* History Book of the Year and was described as "first-class narrative history" in the *Daily Telegraph*.

Further praise for *Constantinople*:

'Moving and convincing . . . Crowley gets you by the throat, switching back and forth between the Ottoman and the Byzantine camps as he leads his story to a nail-biting close.'
Jason Goodwin, *Literary Review*

'A powerful telling of an extraordinary story, presented with a clarity and a confidence that most academic historians would envy.'
Noel Malcolm, *Sunday Telegraph*

'More comprehensive and more leisurely than its immediate predecessor in English, Sir Steven Runciman's *The Fall of Constantinople* . . . Roger Crowley's *Constantinople: The Last Great Siege, 1453* tells an old story, but tells it well, with great flair and authority. A carefully paced, compelling and ultimately fair narrative, it is firmly grounded in the original Italian, Greek and (in lesser number) Ottoman accounts.'
Christine Woodhead, *Times Literary Supplement*

'Gripping . . . Mixes intriguing details of military history with rich references to the religious imagery that influenced both parties.'
The Economist

'Crowley's fascinating account of the years leading up to and the final sacking of Constantinople by the Ottoman Empire reads more like lively fiction than dry recounting of historical events. The characters, led by Mehmet II, the young leader of the Ottoman Turks, and Constantine XI, the wearying fifty-seventh emperor of a weakening Byzantium, are drawn in great detail.'
Michael Standaert, *Los Angeles Times*

by the same author

EMPIRES OF THE SEA

CONSTANTINOPLE

The Last Great Siege
1453

ROGER CROWLEY

ff
faber and faber

First published in 2005
by Faber and Faber Limited
Bloomsbury House
74–77 Great Russell Street
London WC1B 3DA
This paperback edition first published in 2006

Typeset by Faber and Faber Limited
Printed in the UK byCPI Bookmarque, Croydon

A CIP record for this book
is available from the British Library

ISBN 978-0-571-22186-8

6 8 10 9 7 5

For Jan with love, wounded at the sea wall
in pursuit of the siege

Constantinople is a city larger than its renown proclaims. May God in his grace and generosity deign to make it the capital of Islam.

Hasan Ali Al-Harawi, twelfth-century Arab writer

I shall tell the story of the tremendous perils . . . of Constantinople, which I observed at close quarters with my own eyes.

Leonard of Chios

Contents

List of Illustrations

Illustrations in the plate section are reproduced by kind permission of the following: The British Library, London (1); Topkapi Palace Museum, Istanbul/ Giraudon/ www.bridgeman.co.uk (2); www.bridgeman.co.uk (3); The British Museum, Department of Prints and Drawings, No Pp, 1-19 (8); La Bibliothèque Nationale, Paris (9); Musée des Augustins, Toulouse/ www.bridgeman.co.uk (10); Private Collection, Archives Charmet/ www.bridgeman.co.uk (11); National Gallery, London/ www.bridgeman.co.uk (12); Ruggero Vanni/Corbis (13)

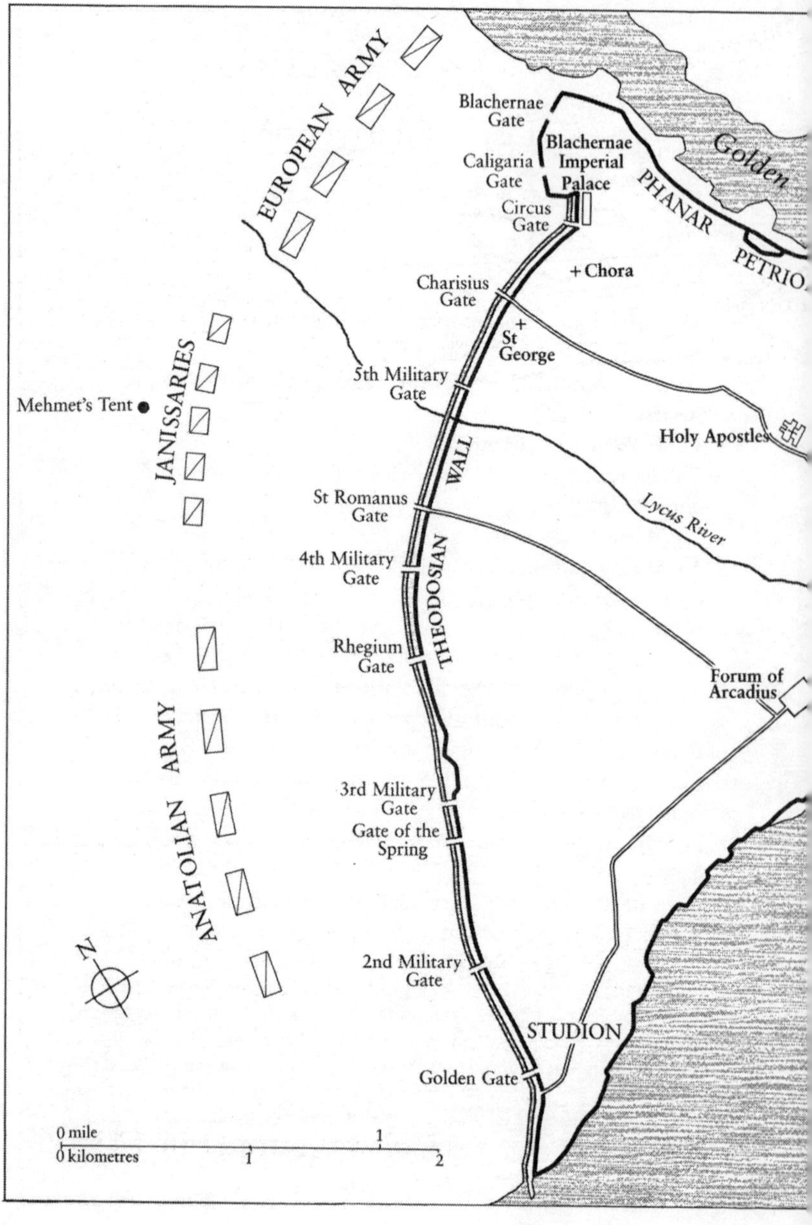
EUROPEAN ARMY
Blachernae Gate
Blachernae Imperial Palace
Golden
Caligaria Gate
PHANAR
Circus Gate
PETRIO
+ Chora
Charisius Gate
+ St George
5th Military Gate
JANISSARIES
Mehmet's Tent
Holy Apostles
WALL
St Romanus Gate
Lycus River
4th Military Gate
THEODOSIAN
Rhegium Gate
Forum of Arcadius
ANATOLIAN ARMY
3rd Military Gate
Gate of the Spring
N
2nd Military Gate
STUDION
Golden Gate
0 mile
1
0 kilometres
1
2

Constantinople in 1453

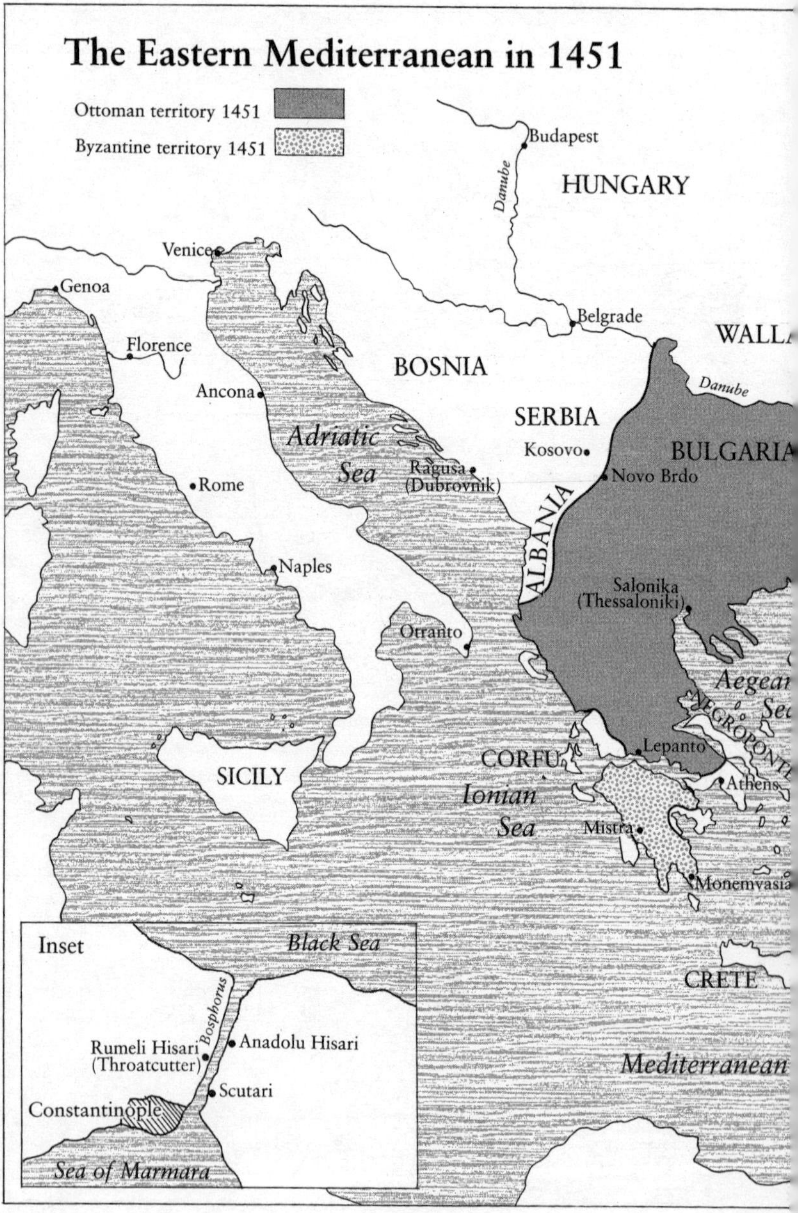
The Eastern Mediterranean in 1451
Ottoman territory 1451
Byzantine territory 1451
Budapest
Danube
HUNGARY
Venice
Genoa
Belgrade
WALLA
Florence
BOSNIA
Danube
Ancona
SERBIA
Adriatic
Sea
Kosovo
BULGARIA
Ragusa
(Dubrovnik)
Novo Brdo
Rome
ALBANIA
Naples
Salonika
(Thessaloniki)
Otranto
Aegean
Sea
NEGROPONTE
Lepanto
CORFU
SICILY
Athens
Ionian
Sea
Mistra
Monemvasia
Inset
Black Sea
Bosphorus
CRETE
Rumeli Hisari
(Throatcutter)
Anadolu Hisari
Mediterranean
Scutari
Constantinople
Sea of Marmara

Tana
Kaffa
GEORGIA
HIA
Black Sea
Varna
Constantinople
Sinop
Trebizond
Manzikert
dirne
See Inset
Amasya
Izmit (Nicomedia)
Dardanelles
Iznik
(Nicaea)
Ankara
Bursa
Gallipoli
LESBOS
ANATOLIA
Manisa
Izmir (Smirna)
Konya
IOS
KARAMAN
N
RHODES
CYPRUS
MAMLUKS
Sea
0
200 miles
0
300 kilometres

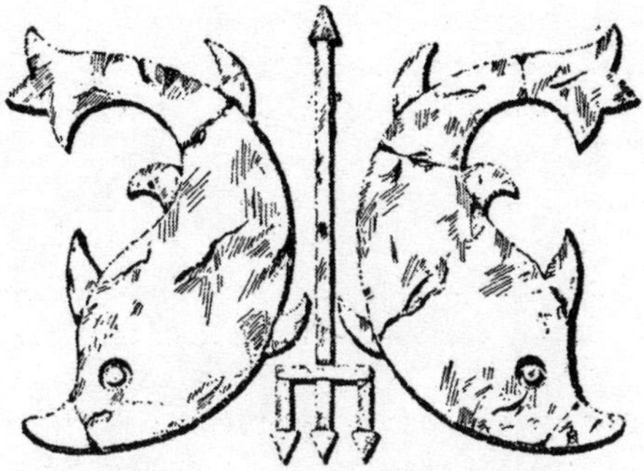

Prologue: The Red Apple

A red apple invites stones.
Turkish proverb

Early spring. A black kite swings on the Istanbul wind. It turns lazy circles round the Suleymaniye mosque as if tethered to the minarets. From here it can survey a city of fifteen million people, watching the passing of days and centuries through imperturbable eyes.

When some ancestor of this bird circled Constantinople on a cold day in March 1453, the layout of the city would have been familiar, though far less cluttered. The site is remarkable, a rough triangle upturned slightly at its eastern point like an aggressive rhino's horn and protected on two sides by sea. To the north lies the sheltered deep-water inlet of the Golden Horn; the south side is flanked by the Sea of Marmara that swells westward into the Mediterranean through the bottleneck of the Dardanelles. From the air one can pick out the steady, unbroken line of fortifications that guard these two seaward sides of the triangle and see how the sea currents rip past the tip of the rhino horn at seven knots: the city's defences are natural as well as man made.

But it is the base of the triangle that is most extraordinary. A complex, triple collar of walls, studded with closely spaced towers and flanked by a formidable ditch, it stretches from the Horn to the Marmara and seals the city from attack. This is the thousand-year-old land wall of Theodosius, the most formidable defence in the medieval world. To the Ottoman Turks of the fourteenth and fifteenth centuries

Dolphin emblem from Constantinople

An imaginative view of the city in the fifteenth century. Galata is on the far right

it was 'a bone in the throat of Allah'– a psychological problem that taunted their ambitions and cramped their dreams of conquest. To Western Christendom it was the bulwark against Islam. It kept them secure from the Muslim world and made them complacent.

Looking down on the scene in the spring of 1453 one would also be able to make out the fortified Genoese town of Galata, a tiny Italian city state on the far side of the Horn, and to see exactly where Europe ends. The Bosphorus divides the continents, cutting like a river through low wooded hills to the Black Sea. On the other side lies Asia Minor, Anatolia – in Greek literally the East. The snow-capped peaks of Mount Olympus glitter in the thin light sixty miles away.

Looking back into Europe, the terrain stretches out in gentler, undulating folds towards the Ottoman city of Edirne, 140 miles west. And it is in this landscape that the all-seeing eye would pick out something significant. Down the rough tracks that link the two cities, huge columns of men are marching; white caps and red turbans advance in clustered masses; bows, javelins, matchlocks and shields catch the low sun; squadrons of outriding cavalry kick up the mud as they pass; chain mail ripples and chinks. Behind come the lengthy baggage trains of mules, horses and camels with all the paraphernalia of warfare and the personnel who supply it – miners, cooks, gunsmiths, mullahs, carpenters and booty hunters. And further back something else still. Huge teams of oxen and hundreds of men are hauling guns with immense difficulty over the soft ground. The whole Ottoman army is on the move.

The wider the gaze, the more details of this operation unfold. Like the backdrop of a medieval painting, a fleet of oared ships can be seen moving with laborious sloth against the wind, from the direction of the Dardanelles. High-sided transports are setting sail from the Black Sea with cargoes of wood, grain and cannon balls. From Anatolia, bands of shepherds, holy men, camp followers and vagabonds are slipping down to the Bosphorus out of the plateau, obeying the Ottoman call to arms. This ragged pattern of men and equipment constitutes the co-ordinated movement of an army with a single objective: Constantinople, capital of what little remains in 1453 of the ancient empire of Byzantium.

The medieval peoples about to engage in this struggle were intensely superstitious. They believed in prophecy and looked for omens. Within Constantinople, the ancient monuments and statues were sources of magic. People saw there the future of the world encrypted in the narratives on Roman columns whose original stories had been lost. They read signs in the weather and found the spring of 1453 unsettling. It was unusually wet and cold. Banks of fog hung thickly over the Bosphorus in March. There were earth tremors and unseasonal snow. Within a city taut with expectation it was an ill omen, perhaps even a portent of the world's end.

The approaching Ottomans also had their superstitions. The object of their offensive was known quite simply as the Red Apple, a symbol of world power. Its capture represented an ardent Islamic desire that stretched back 800 years, almost to the Prophet himself, and it was hedged about with legend, predictions and apocryphal sayings. In the imagination of the advancing army, the apple had a specific location within the city. Outside the mother church of St Sophia on a column 100 feet high stood a huge equestrian statue of the Emperor Justinian in bronze, a monument to the might of the early Byzantine Empire and a symbol of its role as a Christian bulwark against the East. According to the sixth century writer Procopius, it was astonishing.

> The horse faces East and is a noble sight. On this horse is a huge statue of the Emperor, dressed like Achilles . . . his breastplate is in the heroic style; while the helmet covering his head seems to move up and down and it gleams dazzlingly. He looks towards the rising sun, riding, it seems to me towards the Persians. In his left

hand he carries a globe, the sculptor signifying by this that all earth and sea are subject to him, though he has neither sword nor spear nor other weapon, except that on the globe stands the cross through which alone he has achieved his kingdom and his mastery of war.

The statue of Justinian

It was in the globe of Justinian surmounted by a cross that the Turks had precisely located the Red Apple and it was this they were coming for: the reputation of the fabulously old Christian empire and the possibility of world power that it seemed to contain.

Fear of siege was etched deep in the memory of the Byzantines. It was the bogeyman that haunted their libraries, their marble chambers and their mosaic churches, but they knew it too well to be surprised. In the 1,123 years up to the spring of 1453 the city had been besieged some twenty-three times. It had fallen just once – not to the Arabs or the Bulgars but to the Christian knights of the Fourth Crusade in one of the most bizarre episodes in Christian history. The land walls had never been breached, though they had been flattened by earthquake in the fifth century. Otherwise they had held firm, so that when the army of Sultan Mehmet finally reined up outside the city on 6 April 1453, the defenders had reasonable hopes of survival.

What led up to this moment and what happened next is the subject of this book. It is a tale of human courage and cruelty, of technical ingenuity, luck, cowardice, prejudice and mystery. It also touches on many other aspects of a world on the cusp of change: the development of guns, the art of siege warfare, naval tactics, the religious beliefs, myths and superstitions of medieval people. But above all it is the story of a place – of sea currents, hills, peninsulas and weather – the way the land rises and falls and how the straits divide two continents so narrowly 'they almost kiss', where the city is strong, defended by rocky shores, and the particular features of geology that render it vulnerable to attack. It was the possibilities of this site – what it offered for trade, defence and food – that made Constantinople the key to imperial destinies and brought so many armies to its gate. 'The seat of the Roman Empire is Constantinople', wrote George Trapezuntios, 'and he who is and remains Emperor of the Romans is also the Emperor of the whole earth.'

Modern nationalisms have interpreted the siege of Constantinople as a struggle between the Greek and Turkish peoples, but such simplifications are misleading. Neither side would have readily accepted or even understood these labels, though each used them of the other. The Ottomans, literally the tribe of Osman, called themselves just that, or simply Muslims. 'Turk' was a largely pejorative term applied by the nation states of the West, the name 'Turkey' unknown to them until borrowed from Europe to create the new Republic in 1923. The Ottoman Empire in 1453 was already a multicultural creation that sucked in the peoples it conquered with little concern for ethnic identity. Its crack troops were Slavs, its leading general Greek, its admiral Bulgarian, its sultan probably half Serbian or Macedonian. Furthermore under the complex code of medieval vassalage, thousands of Christian troops accompanied him down the road from Edirne. They had come to conquer the Greek-speaking inhabitants of Constantinople, whom we now call the Byzantines, a word first used in English in 1853, exactly 400 years after the great siege. They were considered to be heirs to the Roman Empire and referred to themselves accordingly as Romans. In turn they were commanded by an emperor who was half Serbian and a quarter Italian, and much of the defence was undertaken by people from Western Europe whom the Byzantines called 'Franks': Venetians, Genoese and Catalans, aided by some ethnic Turks, Cretans – and one Scotsman. If it is difficult to fix simple identities or loyalties to the participants at the siege, there was one dimension of the struggle that all the contemporary chroniclers never forgot – that of faith. The Muslims referred to their adversary as 'the despicable infidels', 'the wretched unbelievers', 'the enemies of the Faith'; in response they were called 'pagans', 'heathen infidels', 'the faithless Turks'. Constantinople was the front line in a long-distance struggle between Islam and Christianity for the true faith. It was a place where different versions of the truth had confronted each other in war and truce for 800 years and it was here in the spring of 1453 that new and lasting attitudes between the two great monotheisms were to be cemented in one intense moment of history.

I The Burning Sea 629–717

O Christ, ruler and master of the world, to You now I dedicate this subject city, and these sceptres and the might of Rome.

Inscription on the column of Constantine the Great in Constantinople

Islam's desire for the city is almost as old as Islam itself. The origin of the holy war for Constantinople starts with the Prophet himself in an incident whose literal truth, like so much of the city's history, cannot be verified.

In the year 629, Heraclius, 'Autocrat of the Romans' and twenty-eighth Emperor of Byzantium, was making a pilgrimage on foot to Jerusalem. It was the crowning moment of his life. He had shattered the Persians in a series of remarkable victories and wrested back Christendom's most sacred relic, the True Cross, which he was triumphantly restoring to the Church of the Holy Sepulchre. According to Islamic tradition, when he had reached the city he received a letter. It said simply: 'In the name of Allah the most Beneficent, the most Merciful: this letter is from Muhammad, the slave of Allah, and His Apostle, to Heraclius, the ruler of Byzantines. Peace be upon the followers of guidance. I invite you to surrender to Allah. Embrace Islam and Allah will bestow on you a double reward. But if you reject this invitation you will be misguiding your people.' Heraclius had no idea who the writer of this letter might have been, but he is reported to have made inquiries and to have treated its contents with some

An emperor at the Hippodrome

Heraclius rides in triumph with the true cross

respect. A similar letter sent to the 'King of Kings' in Persia was torn up. Muhammad's reply to this news was blunt: 'Tell him that my religion and my sovereignty will reach limits which the kingdom of Chosroes never attained.' For Chosroes it was too late – he had been slowly shot to death with arrows the year before – but the apocryphal letter foreshadowed an extraordinary blow about to fall on Christian Byzantium and its capital, Constantinople, that would undo all the emperor ever achieved.

In the previous ten years Muhammad had succeeded in unifying the feuding tribes of the Arabian Peninsula around the simple message of Islam. Motivated by the word of God and disciplined by communal prayer, bands of nomadic raiders were transformed into an organized fighting force, whose hunger was now projected outwards beyond the desert's rim into a world sharply divided by faith into two distinct zones. On the one side lay the *Dar al-Islam,* the House of Islam; on the other, the realms still to be converted, the *Dar al-Harb,* the House of War. By the 630s Muslim armies started to appear on the margins of the Byzantine frontier, where the settled land gives way to desert, like ghosts out of a sandstorm. The Arabs were agile, resourceful and hardy. They totally surprised the lumbering mercenary armies in Syria. They attacked then retreated into the desert, lured their opponents out of their strongholds into the barren wilderness, surrounded and massacred them. They traversed the harsh empty quarters, killing their camels as they went and drinking the water from their stomachs – to emerge again unexpectedly behind their enemy. They besieged cities and learned how to take them. Damascus fell, then Jerusalem itself; Egypt surrendered in 641, Armenia in 653; within twenty years the Persian Empire had collapsed and converted to Islam. The velocity of conquest was staggering, the ability to adapt extraordinary. Driven by the word of God and divine conquest, the people of the desert constructed navies 'to wage the holy war by sea' in the dockyards of Egypt and Palestine with the help of native Christians and took Cyprus in 648, then defeated a Byzantine fleet at the Battle of the Masts in 655. Finally in 669, within forty years of Muhammad's death, the Caliph Muawiyyah dispatched a huge amphibious force to strike a knockout blow at Constantinople itself. On the following wind of victory, he had every anticipation of success.

To Muawiyyah it was to be the culmination of an ambitious long-term plan, conceived and executed with great care and thoroughness. In 669 Arab armies occupied the Asian shore opposite the city. The following year a fleet of 400 ships sailed through the Dardanelles and secured a base on the peninsula of Cyzicus on the south side of the Sea of Marmara. Supplies were stockpiled, dry dock and maintenance facilities created to support a campaign that would last as long as was necessary. Crossing the straits west of the city, Muslims set foot on the shores of Europe for the first time. Here they seized a harbour from which to conduct the siege and mounted large-scale raids around the hinterland of the city. Within Constantinople itself, the defenders sheltered behind their massive walls, while their fleet, docked in the Golden Horn, prepared to launch counter-attacks against the enemy.

For five successive years between 674 and 678 the Arabs conducted the campaign on a steady pattern. Between spring and autumn each year they besieged the walls and mounted naval operations in the straits that involved running battles with the Byzantine fleet. Both sides fought with the same types of oared galleys and largely with the same crews, as the Muslims had access to the seafaring skills of Christians from the conquered Levant. In winter the Arabs regrouped at their base at Cyzicus, repaired their ships and prepared to tighten the screw the following year. They were in the siege for the long haul, secure in the belief that victory was inevitable.

And then in 678 the Byzantine fleet made a decisive move. They launched an attack on the Muslim fleet, probably in their base at

Cyzicus at the end of the campaigning season – the details are either unclear or were deliberately suppressed – spearheaded by a squadron of fast *dromons*: light, swift-sailing, many-oared galleys. There are no contemporary versions of what happened next, though the details can be deduced from later accounts. As the attack ships closed on their opponents, they unleashed, behind the conventional volley of winged missiles, an extraordinary stream of liquid fire from nozzles mounted high on their prows. Jets of fire burned the surface of the sea between the closing vessels, then caught hold of the enemy ships, falling 'like a flash of lightning on the faces in front of it'. The explosion of flame was accompanied by a noise like thunder; smoke darkened the sky and steam and gas suffocated the terrified sailors on the Arab ships. The fire storm seemed to defy the laws of nature: it could be directed sideways or downwards in whatever direction the operator wished; where it touched the surface of the sea, the water ignited. It seemed to have adhesive properties too, sticking to the wooden hulls and masts and proving impossible to extinguish, so that the ships and their crews were rapidly engulfed in a propulsive torrent of fire that seemed like the blast of an angry god. This extraordinary inferno 'burned the ships of the Arabs and their crews alive'. The fleet was destroyed and the traumatized survivors, 'having lost many fighting men and received great injury', lifted the siege and sailed home. A winter storm wrecked most of the surviving ships while the Arab army was ambushed and destroyed on the Asian shore. Discouraged, Muawiyyah accepted a thirty-year truce on unfavourable terms in 679, and died, a broken man, the following year. For the first time the Muslim cause had received a major setback.

The chroniclers presented the episode as clear evidence that 'the Roman Empire was guarded by God', but it had, in truth, been saved by a new technology: the development of Greek fire. The story of this extraordinary weapon remains the subject of intense speculation even now – the formula was regarded as a Byzantine state secret. It seems that at about the time of the siege, a Greek fugitive called Kallinikos came to Constantinople from Syria bringing with him a technique for projecting liquid fire through siphons. If so, it is likely that he built on techniques of incendiary warfare widely known throughout the Middle East. The core ingredient of the mixture was almost certainly crude oil from natural surface wells on the Black Sea, mixed with powdered wood resin that gave it adhesive properties. What was probably perfected in the secret military arsenals of the city over the length of the siege was a technology for projecting this material. The Byzantines, who were heirs to the practical engineering skills of the Roman Empire, seem to have developed a technique for heating the mixture in sealed bronze containers, pressurizing it by means of a hand pump then emitting it through a nozzle, where the liquid could be ignited by a flame. To handle inflammable material, pressure and fire on a wooden boat required precision manufacturing techniques and highly skilled men, and it was this that comprised the true secret of Greek fire and destroyed Arab morale in 678.

For forty years the setback at Constantinople rankled with the Umayyad caliphs in Damascus. It remained inconceivable within Islamic theology that the whole of humankind would not, in time, either accept Islam or submit to Muslim rule. In 717 a second and even more determined attempt was made to overcome the obstacle that hindered the spread of the Faith into Europe. The Arab attack came at a time of turmoil within the empire. A new emperor, Leo II, had been crowned on 25 March 717; five months later he found an army of 80,000 men dug in the length of the land walls and a fleet of 1,800 ships controlling the straits. The Arabs had advanced their strategy from the previous siege. It was quickly realized by the Muslim general Maslama that the walls of the city were invulnerable to siege machines; this time there was to be a total blockade. The seriousness of his intentions was underlined by the fact that his army brought wheat seed with them. In the autumn of 717 they ploughed the ground and planted a food supply outside the walls for harvesting the following spring. Then they settled down to wait. A foray by the Greek fire ships had some success but failed to break the stranglehold. Everything had been carefully planned to crush the infidels.

What actually ensued for the Arabs was an unimaginable catastrophe that unfolded in inexorable stages. According to their own chroniclers, Leo managed to deceive his enemies by an extraordinary diplomatic double-cross that was impressive even by the standards of the Byzantines. He persuaded Maslama that he could get the city to surrender if the Arabs both destroyed their own food stores and gave the defenders some grain. Once done, Leo sat tight behind the walls and refused to parley. The tricked army was then subjected to a winter of freak severity for which they were ill prepared. Snow lay on the ground for a hundred days; the camels and horses started to perish in the cold. As they died, the increasingly desperate soldiers had no option but to eat them. The Greek chroniclers, not known for their objectivity, hinted at darker horrors. 'It is said', wrote Theophanes the Confessor a hundred years later, 'that they even cooked in ovens and ate dead men and their dung which they leavened.' Famine was followed by disease; thousands died in the cold. The Arabs had no experience of the surprising severity of winters on the Bosphorus: the ground was too hard to bury the dead; hundreds of corpses had to be thrown into the sea.

The following spring a large Arab fleet arrived with food and equipment to relieve the stricken army but failed to reverse the downward spiral of fortune. Warned of the dangers of Greek fire, they hid their ships on the Asian coast after they had unloaded. Unfortunately some of the crews, who were Egyptian Christians, defected to the emperor and revealed the position of the fleet. An imperial force of fire ships fell on the unprepared Arab vessels and destroyed them. A parallel relief army dispatched from Syria was ambushed and cut to pieces by Byzantine infantry. Meanwhile Leo, whose determination and cunning seem to have been indefatigable, had been negotiating with the pagan Bulgars. He persuaded them to attack the infidels outside the walls; 22,000 Arabs were killed in the ensuing battle. On 15 August 718, almost a year to the day from their arrival, the armies of the caliph lifted the siege and straggled home by land and sea. While the retreating soldiers were harassed across the Anatolian plateau, there was one further calamity in store for the Muslim cause. Some ships were destroyed by storms in the Sea of Marmara; the rest were overwhelmed by an underwater volcanic eruption in the Aegean which 'brought the sea water to a boil, and as the pitch of their keels dissolved, their ships sank in the deep, crews and all'. Of the vast fleet that had set sail, only five ships made it back to Syria 'to announce God's mighty deeds'. Byzantium had buckled but not collapsed under the onslaught of Islam. Constantinople had survived through a mixture of technological innovation, skilful diplomacy, individual brilliance, massive fortifications – and sheer luck: themes that were to be endlessly repeated in the centuries ahead. Not surprisingly under the circumstances, the Byzantines had their own explanation: 'God and the all-holy Virgin, the Mother of God, protect the City and the Christian Empire, and . . . those who call upon God in truth are not entirely forsaken, even if we are chastised for a short time on account of our sins.'

The failure of Islam to take the city in 717 had far-reaching consequences. The collapse of Constantinople would have opened the way for a Muslim expansion into Europe that might have reshaped the whole future of the West; it remains one of the great 'what ifs' of history. It blunted the first powerful onslaught of Islamic jihad that reached its high water mark fifteen years later at the other end of the Mediterranean when a Muslim force was defeated on the banks of the Loire, a mere 150 miles south of Paris.

For Islam itself the significance of resounding defeat at Constantinople was rather more theological than military. In the first century of its existence there had been little reason to doubt final victory for the Faith. The law of jihad dictated inevitable conquest. But under the walls of Constantinople, Islam had been repulsed by the mirror image of its own faith; Christianity was a rival monotheism with a matching sense of mission and desire to win converts. Constantinople had defined the front line in a long running struggle between two closely related versions of the truth that was to be pursued for hundreds of years. In the interim, Muslim thinkers were forced to recognize a practical change in the relationship between the House of Islam and the House of War; the final conquest of the non-Muslim world would have to be postponed, perhaps until the end of the world. Some jurists conceived of a third state, the House of Truce, to express postponement of final victory. The age of jihad seemed to be over.

Byzantium had proved the most obdurate of enemies and Constantinople itself remained for Muslims both a scar and a source of deep longing. Many martyrs had perished at its walls, including the Prophet's standard-bearer Ayyub in 669. Their deaths designated the city as a holy place for Islam and imparted a messianic significance to the project of its capture. The sieges left a rich legacy of myth and folklore that was handed down the centuries. It included amongst the Hadith, the body of sayings attributed to Muhammad, prophecies that foretold a cycle of defeat, death and final victory for the warriors of the Faith: 'In the jihad against Constantinople, one third of Muslims will allow themselves to be defeated, which Allah cannot forgive; one third will be killed in battle, making them wondrous martyrs; and one third will be victorious.' It was to be a long-range struggle. So huge was the architecture of the conflict between Islam and Byzantium that no Muslim banners would be unfurled again before the city walls for another 650 years – a span of time greater than that separating us from 1453 – but prophecy decreed that they would return.

Constantinople, constructed on the site of a settlement raised by the legendary Greek Byzas a thousand years earlier, had already been a Christian city for 400 years when Maslama's forces straggled home. The place chosen by the Emperor Constantine for his new Christian capital in AD 324 possessed the formidable natural advantages of its site. Once the land walls had been built in the fifth century, the city was virtually impregnable to attack as long as siege equipment was limited to the power of catapults. Within the twelve miles of perimeter wall, Constantinople rose on a series of steep hills that afforded natural vantage points over the surrounding sea, while on the east side the inlet of the Golden Horn, shaped like a curved antler, provided a safe deep-water harbour. The only drawback was the barrenness of the promontory, a problem that Roman water engineering would solve with an elaborate series of aqueducts and cisterns.

The site was uniquely positioned at the crossroads of trade routes and military corridors; the history of its earlier settlement echoes with the sound of marching feet and splashing oars – Jason and the Argonauts sailed past to seek fleeces from gold-panners at the mouth of the Dneiper; the Persian king Darius marched 700,000 men across on a bridge of boats to fight the Scythians; the Roman poet Ovid looked up wistfully at 'the place that's the vast doorway of two seas' on his way to exile on the shores of the Black Sea. At this crossroads the Christian city came to control the wealth of a huge hinterland. To the east, the riches of Central Asia could be funnelled through the Bosphorus into the go-downs of the imperial city: barbarian gold, furs and slaves from Russia, caviar from the Black Sea, wax and salt, spices, ivory, amber and pearls from the far Orient. To the south, routes led overland to the cities of the Middle East: Damascus, Aleppo and Baghdad; and to the west, the sea lanes through the Dardanelles opened up the whole of the Mediterranean: the routes to Egypt and the Nile delta, the rich islands of Sicily and Crete, the Italian peninsula, and everything beyond to the Gates of Gibraltar. Nearer to hand lay the timber, limestone and marble to build a mighty city and all the resources to sustain it. The strange currents of the Bosphorus brought a rich seasonal harvest of fish, while the fields of European Thrace and the fertile lowlands of the

Anatolian plateau provided olive oil, corn and wine in rich abundance.

The prosperous city that arose in this place was an expression of imperial splendour, ruled by a Roman emperor and inhabited by Greek-speaking people. Constantine laid out a grid of colonnaded streets, flanked by porticoed public buildings, great squares, gardens, columns and triumphal arches that were both pagan and Christian. There were statues and monuments looted from the classical world (including the fabulous bronze horses perhaps made for Alexander the Great by the Greek sculptor Lysippos, now the icon of Venice), a hippodrome to rival that of Rome, imperial palaces and churches 'more numerous than days of the year'. Constantinople became a city of marble and porphyry, beaten gold and brilliant mosaics, whose population at its height topped 500,000. It astounded the visitors who came to trade or pay homage to the emperors of the eastern Roman Empire. Barbarians from benighted Europe gazed open-mouthed at 'the city of the world's desire'. The reaction of Fulcher of Chartres who came in the eleventh century is typical of many that ring across the ages: 'O what a splendid city, how stately, how fair, how many monasteries therein, how many palaces raised by sheer labour in its broadways and streets, how many works of art, marvellous to behold: it would be wearisome to tell of the abundance of all good things; of gold and silver, garments of manifold fashion and such sacred relics. Ships are at all times putting in at this port, so that there is nothing that men want that is not brought hither.'

Byzantium was not only the last heir to the Roman Empire, it was also the first Christian nation. From its founding, the capital city was conceived as the replica of heaven, a manifestation of the triumph of Christ, and its emperor was considered God's vice-regent on earth. Christian worship was evident everywhere: in the raised domes of the churches, the tolling of bells and wooden gongs, the monasteries, the huge number of monks and nuns, the endless parade of icons around the streets and walls, the ceaseless round of prayer and Christian ceremony within which the devout citizens and their emperor lived. Fasts, feast days and all-night vigils provided the calendar, the clock and the framework of life. The city became the storehouse of the relics of Christendom, collected from the Holy Land and eyed with envy by Christians in the West. Here they had the head of John the Baptist, the crown of thorns, the nails from the cross and the stone from the tomb, the relics of the apostles and a thousand other miracle-working artefacts encased in reliquaries of gold and studded with gems. Orthodox religion worked powerfully on the emotions of the people through the intense colours of its mosaics and icons, the mysterious beauty of its liturgy rising and falling in the darkness of lamplit churches, the incense and the elaborate ceremonial that enveloped church and emperor alike in a labyrinth of gorgeous ritual designed to ravish the senses with its metaphors of the heavenly sphere. A Russian visitor who witnessed an imperial coronation in 1391 was astonished by the slow-motion sumptuousness of the event:

> during this time, the cantors intoned a most beautiful and astonishing chant, surpassing understanding. The imperial cortège advanced so slowly that it took three hours from the great door to the platform bearing the throne. Twelve men-at-arms, covered with mail from head to foot, surrounded the Emperor. Before him marched two standard-bearers with black hair: the poles of their standards, their costume, and their headdress were red. Before these standard-bearers went heralds: their rods were plated with silver . . . Ascending the platform, the Emperor put on the imperial purple and the imperial diadem and the crenated crown . . . Then the holy liturgy began. Who can describe the beauty of it all?

Anchored in the centre of the city, like a mighty ship, was the great church of St Sophia, built by Justinian in only six years and dedicated in 537. It was the most extraordinary building in late antiquity, a structure whose immensity was matched only by its splendour. The huge levitated dome was an incomprehensible miracle to eyewitnesses. 'It seems', said Procopius, 'not to rest upon solid masonry but to cover the space beneath as though suspended from heaven.' It encased a volume of space so vast that those seeing it for the first time were left literally speechless. The vaulting, decorated with four acres of gold mosaic, was so brilliant, according to Paul the Silentiary, that 'the golden stream of rays pours down and strikes the eyes of men, so that they can scarcely bear to look', while its wealth of coloured marbles moved him to poetic trance. They looked as though they were 'powdered with stars . . . like milk splashed over a surface of shining black . . . or like the sea or emerald stone, or again like blue cornflowers in grass, with here and there a drift of snow'. It was the beauty of the liturgy in St Sophia that converted Russia to Orthodoxy after a fact-finding mission from Kiev in the tenth century experienced the service and reported back: 'We knew not whether we were in Heaven or earth. For on earth there is no such splendour and beauty, and we are

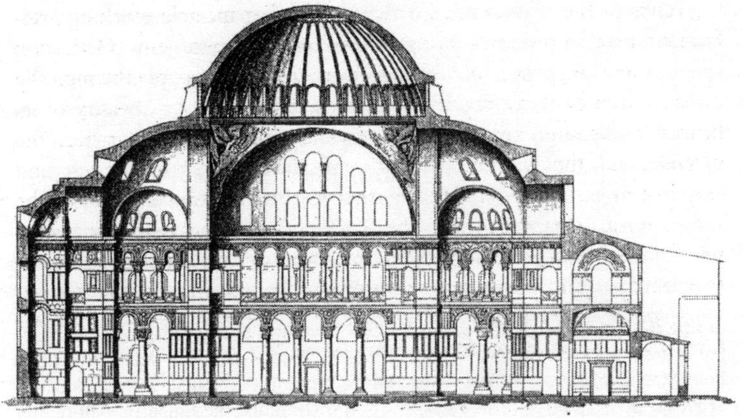

St Sophia in cross-section

at a loss how to describe it. We only know that there God dwells among men.' The detailed gorgeousness of Orthodoxy was the reversed image of the sparse purity of Islam. One offered the abstract simplicity of the desert horizon, a portable worship that could be performed anywhere as long as you could see the sun, a direct contact with God, the other images, colours and music, ravishing metaphors of the divine mystery designed to lead the soul to heaven. Both were equally intent on converting the world to their vision of God.

The Byzantines lived their spiritual life with an intensity hardly matched in the history of Christendom. The stability of the empire was at times threatened by the number of army officers who retired to monasteries and theological issues were debated on the streets with a passion that led to riots. 'The city is full of workmen and slaves who are all theologians,' reported one irritated visitor. 'If you ask a man to change money he will tell you how the Son differs from the Father. If you ask the price of a loaf he will argue that the Son is less than the Father. If you want to know if the bath is ready you are told that the Son was made out of nothing.' Was Christ one or many? Was the Holy Spirit descended just from the Father or from the Father and the Son? Were icons idolatrous or holy? These were not idle questions: salvation or damnation hung on the answers. Issues of orthodoxy and heresy were as explosive as civil wars in the life of the empire and they undermined its unity just as effectively.

The world of Byzantine Christianity was also strangely fatalistic. Everything was ordained by God, and misfortune on any scale, from the loss of a purse to a major siege, was considered to be the result of personal or collective sin. The emperor was appointed at God's bidding, but if he were overthrown in a palace coup – hacked to death by plotters or stabbed in his bath or strangled or dragged along behind horses or just blinded and sent into exile (for imperial fortunes were notoriously unstable) – this was God's will too and betokened some hidden sin. And because fortune was foretold, the Byzantines were superstitiously obsessed with prophecy. It was common for insecure emperors to open and read the Bible at random to get clues to their fate; divination was a major preoccupation, often railed against by the clergy, but too deeply ingrained to be expunged from the Greek soul. It took some bizarre forms. An Arab visitor in the ninth century witnessed a curious use of horses to report on the progress of a distant army campaign: 'They are introduced into the church where bridles have been suspended. If the horse takes the bridle in its mouth, the people say: "We have gained a victory in the land of Islam." [Sometimes] the horse approaches, smells at the bridle, comes back and does not draw near any more to the bridle.' In the latter case, the people presumably departed in gloomy expectation of defeat.

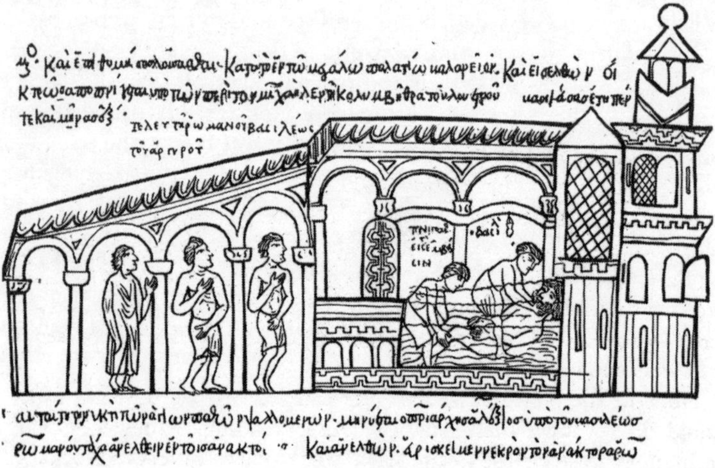

The perils of high office: the Emperor Romanus Augustus Argyrus drowned in his bath, 1034

For long centuries the image of Byzantium and its capital city, brilliant as the sun, exercised a gravitational pull on the world beyond its frontiers. It projected a dazzling image of wealth and longevity. Its currency, the bezant, surmounted by the head of its emperors, was the gold standard of the Middle East. The prestige of the Roman Empire attached to its name; in the Muslim world it was known simply as *Rum,* Rome, and like Rome it attracted the desire and envy of the nomadic semi-barbarous peoples beyond its gates. From the Balkans and the plains of Hungary, from the Russian forests and the Asian steppes turbulent waves of tribal wanderers battered at its defences: the Huns and the Goths, the Slavs and the Gepids, the Tartar Avars, the Turkic Bulgars and the wild Pechenegs all wandered across the Byzantine world.

The empire at its height ringed the Mediterranean from Italy to Tunis, but expanded and contracted continuously under the pressure of these neighbours like an enormous map forever curling at the edges. Year after year imperial armies and fleets departed from the great harbours on the Marmara shore, banners flying and trumpets sounding, to regain a province or secure a frontier. Byzantium was an empire forever at war and Constantinople, because of its position at the crossroads, was repeatedly pressurized from both Europe and Asia. The Arabs were merely the most determined in a long succession of armies camped along the land walls in the first five hundred years of its existence. The Persians and the Avars came in 626, the Bulgars repeatedly in the eighth, ninth, and tenth centuries, Prince Igor the Russian in 941. Siege was a state of mind for the Greek people and their oldest myth: after the Bible, people knew Homer's tale of Troy. It made them both practical and superstitious. The maintenance of the city walls was a constant civic duty; granaries were kept stocked and cisterns filled, but psychic defences were also held to be of supreme importance by the Orthodox faithful. The Virgin was the protector of the city; her icons were paraded along the walls at times of crisis and were considered to have saved the city during the siege of 717. They provided a confidence to equal the Koran.

None of the besieging armies that camped outside the land walls could break down these physical and psychological defences. The technology to storm the fortifications, the naval resources to blockade the sea and the patience to starve the citizens were not available to any would-be conqueror. The empire, though frequently stretched to breaking point, showed remarkable resilience. The infrastructure of the city, the strength of the empire's institutions and the lucky coincidence of outstanding leaders at moments of crisis made the eastern Roman Empire seem to both its citizens and its enemies likely to continue for ever.

Yet the experience of the Arab sieges marked the city deeply. People recognized in Islam an irreducible counterforce, something qualitatively different to other foes; their own prophecies about the Saracens – as the Arabs came to be known in Christendom – articulated their forebodings about the future of the world. One writer declared them to be the Fourth Beast of the Apocalypse that 'will be the fourth kingdom on the earth, that will be most disastrous of all kingdoms, that will transform the entire earth into a desert'. And towards the end of the eleventh century, a second blow fell upon Byzantium at the hands of Islam. It happened so suddenly that no one at the time quite grasped its significance.

2 Dreaming of Istanbul
1071–1422

I have seen that God caused the sun of empire to shine in the mansion of the Turks, and turned the heavenly spheres around their dominion, and named them Turk, and gave them sovereignty, and made them kings of the age, and placed the reins of the people of the time in their hands.
Al-Kashgari

It was the emergence of the Turks that reawakened the slumbering spirit of jihad. They had first appeared on the Byzantine horizon as early as the sixth century when they sent ambassadors to Constantinople to seek alliance against the Persian Empire. To the Byzantines they were just one of an endless succession of peoples beating a path to the great city; their homeland was beyond the Black Sea and stretched as far as China. They were pagan steppe dwellers of the rolling grasslands of Central Asia, from whose epicentre shock waves of nomadic raiders poured out at periodic intervals to ravage the settled peoples beyond. They have left us their word *ordu* – 'horde'– as a memory of this process, like a faint hoof print in the sand.

Byzantium suffered the repeated depredations of these Turkic nomads long before it knew the name. The earliest Turks to impact on settled Greek speakers were probably the Huns, who surged across the Christian world in the fourth century; they were followed in turn by the Bulgars, each successive wave inexplicable as a plague of locusts devastating the land. The Byzantines attributed these visitations to

The clash of Islam and Christianity: Muslims and crusaders

God's punishment for Christian sin. Like their cousins the Mongols, the Turkic peoples lived in the saddle between the great earth and the greater sky and they worshipped both through intermediary shamans. Restless, mobile and tribal, they lived by herding flocks and raiding their neighbours. Booty was a raison d'etre, cities their enemy. Their use of the composite bow and the mobile tactics of horse warfare gave them a military superiority over settled peoples that the Arab historian Ibn Khaldun saw as the key process of history. 'Sedentary people have become used to laziness and ease,' he wrote. 'They find full assurance of safety in the walls that surround them, and the fortifications that protect them. The Bedouins have no gates and walls. They always carry weapons. They watch carefully all sides of the road. They take hurried naps only . . . when they are in the saddle. They pay attention to every faint barking and noise. Fortitude has become a character quality of theirs, and courage their nature.' It was a theme that would soon re-echo in both the Christian and the Islamic worlds.

Repeated convulsions in the heart of Asia continued to propel these Turkish tribes westward; by the ninth century they were in touch with the Muslim populations of Iran and Iraq. The Caliph of Baghdad recognized their fighting qualities and recruited them into his armies as military slaves; by the end of the tenth century Islam was firmly established among the Turks on the frontier zone, yet they maintained their racial identity and language and were soon to usurp power from their masters. By the middle of the eleventh century a Turkish dynasty, the Seljuks, had emerged as sultans in Baghdad, and by its end the Islamic world, from Central Asia to Egypt, was largely ruled by Turks.

The speed of their rise in the Islamic world, far from being resented, came to be widely held as a providential miracle, brought about by God 'to revive the dying breath of Islam and restore the unity of Muslims'. It coincided with the presence of an unorthodox Shia dynasty in Egypt, so that the Turkish Seljuks, who had chosen to conform to the orthodox Sunni tradition, were able to gain legitimacy as true *gazis* – warriors of the Faith waging jihad against the infidel and unorthodox Islam. The spirit of militant Islam suited the Turkish fighting spirit perfectly; the desire for plunder was legitimized by pious service to Allah. Under Turkish influence, Islam regained the zeal of the early Arab conquests and reopened holy war against its Christian foes on a significant scale. Though Saladin himself was a Kurd, he and his successors led armies whose ethos was Turkish. 'God be praised,' wrote Al-Rawandi in the thirteenth century, 'the support of Islam is strong . . . In the lands of the Arabs, the Persians, the Romans and the Russians, the sword is in the hands of the Turks and the fear of their swords is rooted in men's hearts.'

It was not long before the war that had smouldered quietly for centuries between Christians and Muslims along the southern frontiers of Anatolia flared back into life under this new impetus. The Seljuks in Baghdad were troubled by unruly nomadic tribesmen – the Turkmen – whose desire for plunder was a discordant note in the Islamic heartlands. They encouraged these tribal fighters to turn their energy west on Byzantium – the kingdom of *Rum*. By the middle of the eleventh century marauding *gazi* warriors were raiding Christian Anatolia in the name of holy war so frequently that it became essential for the emperor in Constantinople to take decisive action.

In March 1071, the Emperor Romanus IV Diogenes set out personally to the east to repair this situation. In August he met, not the Turkmen, but a Seljuk army led by its brilliant commander Sultan Alp Arslan, 'the heroic lion', at Manzikert in eastern Anatolia. It was a curious affair. The sultan was unwilling to fight. His key objective was not war against Christians but the destruction of the detested Shiite regime in Egypt. He proposed a truce, which Romanus refused. The ensuing battle was a shattering Muslim victory, decided by classic nomad ambush tactics and the defection of Byzantine mercenary troops. Romanus survived to kiss the ground in front of the conquering sultan, who planted a foot on his bent neck in a symbolic show of triumph and submission. It was to prove a tipping point in world history – and a disaster for Constantinople.

For the Byzantines the Battle of Manzikert was 'the Terrible Day', a defeat of seismic proportions that was to haunt their future. The effects were catastrophic, though not immediately understood in Constantinople itself. The Turkmen poured into Anatolia unopposed; where they had previously raided and retired again, they now stayed, pushing further and further west into the lion's head of Anatolia. After the hot deserts of Iran and Iraq, the high rolling plateau was a landscape that suited these nomads from central Asia with their yurts and two-humped camels. With them came both the structure of Orthodox Sunni religion and more fervent Islamic strands: Sufis, dervishes, wandering holy men who preached both jihad and a mystical reverence for saints that appealed to the Christian peoples. Within twenty years of

Manzikert the Turks had reached the Mediterranean coasts. They were largely unresisted by a mixed Christian population, some of whom converted to Islam, while others were only too glad to be rid of taxation and persecution from Constantinople. Islam held Christians to be 'People of the Book'; as such they were afforded protection under the law and freedom of worship. Schismatic Christian sects even gave Turkish rule a positive welcome: 'On account of its justice and good government, they prefer to live under its administration,' wrote Michael the Syrian. 'The Turks, having no idea of the sacred mysteries . . . were in no way accustomed to inquire into professions of faith or to persecute anyone on their account, in contrast to the Greeks,' he went on, 'a wicked and heretical people.' Internal quarrels in the Byzantine state encouraged the Turks; they were soon invited to help in the civil wars that were fragmenting Byzantium. The conquest of Asia Minor happened so easily and with so little resistance that by the time another Byzantine army was defeated in 1176, the possibility of driving back the incomers had gone for ever. Manzikert was irreversible. By the 1220s Western writers were already referring to Anatolia as *Turchia*. Byzantium had lost its resources of food and manpower for good. And at almost the same moment a matching catastrophe overwhelmed Constantinople from a more unexpected quarter – the Christian West.

The matter of the crusades had been conceived as a project to check the militant advance of Turkish Islam. It was against the Seljuks, 'an accursed race, a race utterly alienated from God', that Pope Urban II preached his fateful sermon at Clermont in 1095 'to exterminate this vile race from our lands' and set in motion 350 years of crusader warfare. Despite the support of their Christian brothers in the West, this enterprise was to prove a lasting torment for the Byzantines. From 1096 onwards they were visited by successive waves of marauding knights, who expected support, sustenance and thanks from their Orthodox brethren as they blundered south across the empire towards Jerusalem. Contact brought mutual incomprehension and distrust. Each side had the opportunity closely to observe differences in customs and forms of worship. The Greeks came to see their heavily mailed Western brethren as little more than uncouth barbarian adventurers; their mission a hypocritical exercise in imperial conquest disguised as piety: 'they are indomitable in pride, cruel in character . . .

and inspired by an inveterate hatred of the Empire,' complained Nicetas Chroniates. In truth the Byzantines often preferred their settled Muslim neighbours, proximity with whom had bred a certain familiarity and respect over the centuries following the initial burst of holy war: 'we must live in common as brothers, although we differ in customs, manners and religion,' a patriarch in Constantinople once wrote to a caliph in Baghdad. The crusaders, for their part, saw the Byzantines as depraved heretics who were dangerously oriental in outlook. Seljuk and Turkish soldiers regularly fought for the Byzantines; the crusaders were also appalled to discover that the city dedicated to the Virgin contained a mosque. 'Constantinople is arrogant in her wealth, treacherous in her practices, corrupt in her faith,' declared the crusader, Odo de Deuil. More ominously, the wealth of Constantinople and its fabulous treasury of gem-studded relics left the crusaders open-mouthed. An oblique note of jealousy crept into the reports sent back to the small towns of Normandy and the Rhine: 'since the beginning of the world', wrote the Marshal of Champagne, 'never was so much riches seen collected in a single city'. It was a vivid temptation.

Military, political and commercial pressure from the west had been building on the Byzantine Empire for a long time, but by the end of the twelfth century it had taken on a very visible shape in Constantinople. A large Italian trading community had been established in the city – the Venetians and Genoese were accorded special privileges and benefited accordingly. The profiteering, materialistic Italians were not popular: the Genoese had their own colony at Galata, a walled town across the Horn; the Venetian colony was considered 'so insolent in its wealth and prosperity as to hold the imperial power in scorn'. Waves of xenophobia swept the populace; in 1171 Galata was attacked and destroyed by the Greeks. In 1183 the entire Italian community was massacred under the eye of the Byzantine general Andronikos 'the Terrible'.

In 1204 this history of mutual suspicion and violence returned to haunt Constantinople in a catastrophe for which the Greeks have never fully forgiven the Catholic West. In one of the most bizarre events in the history of Christendom, the Fourth Crusade, embarked on Venetian ships and nominally bound for Egypt, was diverted to attack the city. The architect of this operation was Enrico Dandolo, the apparently blind, eighty-year-old Venetian doge, a man of infinite guile, who personally led the expedition. Sweeping up a convenient pretender to the imperial throne, the huge fleet sailed up the Marmara in June 1203; the crusaders themselves were perhaps startled to see Constantinople, a city of great Christian significance, forming on the port bow rather than the shores of Egypt. Having smashed their way through the chain that protected the Golden Horn, the Venetian ships rode up onto the foreshore and attempted to breach the sea walls; when the attack faltered the octogenarian doge leaped down onto the beach with the flag of St Mark in his hand and exhorted the Venetians to show their valour. The walls were stormed and the pretender, Alexios, duly enthroned.

The following April, after a winter of murky internal intrigue during which the crusaders became increasingly restive, Constantinople was comprehensively sacked. An appalling massacre ensued and huge portions of the city were destroyed by fire: 'More houses were burned than there are to be found in the three greatest cities of the Kingdom of France,' declared the French knight Geoffrey de Villehardouin. The city's great heritage of art was vandalized and St Sophia profaned and ransacked: 'They brought horses and mules into the Church', wrote the chronicler Nicetas, 'the better to carry off the holy vessels and the engraved silver and gold that they had torn from the throne and the pulpit, and the doors, and the furniture wherever it was to be found; and when some of these beasts slipped and fell, they ran them through with their swords, fouling the Church with their blood and ordure.' The Venetians made off with a great trove of statuary, relics and precious objects to adorn their own church of St Mark, including the four bronze horses that had stood in the Hippodrome since the time of Constantine the Great. Constantinople was left a smoking ruin. 'Oh city, city, eye of all cities,' howled the chronicler Nicetas, 'you have drunk to the dregs the cup of the anger of the Lord.' It was a typical Byzantine response; but whether the agent of this disaster was human or divine, the consequences were the same: Constantinople was reduced to a shadow of its former greatness. For nearly sixty years the city became the 'Latin Empire of Constantinople', ruled by the Count of Flanders and his successors. The Byzantine empire was dismembered into a scattered collection of Frankish states and Italian colonies, whilst a large part of the population fled to Greece. The Byzantines established a kingdom in exile at Nicaea in Anatolia and were relatively successful in barring further Turkish incursions. When they recaptured Constantinople in 1261 they found the city's infrastructure close to ruin and its dominions shrunk to a few dispersed fragments. As they tried to restore their fortunes and to face new dangers from the West, the Byzantines again turned their back on Islamic Anatolia, and paid an ever-deepening price.

Anatolia continued to be convulsed by seismic population shifts further east. Two years after the sack of Constantinople, a tribal leader called Temuchin succeeded in uniting the feuding nomads of inner Mongolia into an organized war band and received the title Genghis Khan – the Universal Ruler. The long-haired, sky-worshipping Mongols descended on the Islamic world with terrifying ferocity. As chaos enveloped Persia, a further tidal wave of displaced people streamed west into Anatolia. The continent was a melting pot of ethnic destinies: Greek, Turkish, Iranian, Armenian, Afghani, Georgian. When the Mongols defeated its most coherent principality, that of the Seljuks of Rum, in 1243, Anatolia collapsed into a mosaic of small kingdoms. The wandering Turkish tribes had nowhere further west to migrate; there were no infidel neighbours left to provide legitimate Islamic conquests. Where they met the sea, some acquired fleets and raided Byzantine coastal territories. Others fought amongst themselves. Anatolia was chaotic, fragmented and dangerous – a wild west of raiders, plunderers and religious visionaries, inspired by a combustible mixture of mystical Sufism and orthodox Sunnism. The Turkmen still rode the long horizons in their deep embroidered saddles, seeking plunder and perpetual motion in the *gazi* tradition but now only one insignificant kingdom, the tribe of Osman, still touched the infidel lands of Byzantium in north-western Anatolia.

No one knows the true origins of these people, whom we now call Ottomans. They emerge from among the anonymous wandering Turkmen some time around 1280, a caste of illiterate warriors living amongst tents and wood smoke, who ruled from the saddle and signed with a thumbprint and whose history was subsequently reconstructed by imperial myth-making. Legend tells that Osman was always destined for greatness. One night he fell asleep and had a dream, in which he saw Constantinople, which, 'situated at the junction of two seas and two continents, seemed like a diamond mounted between two sapphires and two emeralds, and appeared thus to form the precious stone of the ring of a vast dominion which embraced the entire world'. Osman took upon himself the mantle of the *gazis*, which his tribe was poised to exploit. Luck and quick-wittedness in equal measure were to transform the realm of Osman from a tiny principality to the world power of the dream.

The domain of Osman, in north-western Anatolia, directly confronted the Byzantine defensive perimeter that guarded Constantinople. Facing unconquered infidel land, it became a magnet for *gazis*, adventurers and land hungry refugees who wanted to try their luck under his command. Osman ruled as a tribal leader in touch with his people. At the same time the Ottomans had a unique opportunity to study the neighbouring Byzantine state and to imitate its structures. The tribe learned literally 'on the hoof', absorbing technologies, protocols and tactics at an extraordinary rate. In 1302 Osman won a first victory over the Byzantines that brought prestige and recruits to his cause. Pushing forward against the crumbling imperial defences, he managed to isolate the city of Bursa; as he lacked the technology for sieges it took a patient seven years of blockade before his son Orhan captured the city in 1326 and secured a capital for his small kingdom. In 1329 Orhan defeated the Emperor Andronikos III at Pelekanos, ending all Byzantine attempts to support its remaining Anatolian cities. They fell in quick succession – Nicaea in 1331, Nicomedia in 1337, Scutari the following year. Muslim warriors were now able to ride their horses to the sea's edge on their own lands and look out across the Bosphorus at Europe. On the far side they could make out Constantinople: the marching line of its sea walls, the enormous dome of St Sophia, imperial banners fluttering from turrets and palaces.

As they advanced, the conquerors smoothed the Greek placenames of captured cities to the vowel harmonies of Turkish. Smyrna became Izmir, Nicaea – home of the Nicene Creed – Iznik; Brusa shifted consonants into Bursa. Constantinople, though the Ottomans would continue to refer to it officially by the Arabic name *Kostantiniyye*, evolved in everyday Turkish into Istanbul by a mutation which is still unclear. The word may be a simple corruption of Constantinople, or it could be derived quite differently. Greek speakers would refer to Constantinople familiarly as *polis*, the city. A man going there would say he was going '*eis tin polin*' – 'into the city' – which could have been interpreted by Turkish ears as *Istanbul*.

The speed of the Ottoman advance seemed as providential as that of the Arabs seven centuries earlier. When the great Arab traveller Ibn Battutah visited Orhan's principality in 1331 he was impressed by the restless energy of the place: 'It is said that he has never stayed for a whole month in any one town. He fights with the infidels continually and keeps them under siege.' The early Ottomans styled themselves as

The tombs of Osman and Orhan at Bursa

gazis; they wrapped the title of warriors of the Faith around them like the green flag of Islam. Soon they were sultans too. In 1337 Orhan set up an inscription in Bursa, styling himself 'Sultan, son of the Sultan of the Gazis, Gazi, son of the Gazi, marquis of the horizons, hero of the world'. It was indeed a new heroic age of Muslim conquest and it quickened the pulse of militant Islam. 'The Gazi is the sword of God,' wrote the chronicler Ahmeti around 1400, 'he is the protector and refuge of the believers. If he becomes a martyr in the ways of God, do not believe that he has died – he lives in beatitude with Allah, he has eternal life.' The conquests aroused wild expectations amongst the free-riding nomadic raiders and the dervish mystics in tattered cloaks who travelled with them across the dusty roads of Anatolia. The air was thick with prophecy and heroic song. They remembered the Hadith about conquering Constantinople and the legends of the Red Apple. When the Emperor John Cantacuzenos invited Orhan's war band across the Dardanelles in the 1350s to help in the interminable civil wars of the Byzantine state, Muslims set foot in Europe for the first time since 718. When an earthquake wrecked the walls of Gallipoli in 1354, the Ottomans promptly declared it to be a sign from God to the Muslims and occupied the town. A steady stream of fighters and holy men followed them into Europe. In 1359 an Islamic army appeared outside the city walls for the first time in 650 years. A note of millennial prophecy creeps into the atmosphere. 'Why have the Gazis appeared at the last?' asked Ahmeti. 'Because the best always comes at the end. Just as the definitive prophet Muhammad came after the others, just as the Koran came down from heaven after the Torah, the Psalms and the Gospels, so also the Gazis appeared in the world at the last.' The capture of Constantinople must have seemed a dream on the edge of possibility.

The speed of the Ottoman advance seemed nothing short of miraculous – as if ordained by God. By geography, custom and luck, the Ottomans were best placed to prosper from the disintegration of the Byzantine state. The early sultans, living close to their men and to nature, were attentive to circumstance and possibility in the shifting political environment around them. Where the Byzantines were hidebound by a thousand years of ceremony and tradition, the Ottomans were quick-witted, flexible and open. The laws of Islam required mercy to conquered peoples and the Ottomans ruled their subjects with a light hand that seemed frequently preferable to European feudalism. No attempt was made to convert Christians, who formed the bulk of the population, to Islam – in fact it was largely thought undesirable by a dynasty with a taste for empire. Under sharia law it was not possible to tax Muslims as heavily as infidels, though in any case their burden was not heavy. The peasants of the Balkans welcomed release from the weightier yoke of feudal servitude. At the same time the Ottomans inbuilt dynastic advantages for themselves. Unlike other Turkish principalities, the early sultans never divided the succession of the kingdom; nor did they designate a successor. All sons were groomed to rule but only one could take the throne – a method that seemed brutally designed to ensure the survival of the fittest. Most startling of all for westerners, they paid no attention to succession through marriage. Where the Byzantine Emperors, like all the ruling houses of Europe, went to exhaustive lengths to secure dynastic marriages and legitimate succession through approved bloodlines, the Ottomans hardly bothered. A sultan's father would naturally be the previous sultan, but his mother might be a concubine or a slave, possibly not a born Muslim, and from one of a dozen subject peoples. This genetic inclusiveness was to provide the Ottomans with extraordinary resources.

Of all Ottoman innovations none was perhaps more significant than the creation of a regular army. The enthusiastic bands of *gazi* warriors were too undisciplined to fulfil the now growing ambitions of the Ottoman sultans; besieging well-defended cities required patience, methodology and a particular set of craft skills. Towards the end of the fourteenth century Sultan Murat I formed a new military force, comprised of slaves captured from the Balkan states. A levy of Christian youths was taken at regular intervals, converted to Islam and taught Turkish. Removed from their families, these new recruits owed their loyalty only to the sultan. They were his private force: the 'slaves of the Gate'. They were organized into infantry units, the *Yeni Cheri* or Janissaries, and the cavalry, which together comprised the first professional paid army in Europe since the time of the Romans. It was to play a critical role in the development of the Ottoman state. This was a custom drawn straight out of the Ottomans' own history: the Turks themselves had been enrolled as military slaves at the frontiers of the Islamic world. It had been their passport to advancement. But to Christians watching the process from afar, it evoked rigid horror: with different images of slavery, the prospect of turning captured Christian children against Christians was fiendish and inhuman. It was to form a powerful ingredient in the myth of the Savage Turk.

This notion of 'the Turk' was seized on early in the West. It was largely a European construct, a term matched to Western identities that was hardly used by the Ottomans. They considered it derogatory. Instead, they chose titles that were neither ethnic nor territorial and reflected both their nomadic heritage, unconfined by fixed territories, and its multi-ethnic composition. Identity was primarily religious: the Ottoman sultans came to describe themselves in increasingly ornate terms as Lords of Islam, their empire as the Refuge of the Faith or the Defended Lands, their people as either Muslims or Ottomans. The Ottoman make-up was a unique assemblage of different elements and peoples: Turkish tribalism, Sunni Islam, Persian court practices, Byzantine administration, taxation and ceremonial, and a high-flown court language that combined Turkish structure with Arabic and Persian vocabulary. It had an identity all of its own.

The rising arc of the Ottomans was mirrored by a corresponding and unhalted decline in the fortunes of Byzantium. The factors that went to make the years after 1300 'the calamitous century' in Europe played out in the eastern empire too. Fragmentation, civil war, population decline and impoverishment stalked Constantinople. There were telling symbolic moments. In 1284, the Emperor Andronikos II took the suicidal decision to abolish the imperial navy. The workless sailors defected to the Ottomans and helped them build a fleet.

The double-headed eagle of the house of Palaiologos

Sometime around 1325 the emperors of the House of Palaiologos adopted the double-headed eagle as their emblem; it did not, as has sometimes been supposed, represent a mighty empire that looked both east and west, but rather symbolized a division of authority between two quarrelsome emperors of the same family. The eagle was prophetic. The years 1341 to 1371 were racked by a ruinous sequence of civil wars, invasion of imperial territory by both the Ottomans and the powerful Serbian state, religious controversy and plague. Constantinople was the first European city to experience the Black Death: rats that scurried up the gangplanks in the Black Sea port of Kaffa jumped ship there in 1347. The population shrank to little more than 100,000. A series of earthquakes devastated Constantinople – the dome of St Sophia collapsed in 1346 – and the city 'of pure gold' became increasingly destitute and forlorn, its inhabitants prone to religious pessimism. Travellers to the city remarked on the melancholy appearance of the place. Ibn Battutah saw, not a city, but thirteen villages separated by fields. When the Spaniard Pero Tafur visited he found even the emperor's palace 'in such a state that both it and the city show well the evils which the people have suffered and still endure . . . the city is sparsely populated . . . the inhabitants are not well clad, but sad and poor, showing the hardship of their lot', before adding with true Christian charity, 'which is, however, not as bad as they deserve, for they are a vicious people, steeped in sin'. The city was shrinking inside its walls like an old man in the clothes of his youth, and its emperors were paupers in their own house. At the coronation of the Emperor John VI Cantacuzenos in 1347, observers noticed that the crown jewels were made of glass, the banqueting plates of clay and pewter. The golden dishes had been sold to pay for civil war; the jewels pawned to the Venetians – they were in the treasury of St Mark's.

In this confusion, the Ottoman advance into Europe continued unchecked. In 1362 they virtually encircled Constantinople from the rear when they took the city of Adrianople – Edirne in Turkish – 140 miles to the west, and moved their imperial capital into Europe. When they shattered the Serbs in battle in 1371 the Emperor John was isolated from all Christian support and had little option but to become a vassal of the sultans, contributing troops on demand and seeking permission for imperial appointments. The advance of the Ottomans seemed unstoppable: by the end of the fourteenth century their terrain stretched from the Danube to the Euphrates. 'Turkish or heathen expansion is like the sea,' wrote the Serbian, Michael 'the Janissary', 'it never has peace but always rolls . . . until you smash a snake's head it is always worse.' The Pope issued a bull proclaiming crusade against the Ottomans in 1366, and in vain threatened excommunication against the trading states of Italy and the Adriatic for supplying them with arms. The next fifty years were to see three crusades against the infidel, all led by the Hungarians, the most threatened state in Eastern Europe. They were to be the swan song of a united Christendom. Each one ended in punishing defeat, the causes of which were not hard to find. Europe was divided, poverty stricken, wracked by its own internal disputes, weakened by the Black Death. The armies themselves were lumbering, quarrelsome, ill disciplined and tactically inept, in comparison with the mobile and well organized Ottomans, unified around a common cause. The few Europeans who saw them up close could not but profess a sneaking admiration for 'Ottoman order'. The French traveller Bertrandon de la Brocquière observed in the 1430s:

> They are diligent, willingly rise early, and live on little . . . they are indifferent as to where they sleep, and usually lie on the ground . . . their horses are good, cost little in food, gallop well and for a long time . . . their obedience to their superiors is boundless . . . when the signal is given, those who are to lead march quietly off, followed by the others with the same silence . . . ten thousand Turks on such an occasion will make less noise than 100 men in the Christian armies . . . I must own that in my various experiences I have always found the Turks to be frank and loyal, and when it was necessary to show courage, they have never failed to do so.

Against this background the start of the fifteenth century looked bleak for Constantinople. Siege by the Ottomans had become a recurring feature of life. When the Emperor Manuel broke his oath of vassalage in 1394, Sultan Bayezit subjected the city to a series of assaults, only called off when Bayezit was himself defeated in battle by the Turkic Mongol, Timur – the Tamburlaine of Marlowe's play – in 1402. Thereafter the emperors sought increasingly desperate help from the west – Manuel even came to England in 1400 – whilst pursuing a policy of diplomatic intrigue and support for pretenders to the Ottoman throne. Sultan Murat II besieged Constantinople in 1422 for encouraging pretenders but the city still held out. The Ottomans had neither the fleet to close off the city nor the technology quickly to storm its massive land walls and Manuel, by now an old man but still one of the most astute of all diplomats, managed to conjure up another claimant to the Ottoman throne to threaten civil war. The siege was lifted, but Constantinople was hanging on by the skin of its teeth. It seemed only a matter of time before the Ottomans came for the city again and in force. It was only the fear of a concerted European crusade that restrained them.

The tugra, the imperial cipher, of Orhan, the first sultan to take a city by siege

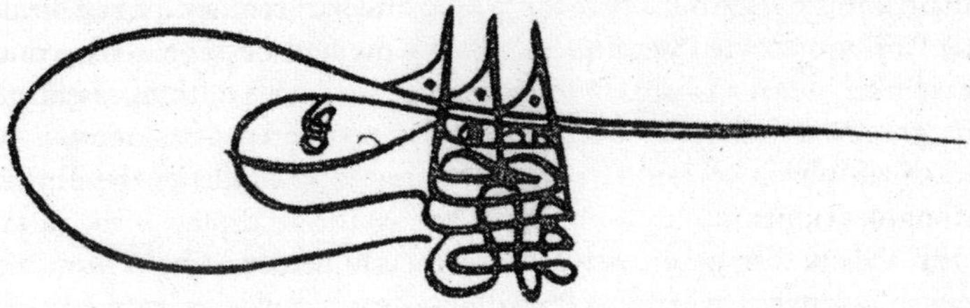

3 Sultan and Emperor 1432–1451

Mehmet Chelebi – Sultan – may God fasten the strap of his authority to the pegs of eternity and reinforce the supports of his power until the predestined day!
Inscription on the tomb of the mother of Mehmet II

Constantine Palaiologos, in Christ true Emperor and Autocrat of the Romans.
Ceremonial title of Constantine XI, eighty-eighth Emperor of Byzantium

The man destined to tighten the Muslim noose on the city was born ten years after Murat's siege. In Turkish legend, 1432 was a year of portents. Horses produced a large number of twins; trees were bowed down with fruit; a long-tailed comet appeared in the noonday sky over Constantinople. On the night of 29 March, Sultan Murat was waiting in the royal palace at Edirne for news of a birth; unable to sleep, he started to read the Koran. He had just reached the Victory suras, the verses that promise triumph over unbelievers, when a messenger brought word of a son. He was called Mehmet, Murat's father's name, the Turkish form of Muhammad.

Like many prophecies, these have a distinctly retrospective feel to them. Mehmet was the third of Murat's sons; both his half-brothers were substantially older and the boy was never his father's favourite. His chances of living to become sultan were slim. Perhaps it is significant of the entry Mehmet made into the world that considerable uncertainty surrounds the identity of his mother. Despite the efforts of some Turkish historians to claim her as an ethnic Turk and a Muslim,

The tugra of Mehmet

the strong probability is that she was a western slave, taken in a frontier raid or captured by pirates, possibly Serbian or Macedonian and most likely born a Christian – a parentage that casts a strange light on the paradoxes in Mehmet's nature. Whatever the genetic cocktail of his origins, Mehmet was to reveal a character quite distinct from that of his father, Murat.

By the middle of the fifteenth century Ottoman sultans were no longer unlettered tribal chieftains who directed war bands from the saddle. The heady mixture of jihad and booty had given way to something more measured. The sultan still derived immense prestige as the greatest leader of holy war in the lands of Islam, but this was increasingly a tool of dynastic policy. Ottoman rulers now styled themselves the 'Sultan of Rum' – a title that suggested a claim to the inheritance of the ancient Christian empire – or 'Padishah', a high-flown Persian formula. From the Byzantines they were developing a taste for the ceremonial apparatus of monarchy; their princes were formally educated for high office; their palaces were high-walled; access to the sultan became carefully regulated. Fear of poison, intrigue and assassination were progressively distancing the ruler from his subjects – a process that had followed the murder of Murat I by a Serbian envoy after the first Battle of Kosovo in 1389. The reign of the second Murat was a fulcrum in this process. He still signed himself 'bey' – the old title for a Turkish noble – rather than the grander 'sultan' and was popular with his people. The Hungarian monk, Brother George, was surprised by the lack of ceremonial surrounding him. 'On his clothing or on his horse the sultan had no special mark to distinguish him. I watched him at his mother's funeral, and if he had not been pointed out to me, I could not have recognised him.' At the same time a distance was starting to be interposed between the sultan and the world around him. 'He never took anything in public', noted Bertrandon de la Brocquière, 'and there are very few persons who can boast of having seen him speak, or having seen him eat or drink.' It was a process that would lead successive sultans to the hermetic world of the Topkapi Palace with its blank outer walls and elaborate ritual.

It was the chilly atmosphere of the Ottoman court that shaped Mehmet's early years. The issue of succession to the throne cast a long shadow over the upbringing of male children. Direct dynastic succession from father to son was critical for the empire's survival – the harem system was instrumental in ensuring an adequate supply of surviving male children to protect it – but comprised its greatest vulnerability. The throne was a contest between the male heirs. There was no law prioritizing the eldest; the surviving princes simply fought it out at the sultan's death. The outcome was considered to be God's will. 'If He has decreed that you shall have the kingdom after me,' a later sultan wrote to his son, 'no man living will be able to prevent it.' In practice, succession often became a race for the centre – the winner would be the heir who secured the capital, the treasury and the support of the army; it was a method that might either favour the survival of the fittest or lead to civil war. The Ottoman state had nearly collapsed in the early years of the fifteenth century in a fratricidal struggle for power in which the Byzantines were deeply implicated. It had become almost state policy in Constantinople to exploit the dynasty's moment of weakness by supporting rival claimants and pretenders.

In order both to guard against pre-emptive strikes and to teach their sons the craft of monarchy, the sultans dispatched their male heirs at a very early age to govern provinces under the watchful eye of carefully chosen tutors. Mehmet spent his first years in the palace harem in Edirne but was sent to the regional capital of Amasya in Anatolia at the age of two to begin the early preparation for his education. His oldest half-brother Ahmet, who was twelve years of age, became governor of the city at the same time. Dark forces stalked the heirs to the throne during the next decade. In 1437 Ahmet died suddenly in Amasya. Six years later, when his other half-brother Ali was governor, a gruesome Ottoman version of 'the Princes in the Tower' mystery took place in the town. A leading noble, Kara Hizir Pasha, was dispatched to Amasya by unknown persons. He managed to steal into the palace at night and strangle Ali in his bed, as well as both his infant sons. A whole branch of the family was snuffed out in a single night; Mehmet remained the only heir to the throne. Rippling like a black shadow behind these murky events was a long-running power struggle within the Ottoman ruling class for the soul of the state. During his reign Murat had strengthened the Janissary corps of slave-recruited troops and elevated some Christian converts to the status of vizier in an attempt to establish a counter-balance to the power of the traditional Turkish nobility and army. It was a contest that would be played out to its final conclusion before the walls of Constantinople nine years later.

Ali had been Murat's favourite son: his death affected the sultan deeply – though at the same time it is not impossible that Murat himself ordered the executions on discovering a plot by the prince. However, he realized that there was now no choice but to recall the young Mehmet to Edirne and to take his education in hand. At that moment the eleven-year-old represented the only future for the Ottoman dynasty. Murat was horrified when he saw the boy again. He was already headstrong, wilful and almost uneducable. Mehmet had openly defied his previous tutors, refusing to be chastised or to learn the Koran. Murat called in the celebrated mullah, Ahmet Gurani, with orders to thrash the young prince into submission. Cane in hand, the mullah went to see the prince. 'Your father', he said, 'has sent me to instruct you, but also to chastise you in case you do not obey.' Mehmet laughed aloud at the threat, at which the mullah delivered such a beating that Mehmet swiftly buckled down to study. Under this formidable tutor, Mehmet began to absorb the Koran, then a widening circle of knowledge. The boy revealed an extraordinary intelligence coupled with an iron will to succeed. He developed fluency in languages – by all accounts he knew Turkish, Persian and Arabic, as well as spoken Greek, a Slavic dialect and some Latin – and became fascinated by history and geography, science, practical engineering and literature. A remarkable personality was starting to emerge.

The 1440s marked a new period of crisis for the Ottomans. The empire was threatened in Anatolia by an uprising by one of its Turkmen vassals, the Bey of Karaman, while a new Hungarian-led crusade was being prepared in the West. Murat appeared to have defused the Christian threat with a ten-year truce and departed to Anatolia to deal with the troublesome Bey. Before he went he took the surprising step of abdicating from the throne. He was fearful of civil war within the state and wanted to confirm Mehmet in power before he himself died; world-weariness too may have been a factor. The burdens of office hung heavily on an Ottoman sultan and Murat may have been depressed by the murder of his favourite son Ali. At the age of twelve Mehmet was confirmed as sultan at Edirne under the guidance of the trustworthy Chief Vizier Halil. Coins were minted in his name and he was mentioned in weekly prayers, according to prerogative.

The experiment was a disaster. Tempted by the opportunity presented by a callow young sultan, the Pope immediately absolved the Hungarian king Ladislas of his oath of truce and the crusader army rumbled forward. In September it crossed the Danube; a Venetian fleet was dispatched to the Dardanelles to block Murat's return. The atmosphere in Edirne became turbulent. In 1444 an inspirational religious fanatic of a heretical Shia sect had appeared in the city. Crowds flocked to the Persian missionary who promised reconciliation between Islam and Christianity, and Mehmet himself, attracted by his teachings, welcomed the man into the palace. The religious authorities were shocked and Halil himself was alarmed by the popular enthusiasm for the heretic. An attempt was made to arrest him. When the missionary sought sanctuary in the palace, Mehmet had to be persuaded to give the man up. He was eventually hauled off to the public prayer site and burned alive; his followers were massacred. The Byzantines also decided to profit from this confusion. A pretender to the Ottoman throne, Prince Orhan, whom they were holding in the city, was released to foment a revolt. Uprisings ensued against the Ottomans in the European provinces. There was panic in Edirne; a large portion of the town was burned down and Turkish Muslims started to flee back to Anatolia. Mehmet's reign was unravelling in chaos.

Murat meanwhile had negotiated a truce with the Bey of Karaman and hurried back to confront the threat. Finding the Dardanelles blocked by Venetian ships, he was ferried across the Bosphorus with his army by their rivals, the Genoese, at the handsome fee of a ducat a head and advanced to meet the crusader army at Varna on the Black Sea on 10 November 1444. The outcome was a crushing victory for the Ottomans. Ladislas's skull was mounted on a lance and sent to the old Ottoman city of Bursa as a triumphal token of Muslim supremacy. It was a significant moment in the holy war between Christianity and Islam. After 350 years the defeat at Varna extinguished the appetite in the West for crusading; never again would Christendom unite to try to drive the Muslims out of Europe. It confirmed the Ottoman presence in the Balkans and left Constantinople emphatically isolated as an enclave within the Islamic world, reducing the likelihood of western help in the event of Ottoman attack. Worse still, Murat held the Byzantines responsible for much of the chaos of 1444, an opinion that would soon shape Ottoman strategy.

Immediately after Varna, and despite the early failure of Mehmet's sultanship, Murat again retired to Anatolia. Halil Pasha remained first vizier, but Mehmet was more influenced by the two men who acted as his governors: the chief eunuch Shihabettin Pasha, lord of the European provinces, and a forceful Christian renegade, Zaganos Pasha. Both these men favoured advancing the plan for taking Constantinople, in the knowledge that the city still held the pretender Orhan; capturing it would stabilize Mehmet's rule and bring the young sultan immense personal kudos. It is clear that even at an early age Mehmet was magnetically attracted to the project of capturing the Christian city and making himself heir to the Roman Empire. In a poem he wrote that 'my earnest desire is to crush the Infidels', yet Mehmet's longing for the city was as much imperial as it was religious, and derived in part from a source that was surprisingly non-Islamic. He was deeply interested in the exploits of Alexander the Great and Julius Caesar. Alexander had been transformed into an Islamic hero by medieval Persian and Turkish epics. Mehmet would have known of Alexander from his early years; he had the Greek biography of the World Conqueror by the Roman writer Arrian read to him daily in the palace. From these influences he conceived for himself twin identities – as the Muslim Alexander whose conquests would reach to the ends of the earth, and as a *gazi* warrior leading jihad against the infidel. He would reverse the flow of world history: Alexander swept east; he in his turn would bring glory to the East and to Islam by conquering the West. It was a heady vision, fuelled by his personal advisers, who saw that their own careers might be made on the wave of conquest.

The precocious Mehmet, supported by his tutors, started to plan a new assault on Constantinople as early as 1445. He was thirteen years old. Halil Pasha was thoroughly alarmed. He disapproved of the young sultan's plan; after the debacle of 1444, he feared such a move would end in further disaster. Despite its formidable resources, the Ottoman Empire had all but collapsed within living memory under civil war, and Halil retained the deep fear of many, that a concerted attempt on Constantinople could provoke a massive Christian response from the West. He had personal motives too: he was concerned for the erosion of his own power and that of the traditional Muslim-Turkish nobility at the expense of the warmongering Christian converts. He decided to engineer Mehmet's deposition by instigating a Janissary revolt and petitioning Murat to return to Edirne to take control again. He was welcomed back with wild enthusiasm; the haughty, aloof young sultan was not popular with either the people or the Janissaries. Mehmet retired to Manisa with his advisers. It was a humiliating rebuff that he would never forgive or forget; one day it would cost Halil his life.

Mehmet remained in the shadows for the rest of Murat's life, though he continued to regard himself as sultan. He accompanied his father to the second Battle of Kosovo in 1448, where the Hungarians made one final bid to break Ottoman power. It was Mehmet's baptism of fire. The outcome, despite huge Ottoman losses, was as decisive as Varna and further served to cement the legend of Ottoman invincibility. A gloomy pessimism started to pervade the West. 'The Turks through such organisation are far ahead', wrote Michael the Janissary. 'If you pursue him, he will flee; but if he pursues you, you will not escape . . . the Tartars have several times won victories over the Turks, but the Christians never, and especially in pitched battle, most of all because they let the Turks encircle them and approach from the flank.'

Murat's final years were spent in Edirne. The sultan seems to have lost the appetite for further military adventure, preferring the stability of peace to the uncertainties of war. As long as he lived, Constantinople breathed in uneasy peace; when he died in February 1451 he was mourned by friend and foe alike. 'The treaties that he had sworn sacredly with the Christians', declared the Greek chronicler Doukas, 'he always kept intact. His anger was short-lived. He was averse to warfare and keen on peace, and for this reason the Father of Peace rewarded him with a peaceful death, rather than being dispatched by the sword.' The Greek chronicler would have been less generous had he known the recommendation Murat left to his successor. Byzantine meddlings in the 1440s had convinced him that the Ottoman state could never be secure as long as Constantinople remained a Christian enclave. 'He left as a bequest to his illustrious successor', said the Ottoman chronicler Sa'd-ud-din, 'the erection of the standards of the jihad for the capture of that city, by the addition of which . . . he might protect the prosperity of the people of Islam and break the back of the wretched misbelievers.'

The death of a sultan always constituted a dangerous moment for the Ottoman state. In accordance with tradition, and to forestall any armed revolt, the news was kept secret. Murat had one other son, a baby called Little Ahmet, who posed no immediate threat to Mehmet's succession, but the pretender Orhan remained in Constantinople, and Mehmet was hardly popular. News of his father's death was dispatched in a sealed letter by flying courier. In it Halil advised Mehmet not to tarry; a swift arrival at Edirne was imperative – any delay might provoke insurrection. According to legend, Mehmet immediately had his horse saddled and called to his retainers, 'Let him who loves me, follow me.' Accompanied by his household troops he made the crossing at Gallipoli in two days. As he rode across the plain to Edirne he was met by a vast throng of officials, viziers, mullahs, state governors and common people, in a ritual harking back to their tribal past on the Asian steppes. When they were a mile off, the welcoming party dismounted and walked towards their new ruler in dead silence. Half a mile distant, they stopped and broke into wild ululations for the dead sultan. Mehmet and his retinue similarly dismounted and joined in the communal lamentation. The winter landscape echoed with mournful cries. The chief officials bowed before the new sultan then the whole gathering remounted and progressed back to the palace.

The following day the official presentation of the ministers took place. It was an edgy occasion, the moment when the viziers of the old sultan discovered their fate. Mehmet was seated on the throne, flanked by his own trusted advisers. Halil Pasha hung back, waiting to see what Mehmet would do. The boy sultan said, 'Why do my father's viziers hang back? Call them forward, and tell Halil to take his usual place.' Halil was restored to the role of chief vizier. It was a typical move by Mehmet: to maintain a status quo while he kept his deeper plans close to his chest and bided his time.

The new sultan was just seventeen years old, a mixture of confidence and hesitancy, ambition and reserve. His early years had evidently marked Mehmet deeply. He had probably been separated from his mother when very young and had survived in the shadow world of the Ottoman court largely through luck. Even as a young man he emerges as deeply secretive and suspicious of others: self-reliant, haughty, distant from human affection and intensely ambitious – a personality of paradox and complexity. The man whom the Renaissance later presented as a monster of cruelty and perversion was a mass of contradictions. He was astute, brave and highly impulsive – capable of deep deception, tyrannical cruelty and acts of sudden kindness. He was moody and unpredictable, a bisexual who shunned close relationships, never forgave an insult but who came to be loved for his pious foundations. The key traits of his mature character were already in place: the later tyrant who was also a scholar; the obsessive military strategist who loved Persian poetry and gardening; the expert at logistics and practical planning who was so superstitious that he relied on the court astrologer to confirm military decisions; the Islamic warrior who could be generous to his non-Muslim subjects and enjoyed the company of foreigners and unorthodox religious thinkers.

A handful of portraits painted over the course of his life provide probably the first authentic likenesses of an Ottoman sultan. A reasonably consistent face emerges – an aquiline profile, the hawk nose protruding over sensual lips like 'a parrot's beak resting on cherries' in the memorable phrase of an Ottoman poet, complemented by a reddish beard on a thrusting chin. In one stylized miniature, he is delicately holding an uncrushed rose to his nose between jewelled fingers. It is the conventional representation of the sultan as aesthete, the lover of gardens and the author of Persian quatrains, but it is informed by a fixed gaze, as if he were looking at some faraway point where the world vanishes. In other mature portraits he is bull-necked and corpulent and in the famous late portrait by Bellini now hanging in the National Gallery in London he just looks grave and ill. All these pictures contain a note of steady authority, the natural assumption of power by 'God's shadow on earth', that assumes the world sits in his hand too naturally to be called arrogance, but there is a chilly melancholy too that recalls the cold and dangerous childhood years.

The pictures are matched by a vivid account of the complex young Mehmet by an Italian, Giacomo de Languschi:

> The sovereign, the Grand Turk Mehmet Bey is a youth . . . well-built, of large rather than medium stature, expert at arms, of aspect more frightening than venerable, laughing seldom, full of circumspection, endowed with great generosity, obstinate in pursuing his plans, bold in all undertakings, as eager for fame as Alexander of Macedon. Daily he has Roman and other historical works read to him. He speaks three languages, Turkish, Greek and Slavic. He is at great pains to learn the geography of Italy . . . where the seat of the pope is and that of the emperor, and how many kingdoms there are in Europe. He possesses a map of Europe with the countries and provinces. He learns of nothing with greater interest and enthusiasm than the geography of the world and of military affairs; he burns with desire to dominate; he is a shrewd investigator of conditions. It is with such a man that we Christians have to deal . . . Today, he says, the times have changed, and declares that he will advance from east to West as in former times the Westerners advanced into the Orient. There must, he says, be only one empire, one faith, and one sovereignty in the world.

It was a vivid snapshot of Mehmet's ambition to reverse the tide of history by carrying Islamic banners into Europe, but at his accession the obsession and intelligence were largely hidden from the West. They saw only a callow and inexperienced youth whose early taste of power had ended in humiliation.

*

Two years before Mehmet's accession to the throne, Constantinople had also welcomed a new emperor, though in very different circumstances. The man destined to oppose Mehmet in the struggle ahead bore the name of the city's founder – a fact that superstitious Byzantines would be quick to recall. Constantine XI was the eighth member of the ruling dynasty of Palaiologos to sit on the throne since 1261. The family had usurped power and their rule coincided with the relentless downward spiral of the empire into anarchy and discord. His own background was typically multi-racial. He was Greek speaking but hardly Greek: his mother was Serbian and Constantine adopted her family name of Dragases, his father was half Italian. He described himself, like all Byzantines, as a Roman, and signed himself with the proud and ancient title of his predecessors: 'Constantine Palaiologos, in Christ true Emperor and Autocrat of the Romans'.

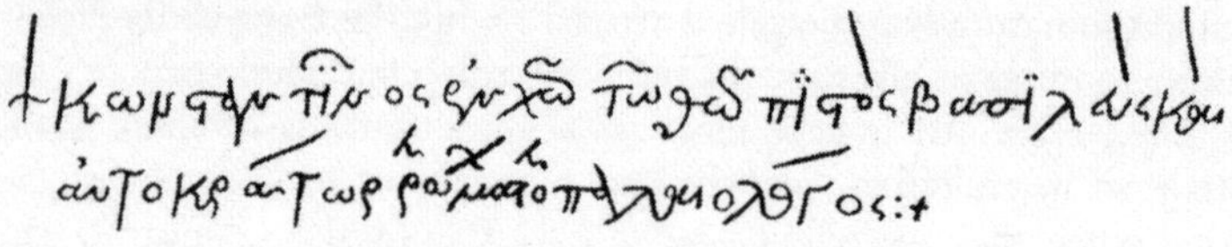

Signature of Constantine as Emperor of the Romans

It was a hollow protocol but typical of the ritual formulae and ceremonial that the Byzantines clung to during their unchecked decline. The empire had a High Admiral, but no fleet, a Commander-in-Chief but few soldiers. Within the Lilliputian world of the court, the nobility jostled and squabbled for absurdly pretentious titles such as Grand Domestic, Grand Chancellor or Lord of the Imperial Wardrobe. Constantine was effectively an emperor without power. His territory had shrunk to the city and its suburbs, a few islands and linked dominions in the Peloponnese, which the Greeks called, rather poetically, the Morea, the Mulberry Leaf: the peninsula was famous for its silk production and its shape reminded them of this food of silk worms.

It is hard to envy Constantine his crown. He inherited bankruptcy, a family with a taste for civil war, a city divided by religious passions and an impoverished and volatile proletariat. The empire was a snake pit of internecine feuding – in 1442 his brother Demetrios marched on the city with Ottoman troops. It lived a half-life as the vassal of the

Ottoman emperor who could lay siege to the city at any time. Nor was Constantine's personal authority particularly secure: a whiff of illegitimacy surrounded his accession to the throne in 1449. He was invested in Mistra in the Peloponnese, a highly unusual protocol for an emperor, and never subsequently crowned in St Sophia. The Byzantines had to ask Murat's approval of their new emperor but were then too poor to provide him with transport home. Humiliatingly, he had to beg passage to his throne on a Catalan ship.

There are no contemporary illustrations of the city he returned to in March 1449. A slightly earlier Italian map shows Constantinople to be a place of empty spaces, while across the Golden Horn, the Genoese trading colony known as Galata, or Pera, was reported to be thriving and prosperous: 'a large town, inhabited by Greeks, Jews and Genoese' according to the traveller Bertrandon de la Brocquière, who declared it to be the handsomest port he had ever seen. The French knight found Constantinople itself fascinating but down at heel. The churches were impressive, particularly St Sophia, where he saw 'the gridiron on which St Lawrence was broiled, and a large stone in the shape of a washstand, on which they say Abraham gave the angels food when they were going to destroy Sodom and Gomorra'. The great equestrian statue of Justinian, which he mistook for Constantine the Great, was still in place: 'He holds a sceptre in his left hand, and holds his right extended towards Turkey in Asia and the road to Jerusalem, as if to denote that the whole of that country was under his rule.' But the truth was obvious – the emperor was scarcely master in his own house.

There are merchants from all nations in this city, but none so powerful as the Venetians, who have a bailey to regulate all their affairs independently of the Emperor and his ministers. The Turks also have an officer to superintend their commerce, who, like the Venetian bailiff, is independent of the Emperor. They have even the privilege, that if one of their slaves should run away and take refuge within the city, on their demanding him, the Emperor is bound to give him up. This prince must be under great subjection to the Turk, since he pays him, I am told, a tribute of ten thousand ducats annually.

De la Brocquière noted everywhere the epitaphs of vanished greatness – none more telling than (apparently) three empty marble plinths in the Hippodrome: 'here stood once three gilt horses, now at Venice'. It seemed only a matter of time before the Ottomans came for the city again and the people just opened the gates for them. They had received

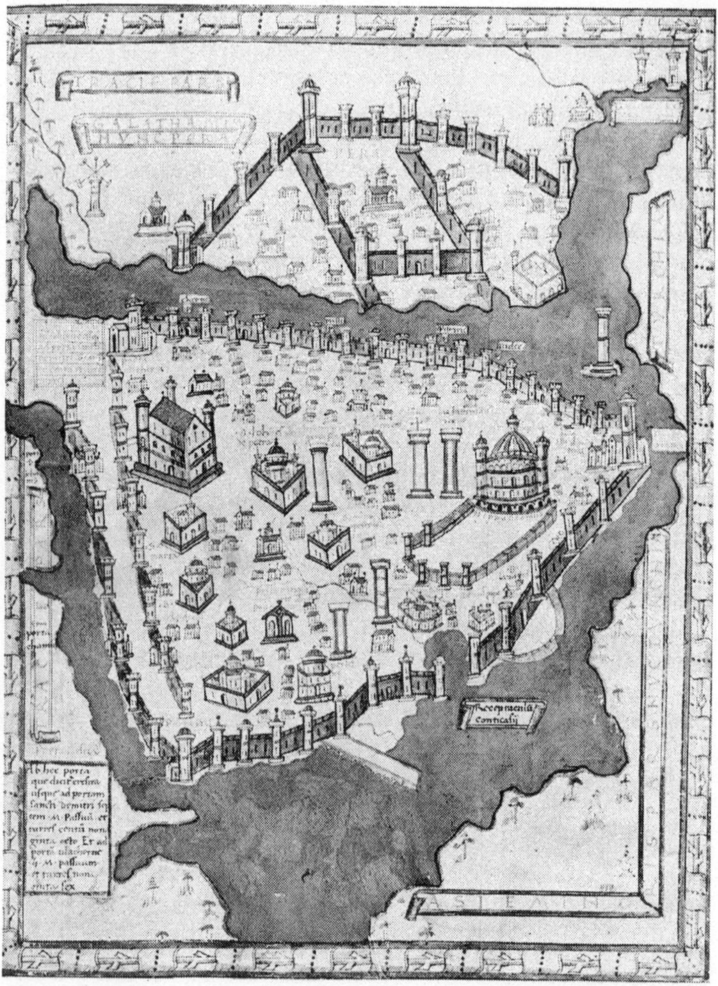

An Italian map of Constantinople from the early fifteenth century. It portrays a sizeable moat on the left-hand side outside the landwalls. Galata is at the top.

a terrible warning of the alternatives in 1430 when Thessaloniki had refused to submit to Murat. It took the Ottomans just three hours to storm the walls; three days of rape and plunder followed; 7,000 women and children were carried off into slavery.

We have little idea what Constantine looks like; his face is almost a blank. He seems to have inherited the strong, regular features and bearing of his father Manuel II, but the empire was too distracted to commission portraits of the new emperor and the gold seal of state that shows a thin hawk-like face is far too schematic to be meaningful. However there is consensus about his personality. Of all the sons of Manuel, Constantine was the most capable and trustworthy, 'a philanthropist and without malice', imbued with resoluteness, courage and a deep patriotism. Unlike his quarrelsome and unprincipled brothers, Constantine was straightforward; he seems to have inspired deep loyalty among those around him. He was by all accounts a man of action rather than a skilled administrator or a deep thinker, adept in horsemanship and the arts of war, courageous and enterprising. Above all, he was resolute in the face of setbacks. A strong sense of responsibility for the Byzantine inheritance ran through his character; he spent a lifetime trying to shore it up.

Constantine was twenty-seven years older than Mehmet; he was born in Constantinople in 1405 and from his early youth can have had few illusions about the city's plight. At seventeen he experienced Murat's siege of 1422; the following year he was appointed regent while his brother John VIII made one of the many fruitless trips around the states of Christendom to seek support for the Byzantine cause. At his accession in 1449, he was forty-four years old and had twenty years of fighting behind him. The majority of this time had been spent trying to regain full Byzantine control of the Peloponnese, with varying success. By 1430 he had cleared most of the small foreign kingdoms out of the peninsula and during the 1440s, as Despot of Morea, he pushed its boundaries forward into Northern Greece. To Murat he was a constant irritant; a rebellious vassal who needed to be cuffed back into line. Definitive retribution came in 1446 after the failed Crusade of Varna. An Ottoman army swept into the Morea devastating the countryside and enslaving 60,000 Greeks. Constantine was forced to conclude a humiliating truce, making vows of vassalage to the sultan and paying a heavy tribute. Failure had dogged the enterprise of rebuilding Byzantine fortunes in Greece, but his spirit, military skill and straightforwardness contrasted with the behaviour of his three brothers Demetrios, Thomas and Theodore – by turns self-seeking, treacherous, quarrelsome and indecisive, they contrived to hinder his attempts to prop up the remnants of empire. Their mother, Helena, had to insist on Constantine's claim to the throne: he alone could be entrusted with the inheritance.

Coin of Constantine

In subsequent Byzantine legend bad luck clung to Constantine like a curse – his well-meaning imperial venture in the Morea had been courageous but ill-starred. He had fought on alone after the catastrophe at Varna, when the Venetian fleet sailed home and the Genoese failed to send their promised aid, but this persistence had visited considerable suffering on the Greek people. His personal life was similarly unlucky. His first wife died childless in 1429; his second in 1442. During the late 1440s he made repeated attempts to forge a dynastic marriage that would shore up the fortunes of his crown and create the possibility of a natural successor. They all failed to come to fruition in the increasingly fraught political atmosphere on the eve of Mehmet's succession.

In February 1451 Mehmet settled into the royal palace at Edirne. His first act was startling and decisive. When he died, Murat had left behind an infant son by another wife – Little Ahmet. A few days later, while the mother was paying an official visit to the throne room to express her grief at his father's death, Mehmet dispatched a minion,

Ali Bey, to the women's quarters to drown Little Ahmet in the bath. The next day he executed Ali Bey for the crime, then married the distraught mother off to one of his nobles. It was an act of ruthless intelligence that carried the struggle for power in the Ottoman court to its logical conclusion: only one could rule, and to avoid the fractious possibilities of civil war, only one could survive – to the Ottomans this seemed preferable to the endless struggles that sapped the lifeblood of Byzantium. Instantly Mehmet had clarified the practice of Ottoman succession, which he was later to codify as a law of fratricide: 'whichever of my sons inherits the sultan's throne, it behooves him to kill his brother in the interest of the world order. Most of the jurists have approved this procedure. Let action be taken accordingly.' Henceforth execution was to stalk the succession as a dreadful certainty. It would reach its apogee with the sultanate of Mehmet III in 1595, when nineteen coffins containing the bodies of his brothers were carried out of the palace. Despite this, the fratricide law failed to prevent civil wars: with it came pre-emptive acts of rebellion by frightened sons, a consequence that would return to haunt Mehmet. In Constantinople the circumstances surrounding Little Ahmet's death should have provided a key to Mehmet's character: it appears they did not.

4 Cutting the Throat

FEBRUARY 1451–NOVEMBER 1452

The Bosphorus with one key opens and closes two worlds, two seas.
Pierre Gilles, sixteenth-century French scholar

Throughout the West news of Murat's death was greeted with relief. In Venice, Rome, Genoa and Paris they were all too ready to accept the opinion set out in a letter from the Italian Francesco Filelfo to King Charles of France a month later, that the young Mehmet was young, inexperienced and simple minded. They would probably have been less interested in his conclusion – that the time was ripe for a decisive military operation to drive the Ottomans, 'a mob of venal corrupt slaves', out of Europe for good. Any immediate appetite for crusading had been firmly scotched by the bloody debacle at Varna in 1444 and the potentates of Europe welcomed the prospect of the callow, and so far disastrous, Mehmet ascending the throne.

Those with a deeper knowledge of the Great Turk knew better. George Sphrantzes, Constantine's most trusted ambassador, was crossing the Black Sea on his way from the King of Georgia to the Emperor of Trebizond at the time of Murat's death. He was engaged in an interminable round of diplomacy, seeking a suitable match for the widowed Constantine with the aim of shoring up his beleaguered position, providing the possibility of an heir and filling his coffers with dowry. At Trebizond the Emperor John Komnenos greeted him jovially with word of Mehmet's accession: 'Come, Mr Ambassador, I have good news for

Rumeli Hisari

you and you must congratulate me.' Sphrantzes' reaction was startling: 'Overcome by grief, as if I had been told of the death of those dearest to me, I stood speechless. Finally, with considerable loss of spirit, I said: "Lord this news brings no joy; on the contrary, it is a cause for grief."' Sphrantzes went on to explain what he knew of Mehmet – that he was 'an enemy of the Christians since childhood' and keen to march against Constantinople. Moreover Constantine was so short of funds that he needed a period of peace and stability to repair the city's finances.

Back in Constantinople ambassadors were hastily dispatched to Edirne to present their respects to the young sultan and seek reassurance. They were pleasantly surprised by the reception. Mehmet exuded sweet reasonableness. He is said to have sworn by the Prophet, the Koran, 'and by the angels and archangels that he would devote himself to peace with the City and the Emperor Constantine for his whole life'. He even granted the Byzantines an annual sum from the tax revenues of some Greek towns in the lower Struma valley that legally belonged to Prince Orhan, the Ottoman pretender. The money was to go towards the upkeep of Orhan so long as he was detained in the city.

The stream of embassies that followed was similarly reassured. In September the Venetians, who had trading interests in Edirne, renewed their peace with Mehmet, while the Serbian despot, George Branković, was soothed by the return of his daughter Mara, who had been married to Murat, and the handing back of some towns. Mehmet, for his part, requested George's help in brokering a deal with the Hungarians, whose brilliant leader, the regent John Hunyadi, presented the most potent threat from Christian Europe. As Hunyadi needed to crush some domestic intrigues of his own, he was willing to agree a three-year truce. Emissaries from the Genoese at Galata, from the Lords of Chios, Lesbos and Rhodes, from Trebizond, Wallachia and Ragusa (Dubrovnik) were similarly able to secure guarantees of peace on reasonable terms. By the autumn of 1451 it was commonly accepted in the West that Mehmet was firmly under the thumb of his peaceable vizier, Halil Pasha, and would pose a threat to no one – and it seems too that many at Constantinople, less wary or less experienced than Sphrantzes, were similarly lulled. It suited kings and potentates across the Christian world to believe that all was well. Mehmet guarded his hand carefully.

Christians were not alone in misreading Mehmet's strength of character. In the autumn of 1451, the troublesome Bey of Karaman tried yet again to wrest back territory in western Anatolia from Ottoman control. He occupied fortresses, reinstated former chieftains and invaded Ottoman land. Mehmet sent his generals to put down the uprising and having concluded his peace treaties at Edirne, appeared on the scene himself. The effect was immediate. The revolt was quickly crushed and Mehmet turned for home. At Bursa he encountered a further test of strength – this time from his own Janissary corps. 'Standing with their arms in two rows on either side of the road, they shouted at him: "This was our sultan's first campaign, and he should reward us with the customary bonus."' On the spot he was forced to accede; ten sacks of coins were distributed among the mutineers, but for Mehmet it was a crucial test of wills that he was determined to win. A few days later he summoned their general, castigated and stripped him of his office; several of the officer corps were similarly punished. This was the second revolt Mehmet had experienced and he recognized the imperative to secure the full loyalty of the Janissary corps if the capture of Constantinople were to be successful. Accordingly the regiment was restructured; he added 7,000 men from his personal household troops and gave command to a new general.

It was at this moment that Constantine and his advisers advanced an initiative of their own that demonstrated how little they understood Mehmet. Prince Orhan, the only other claimant to the Ottoman throne, was lodged in Constantinople, his upkeep paid for out of the tax revenues agreed with the sultan in the summer. The Byzantines dispatched ambassadors to Halil at Bursa with a peremptory demand:

> the Emperor of the Romans does not accept the annual allowance of three hundred thousand aspers. For Orhan, who is equal to your leader as a descendant of Osman, has now come of age. Every day many flock to him. They call him lord and leader. He himself does not have the means to be generous to his followers, so he asks the Emperor, who because he lacks funds, cannot satisfy these requests. Therefore we ask one of two things: either double the allowance, or we will release Orhan.

The implication was clear enough – if the young sultan failed to pay, a rival claimant to the throne would be at large to foment civil war in the empire.

It was a classic ploy. Throughout its history, the exploitation of dynastic rivalry amongst adjacent states had been a cornerstone of Byzantine diplomacy. It had frequently offset periods of military weakness and earned Byzantium an unenviable and unequalled reputation for cunning. The Ottomans had had a prior taste of these tactics under Constantine's father, Manuel II, when the dynasty had almost collapsed in a civil war shrewdly promulgated by the emperor, an episode of which Mehmet was keenly aware. Constantine evidently saw Orhan as a golden card, perhaps the only card left, and decided to play it. Under the circumstances it was a serious blunder – and almost inexplicable, given the knowledge of seasoned diplomats such as Sphrantzes about the politics of the Ottoman court. It may simply have been dictated by the state of the imperial finances rather than any realistic expectation of stirring up insurrection but it confirmed for the war party at the Ottoman court all the reasons why Constantinople must be taken. It was a proposal almost calculated to destroy Halil's attempts at peacekeeping – and to endanger the vizier's own position. The old vizier exploded with anger:

> You stupid Greeks, I have had enough of your devious ways. The late sultan was a lenient and conscientious friend to you. The present sultan is not of the same mind. If Constantine eludes his bold and imperious grasp, it will be only because God continues to overlook your cunning and wicked schemes. You are fools to think that you can frighten us with your fantasies, and that when the ink on our recent treaty is barely dry. We are not children without strength or reason. If you think you can start something, do so. If you want to proclaim Orhan as sultan in Thrace, go ahead. If you want to bring the Hungarians across the Danube, let them come. If you want to recover the places which you lost long since, try this. But know this: you will make no headway in any of these things. All that you will achieve is to lose what little you still have.

Mehmet himself received the news with a poker face. He dismissed the ambassadors with 'affable sentiments' and promised to look into the matter when he returned to Edirne. Constantine had handed him an invaluable pretext for breaking his own word when the time was right.

On his way back to Edirne Mehmet discovered that it was impossible to cross to Gallipoli as he intended. The Dardanelles were blocked by Italian ships. Accordingly he made his way up the straits of the Bosphorus to the Ottoman fortress of Anadolu Hisari – 'the Anatolian castle' – built by his great grandfather Bayezit in 1395 at the time of his siege of the city. At this spot the distance that separates Asia from Europe shrinks to a mere 700 yards, and it affords the best point to cross the fast-flowing and treacherous waters, a fact known to the Persian king, Darius, who moved an army of 700,000 men across on a bridge of boats on his way to battle 2,000 years earlier. As Mehmet's small fleet of ships scuttled back and forth ferrying men across to Europe his fertile mind pondered the Bosphorus and he seems to have come to a number of conclusions. The straits represented an area of vulnerability for the Ottomans: it was impossible to be the secure lord of two continents if crossing between them could not be guaranteed; at the same time, if he could find a way to dominate the Bosphorus, Mehmet could strangle the supply of grain and help to the city from the Greek colonies on the Black Sea and cut off the customs revenues it derived from shipping. The idea came to him to construct a second fortress on the European side, on land belonging to the Byzantines, to secure control of the straits, so that the 'path of the vessels of the infidels may be blocked'. It was probably now that he also recognized the acute need for a larger fleet to counter Christian maritime superiority.

Once back at Edirne he took immediate action over the Byzantine ultimatum, confiscating the taxes from the towns on the Struma intended for Orhan's maintenance and expelling its Greek inhabitants. Perhaps Constantine could already feel pressure tightening on the city; he had dispatched an envoy to Italy in the summer of 1451 who went first to Venice to seek permission to recruit archers from the Venetian colony of Crete and then to Rome with a message to the Pope. More likely, Constantine was still hopeful that positive offensive action could be taken against the new sultan: there was no hint of emergency in the messages sent to the Italian states.

As the winter of 1451 approached Mehmet was in Edirne, restlessly making plans. Here he surrounded himself with a group of Westerners, particularly Italians, with whom he discussed the great heroes of classical antiquity, Alexander and Caesar, his role models for the future that he intended. Remembering the disturbance among the Janissaries at Bursa in the autumn, he carried out further reforms of the army and the administration. New governors were appointed to some provinces, the pay of the palace regiments increased and he began to stockpile armaments and supplies. It is likely that he also embarked on a shipbuilding programme. At the same time the idea of the castle was taking shape in his mind. He sent out proclamations to every province of the empire requisitioning the services of thousands of masons, labourers and limekiln workers the following spring. Arrangements were also made for the collection and transportation of building materials – 'stone and timber and iron and everything else that was useful' . . . 'for the construction of a castle at the Sacred

Mouth above the city' – near the site of the ruined church of St Michael.

The news of this decree swiftly reached Constantinople and the Greek colonies on the Black Sea and the islands of the Aegean. A mood of pessimism swept the people; old prophecies were recalled foretelling the end of the world: 'now you can see the portents of the imminent destruction of our nation. The days of the Antichrist have come. What will happen to us? What should we do?' Urgent prayers were offered up for deliverance in the city churches. At the end of 1451 Constantine dispatched another messenger to Venice with more urgent news: the sultan was preparing a massive build-up against the city and that unless help was sent it would surely fall. The Venetian Senate deliberated at its own speed and delivered their reply on 14 February 1452. It was characteristically cautious; they had no desire to compromise their commercial advantages within the Ottoman Empire. They suggested that the Byzantines should seek the co-operation of other states rather than relying on the Venetians alone, though they did authorize the dispatch of gunpowder and breastplates that Constantine had requested. Constantine meanwhile had no option but to make direct representations to Mehmet. His ambassadors trundled back over the hills of Thrace for another audience. They pointed out that Mehmet was breaking a treaty by threatening to build this new castle without consultation, that when his great grandfather had built the castle at Anadolu Hisari he had made this request of the emperor, 'as a son would beg his father'. Mehmet's response was short and to the point: 'What the city contains is its own; beyond the fosse it has no dominion, owns nothing. If I want to build a fortress at the sacred mouth, it can't forbid me.' He reminded the Greeks of the many Christian attempts to bar Ottoman passage over the straits and concluded in typically forthright style: 'Go away and tell your emperor this: "The sultan who now rules is not like his predecessors. What they couldn't achieve, he can do easily and at once; the things they did not wish to do, he certainly does. The next man to come here on a mission like this will be flayed alive."' It could hardly be clearer.

In mid-March Mehmet set out from Edirne to start the building work. He went first to Gallipoli; from there he dispatched six galleys with some smaller warships, 'well-prepared for a sea battle – in case that should be necessary', and sixteen transport barges to carry equipment. He then made his way to the chosen spot by land with the army. The whole operation was typical of his style. Mehmet's genius at logistical arrangements ensured that men and materials were mobilized on cue and in enormous quantities with the aim of completing the task in the shortest possible time. The governors of provinces in both Europe and Asia gathered their conscripted men and set out for the site. The vast army of workers – 'masons, carpenters, smiths, and lime burners, and also various other workmen needed for that, without any lack, with axes, shovels, hoes, picks, and with other iron tools' – arrived to start the work. Building materials were ferried across the straits in lumbering transport barges: lime and slaking ovens, stone from Anatolia, timber from the forests of the Black Sea and from Izmit, while his war galleys cruised the outer straits. Mehmet personally surveyed the site on horseback and in conjunction with his architects, who were both Christian converts, planned the details of the layout: 'the distance between the outer towers and the main turrets and the gates and everything else he worked out carefully in his head'. He had probably sketched outline plans for the castle over the winter in Edirne. He oversaw the staking out of the ground plan and laid the cornerstone. Rams were killed and their blood mixed with the chalk and mortar of the first layer of bricks for good luck. Mehmet was deeply superstitious and strongly influenced by astrology; there were those who claimed the curious shape of the castle to be cabbalistic; that it represented the interwoven Arabic initials of the Prophet – and of Mehmet himself. More likely the layout was dictated by the steep and difficult terrain of the Bosphorus shore, comprising 'twisting curves, densely wooded promontories, retreating bays and bends' and rising to a height of two hundred feet from the shore to the apex of the site.

The work started on Saturday 15 April and was carefully organized under a system of competitive piecework that relied on Mehmet's characteristic mixture of threats and rewards and involved the whole workforce, from the greatest vizier to the humblest hod carrier. The structure was four sided, with three great towers at its cardinal points linked by massive walls and a smaller fourth tower inserted into the south-west corner. The responsibility for building – and funding – the outer towers was given to four of his viziers, Halil, Zaganos, Shihabettin and Saruja. They were encouraged to compete in the speedy construction of their portion, which given the tense internal power struggles at court and the watchful eye of their imperious sultan who 'gave up all thoughts of relaxation' to oversee their work, was a powerful spur to performance. Mehmet himself undertook the building of the connecting walls and minor towers. The workforce of over 6,000, which comprised 2,000 masons and 4,000 masons' assistants as well as a full complement of other workmen, was carefully subdivided on military principles. Each mason was assigned two helpers, one to work each side of him, and was held responsible for the construction of a fixed quantity of wall per day. Discipline was overseen by a force of *kadis* (judges), gathered from across the empire, who had the power of capital punishment; enforcement and military protection was provided by a substantial army detachment. At the same time Mehmet 'publicly offered the very best rewards to those who could do the work quickly and well'. In this intense climate of competition and fear, according to Doukas even the nobility sometimes found it useful to encourage their workforce by personally carrying stones and lime for the perspiring masons. The scene resembled a cross between a small makeshift town and a large building site. Thousands of tents sprang up nearby at the ruined Greek village of Asomaton; boats manoeuvred their way back and forth across the choppy running currents of the strait; smoke billowed from the smouldering lime pits; hammers chinked in the warm air; voices called. The work went on round the clock, torches burning late into the night. The walls, encased in a lattice work of wooden scaffolding, rose at an astounding speed. Round the site spring unfolded along the Bosphorus: on the densely wooded slopes wisteria and judas trees put out their blossom; chestnut candles flowered like white stars; in the tranquil darkness, when moonlight rippled and ran across the glittering straits, nightingales sang in the pines.

Within the city they watched the preparations with growing apprehension. The Greeks had been stunned by the sudden appearance of a hitherto unknown Ottoman fleet in the straits. From the roof of St Sophia and the top of the Sphendone, the still surviving raised section at the southern end of the Hippodrome, they could glimpse the hive of activity six miles upstream. Constantine and his ministers were at a loss about how to respond but Mehmet went out of his way to tease a reaction. Early in the project Ottoman workmen began to pillage certain ruined monasteries and churches near the castle for building materials. The Greek villagers who lived nearby and the inhabitants of the city still held these places as sacred sites. At the same time Ottoman soldiers and builders started to raid their fields. As the summer wore on and the crops approached harvest, these twin aggravations turned into flashpoints. Workmen were removing columns from the ruined church of Michael the Archangel when some inhabitants of the city tried to stop them; they were captured and executed. If Mehmet was hoping to draw Constantine out to fight, he failed. The emperor may have been tempted to make a sortie, but was talked out of it. Instead he resolved to defuse the situation by offering to send food out to the building workers to prevent them robbing Greek crops. Mehmet responded by encouraging his men to let their animals loose in the fields to graze, while ordering the Greek farmers not to hinder them. Eventually the farmers, provoked beyond endurance by the sight of their crops being ravaged, chased the animals out and a skirmish ensued in which men were killed on both sides. Mehmet ordered his commander, Kara Bey, to punish the inhabitants of the offending village. The following day a detachment of cavalry surprised the farmers as they harvested their fields and put them all to the sword.

When Constantine heard of the massacre he closed the city gates and detained all the Ottoman subjects within. Among these were a number of Mehmet's young eunuchs who were on a visit to the city. On the third day of their captivity they petitioned Constantine for release declaring that their master would be angry with them for not returning. They begged either to be freed at once or executed, on the grounds that release later would still result in their death at the sultan's hand. Constantine relented and let the men go. He sent one more embassy to the sultan with a message of resignation and defiance:

> since you have preferred war to peace and I can call you back to peace neither with oaths or pleas, then follow your own will. I take refuge in God. If He has decreed and decided to hand over this city to you, who can contradict Him or prevent it? If He instills the idea of peace in your mind, I would gladly agree. For the moment, now that you have broken the treaties to which I am bound by oath, let these be dissolved. Henceforth I will keep the city gates closed. I will fight for the inhabitants with all my strength. You may continue in your power until the Righteous Judge passes sentence on each of us.

It was a clear declaration of Constantine's resolve. Mehmet simply executed the envoys and sent a curt reply: 'Either surrender the city or stand ready to do battle.' An Ottoman detachment was dispatched to ravage the area beyond the city walls and carry off flocks and captives, but Constantine had largely removed the population from the nearby villages into the city, together with the harvested crops. The Ottoman chroniclers record that he also sent bribes to Halil to pursue his quest for peace, but this seems more likely to be the propaganda of the vizier's enemies. From midsummer the gates of the city were to remain shut and the two sides were effectively at war.

On Thursday 31 August 1452 Mehmet's new fortress was complete, a bare four and half months after the first stone was laid. It was huge, 'not like a fortress', in the words of Kritovoulos, 'more like a small town' and it dominated the sea. The Ottomans called it *Bogaz Kesen*, the Cutter of the Straits or the Throat Cutter, though in time it would become known as the European castle, Rumeli Hisari. The triangular structure with its four large and thirteen small towers, its curtain walls twenty-two feet thick and fifty feet tall and its towers roofed with lead, represented an astonishing building feat for the time. Mehmet's ability to co-ordinate and complete extraordinary projects at breakneck speed was continually to dumbfound his opponents in the months ahead.

A recreation of Rumeli Hisari, the Throat Cutter

On 28 August Mehmet rode round the top of the Golden Horn with his army and camped outside the city walls, now firmly barred against him. For three days he scrutinized the defences and the terrain in forensic detail, making notes and sketches and analysing potential weaknesses in the fortifications. On 1 September, with autumn coming on, he rode off back to Edirne well satisfied with his summer's work, and the fleet sailed back to its base at Gallipoli. The Throat Cutter was garrisoned with 400 men under its commander Firuz Bey, who was ordered to detain all ships passing up and down the straits on payment of a toll. To add force to this menace, a number of cannon had been constructed and hauled to the site. Small ordnance was mounted on the battlements but a battery of large guns, 'like dragons with fiery throats', was installed on the seashore beneath the castle wall. The guns, which were angled in different directions to command a wide field of fire, were capable of sending huge stone balls weighing 600 pounds whistling low across the surface of the water level with the hulls of passing ships, like stones skimming across a pond. They were matched by other guns at the castle opposite, so that 'not even a bird could fly from the Mediterranean to the Black Sea'. Henceforth no ship could pass up or down to the Black Sea unexamined, either by day or night. 'In this manner', recorded the Ottoman chronicler Sa'd-ud-din, 'the Padishah, the asylum of the world, blockading that strait, closed the way of the vessels of the enemy, and cauterized the liver of the blind-hearted emperor.'

In the city Constantine was gathering his resources against a war that now looked inevitable, and dispatching messengers to the West with increasing urgency. He sent word to his brothers in the Morea, Thomas and Demetrios, asking them to come at once to the city. He made extravagant offers of land to any who would send help: to Hunyadi of Hungary he offered either Selymbria or Mesembria on the Black Sea, to Alfonso of Aragon and Naples the island of Lemnos. He made appeals to the Genoese on Chios, to Dubrovnik, Venice and yet again to the Pope. Practical help was hardly forthcoming but the powers of Christian Europe were reluctantly becoming aware that an ominous shadow was falling over Constantinople. A flurry of diplomatic notes was exchanged. Pope Nicholas had persuaded the Holy Roman Emperor, Frederick III, to send a stern but empty ultimatum to the sultan in March. Alfonso of Naples dispatched a flotilla of ten ships to the Aegean then withdrew them again. The Genoese were troubled by the threat to their colonies at Galata and on the Black Sea but were unable to provide practical help; instead they ordered the Podesta (mayor) of Galata to make the best arrangements he could with

Mehmet should the city fall. The Venetian Senate gave similarly equivocal instructions to its commanders in the eastern Mediterranean: they must protect Christians whilst not giving offence to the Turks. They knew that Mehmet threatened their Black Sea trade almost before the Throat Cutter was finished; soon their spies would be sending back detailed sketch maps of the threatening fortress and its guns. The issue was coming closer to home: a vote in the Senate in August to abandon Constantinople to its fate was easily defeated, but resulted in no more decisive counter-action.

Back in Edirne Mehmet had either predicted, or got wind of, Constantine's appeal to his brothers in the Morea – and moved rapidly to scotch it. On 1 October 1452 he ordered his elderly general Turahan Bey to march into the Peloponnese and attack Demetrios and Thomas. He ravaged the countryside, striking far into the south and making the release of forces back to Constantinople an impossibility. Meanwhile the supply of grain from the Black Sea was starting to dry up. A new embassy was sent to Venice in the autumn. The Senate's reply on 16 November was as vague as before, but the Venetians were shortly to have their attention drawn into sharp focus by events further east.

By November the masters of Italian ships plying the routes between the Black Sea and the Mediterranean found themselves in a quandary as to whether to submit to Mehmet's custom toll at the Throat Cutter or to ignore it and risk the consequences. The force of the current meant that ships travelling downstream had a fair chance of passing through the checkpoint before they could be blasted out of the water. On 26 November a Venetian captain, Antonio Rizzo, came down the Bosphorus from the Black Sea with a cargo of food for the city. Approaching the castle he decided to take the risk. Ignoring warning shouts from the bank to lower his sails, Rizzo pressed on. A volley of shots sped low across the water and one giant stone ball struck the lightweight hull of his galley, shattering it. The captain and thirty survivors were able to make it to the shore in a small boat where they were promptly captured, bound in chains and marched off to face the Sultan's displeasure in the town of Didimotkon near Edirne. While they languished in prison, the Venetian ambassador in Constantinople travelled hotfoot to the imperial court to beg for the sailors' lives. He arrived too late. Mehmet had determined to make an example of the Venetians. Most of the men he beheaded; Rizzo himself was impaled 'by a stake through his anus'. All the bodies were then left to rot outside the town walls as a warning against disobedience. 'I saw them a few days later, when I went there,' the Greek chronicler Doukas recalled. A few of the sailors were returned to Constantinople to ensure the news got back to the city. There was one other survivor: Mehmet took a fancy to the son of Rizzo's clerk and put the boy in the seraglio.

This savage demonstration had the desired effect. It drove the populace of Constantinople into instant panic. Meanwhile, despite Constantine's embassies, there was still no sign of concerted help from the West. Only the Pope could stand above Europe's factional mercantile interests, dynastic feuds and wars, and appeal for help in the name of Christendom, but the papacy itself was involved in an intractable and long-running dispute with the Orthodox Church that cast a shadow over all such dealings. It was about to severely blight Constantine's chances of organizing effective resistance.

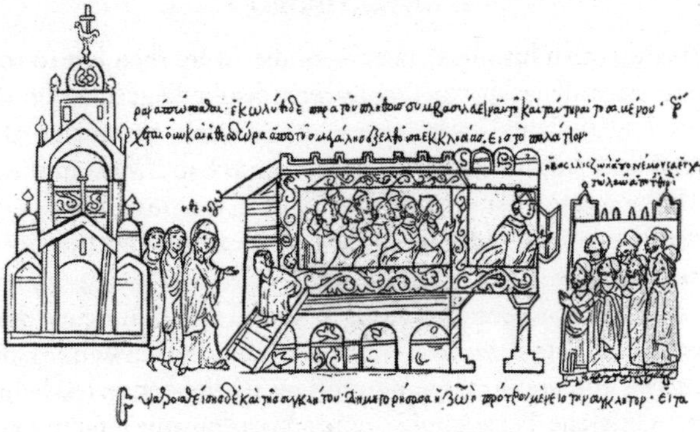

The church of St Sophia

5 The Dark Church

NOVEMBER 1452–FEBRUARY 1453

It is far better for a country to remain under the rule of Islam than be governed by Christians who refuse to acknowledge the rights of the Catholic Church.
Pope Gregory VII, 1073

Flee from the papists as you would from a snake and from the flames of a fire.
St Mark Eugenicus, fifteenth-century Greek Orthodox theologian

The principal source of Constantine's difficulties in mustering help from the West and organizing an effective defence of his city could be pinpointed to a dramatic incident one summer's day nearly 400 years earlier – though its causes were far older even than that.

On 16 July 1054, at about 3 o'clock in the afternoon, as the clergy were preparing for the afternoon liturgy in St Sophia, three prelates, dressed in full canonical robes, stepped into the church through one of the great west doors and walked purposefully towards the altar, watched by the gathering congregation. The men were cardinals of the Catholic Church sent from Rome by the Pope to settle theological disputes with their brothers in the East and led by one Humbert of Mourmoutiers. They had been in the city for some time, but this afternoon, after lengthy and awkward negotiations, they had lost patience and were coming to take decisive action. Humbert carried in his hands a document whose content was to prove explosive for Christian unity. Advancing into the sanctuary, he placed a bull of excommunication on the great altar, turned smartly on his heels and walked out. As the stiff-necked cardinal clopped back into the brilliant summer light he shook the dust from his feet and proclaimed: 'Let God look and judge.' One of the church deacons ran into the street after Humbert waving the bull and beseeching him to take it back. Humbert refused and walked off, leaving the document lying in the dust. Two days later the cardinals took ship back to Rome; violent religious rioting broke out in the streets that was only pacified by pronouncing anathema on the papal delegation; the offending document was publicly burned. This incident was the start of a process known to history as the Great Schism that was to inflict deep wounds on Christendom – the anathemas were not rescinded until 1965, but the scars still remain. And for Constantine in the winter of 1452 they were to pose an intractable problem.

In reality the events of that day were only the culmination of a lengthy process of separation between two forms of worship that had been gathering force for hundreds of years. It was based as much as anything on cultural, political and economic differences. In the East they worshipped in Greek, in the West in Latin; there were different forms of worship, different approaches to church organization and differing views on the role of the Pope. More generally the Byzantines had come to regard their western neighbours as uncouth barbarians; they probably had more in common with the Muslims on their frontier than the Franks across the sea. At the centre of their disagreement, however, were two key issues. The Orthodox were prepared to accept that the Pope had a special place among the patriarchs, but they bridled at the notion articulated by Pope Nicholas I in 865 that his office was endowed with authority 'over all the earth, that is, over every church'. This they perceived as autocratic arrogance.

The second issue was doctrinal. The bull of excommunication had accused the Eastern Church of omitting one word from the creed – a matter of supreme importance to the theologically preoccupied citizens of Byzantium. The apparently innocuous word, in Latin *filioque*, 'and from the Son', had immense significance. Whereas the original Nicene creed ran: 'I believe . . . in the Holy Spirit, the Lord, the Giver of Life, who proceeds from the Father, who with the Father and the Son together is worshipped and together glorified', the Church in the West had come to add the additional word '*filioque*' to make the text read 'who proceeds from the Father *and from the Son*'. In time the upshouldering Roman church even started to accuse the Orthodox of error for omitting the phrase. The Orthodox, in reply, claimed that the addition was theologically untrue; that the Holy Spirit proceeds only from the Father, and to add the name of the Son was heretical. Such issues were the stuff of riots within Constantinople.

With time the rift widened, despite efforts to patch it up. The sack of Constantinople in 1204 by 'Christian' crusaders, which Pope Innocent III himself declared to be 'an example of perdition and the works of darkness', added a wider cultural hatred of all things connected to the West; so did the mercantile power of the Italian city states that grew at Byzantium's expense as a direct result of the plunder. In 1340 Baalaam of Calabria suggested to Pope Benedict XII that it was not so much 'a difference of dogma that turns the hearts of the Greeks against you as the hatred of the Latins which has entered into their spirits, in consequence of the many and great evils which the Greeks have suffered from the Latins at various times, and are still suffering day by day'. It was true up to a point. But dogma was always central to the way ordinary people in the city lived their faith, and their tenacity to its tenets, in the face of attempts over the centuries by their own emperors to impose anything they considered contrary, had been a stubborn and persistent pattern in the mosaic of Byzantine history.

By the fifteenth century the relentless pressure of the Ottoman state was forcing successive emperors westward in a wearying round of pleas for help. When the Emperor John VIII toured Italy and Hungary in the 1420s the Catholic King of Hungary suggested that aid would be more readily forthcoming if the Orthodox united with the Church of Rome and swore loyalty to its Pope and creed. Union had become for the ruling families a potential tool of policy as much as a matter of faith: the threat of a united Christian crusade was used repeatedly to restrain Ottoman aggression against the city. (John's father Manuel had given typically Byzantine advice to his children on his deathbed: 'Whenever the Turks begin to be troublesome, send embassies to the West at once, offer to accept union, and protract negotiations to great length; the Turks so greatly fear such union that they will become reasonable; and still the union will not be accomplished because of the enmity of the Latin nations!') The advice had proved useful in the past but as the Ottomans grew stronger they tended to exactly the opposite course of action: the move towards union became increasingly a spur to armed intervention. For John VIII however, fear of Ottoman displeasure and the distrust of his people were being outweighed by the frequency with which the enemy was knocking on the gates of the city, and when Pope Eugenius IV proposed a council in Italy to accomplish union of the churches he set sail again in November 1437, leaving his brother Constantine as regent to mind the city.

The resulting Council of Florence was a protracted, bitter affair that was not concluded until June 1439. When it finally proclaimed that the union of the two churches had been achieved, church bells rang out across Europe all the way to England. Only one of the Orthodox delegates had refused to sign the document, which had been phrased in a wording designed to fudge some of the key issues: papal claims to supremacy were recognized along with the concept of the *filioque*, though the Orthodox were not actually required to insert it into their creed. But for the Greeks acceptance began to unravel almost before the ink was dry. Back in the city the Orthodox faithful greeted the returning delegation with hostility; many of those who signed immediately revoked their signatures. The Eastern patriarchs refused to accept the decision of their delegates; the next Patriarch of Constantinople, Gregory Mammas, who supported the union, was widely unpopular and it became impossible to celebrate the union in St Sophia. The issue split the city in two: Constantine and most of his immediate circle of nobles, officers and civil servants supported the union; only a fraction of the clergy and people did – they believed that union had been forced on them by the treacherous Franks and that their immortal souls had been imperilled for base and materialistic motives. The people were profoundly anti-papist: they were accustomed to equate the Pope with the Antichrist, 'the wolf, the destroyer'; 'Rum Papa' – the Roman Pope – was a popular choice of name for city dogs. The citizens formed a volatile proletariat: impoverished, superstitious, easily swayed to riot and disorder.

The sea of religious trouble that Constantine inherited with the title of Emperor was not untypical of the whole long history of Byzantium: Constantine the Great had been similarly vexed by doctrinal disputes eleven hundred years earlier. Constantine XI was a soldier rather than a theologian and his view of the union was strictly pragmatic. He was obsessed by only one thing – saving the city whose ancient past had been put in his care. If union presented the only chance of doing this, then so be it, but this did not endear him to his citizens. His constitutional position was also precarious: he had never been formally crowned in Mistra. The ceremony should have taken place in St

Sophia but there was a strong feeling that the coronation of a unionist emperor by a unionist patriarch would risk grave public disorder. It was quietly shelved. Many in the city refused to remember their new emperor in their prayers, and one of the chief doubters at the council, George Scholarios, took to a monastery under the monastic name of Gennadios and started to orchestrate resistance in the form of a synod of anti-unionist clergy. In 1451 the Patriarch Gregory tired of this unremitting hostility and departed for Rome, where he kept Pope Nicholas fully informed of the activities of the anti-unionists. No suitable candidate could be found to replace him. Constantinople henceforth had neither a fully legitimate emperor nor a patriarch.

As the threat of war with Mehmet grew, Constantine addressed a series of increasingly desperate pleas to the Pope; unwisely perhaps he also included a statement from the anti-unionists proposing a new synod. Gregory's briefings about the state of the union in Constantinople had hardened Nicholas's heart and he was in no mood for further prevarication from the backsliding Greeks. The response was frosty: 'If you, with your nobles and the people of Constantinople accept the decree of union, you will find Us and Our venerable brothers, the cardinals of the Holy Roman Church, ever eager to support your honour and your empire. But if you and your people refuse to accept the decree, you will force Us to take such measures as are necessary for your salvation and Our honour.' The threat only stiffened the resolve of the anti-unionists who continued to work to undermine Constantine's position in the city. In September 1452 one of their number wrote: 'Constantine Palaiologos . . . remains uncrowned because the church has no leader and is indeed in disarray as a result of the turmoil and confusion brought upon it by the falsely named union . . . This union was evil and displeasing to God and has instead split the church and scattered its children and destroyed us utterly. Truth to tell, this is the source of all our other misfortunes.'

Back in Rome Pope Nicholas resolved on steps to enforce the decisions taken in Florence. He decided to send a papal legate to Constantinople to ensure that the union was celebrated in St Sophia. The man he chose was Cardinal Isidore, formerly Bishop of Kiev. Isidore was a Byzantine who understood the delicacies of the problem at first hand. He had accepted union at Florence. On his return to Kiev his Orthodox flock had rejected and imprisoned him. He set out for Constantinople in May 1452 with a body of 200 archers, funded by the Pope, as a gesture of military support for his principally theological mission. On route he was joined by Leonard of Chios, the Genoese Archbishop of Lesbos, a man who was to be an engaged and partisan commentator on everything that ensued. Advance warning had reached the anti-unionists of their coming and whipped the city into deeper turmoil. Gennadios delivered a virulent public harangue against union that lasted from midday until evening. He begged the people to hold fast to their faith rather than hope for material assistance that would be of little value. However when Cardinal Isidore stepped ashore at Constantinople on 26 October 1452, the sight of his small body of archers made a favourable impression on the populace. This small troop of men might only be the advance guard of a substantial force: there was a visible shift in favour of union. For a while opinion see-sawed back and forth in the volatile city. The anti-unionists were held to be unpatriotic, but when no further ships arrived, the people again swung back to Gennadios and there were outbreaks of anti-unionist rioting. Leonard demanded in shrill tones that Constantine should imprison the ringleaders. He complained bitterly that 'apart from . . . a certain few monks and laymen, pride had possessed nearly all the Greeks, so that there was no one who, moved by zeal for the true Faith or for his own salvation, would be seen to be the first to be contemptuous of his obstinate opinions'. Constantine refused to act on this advice; he feared the city might descend into chaos. Instead he called the anti-unionist synod to the palace to explain their objections.

Ten days later, the sound of gunfire at the Throat Cutter could be heard in the city. As the fate of Rizzo and his crew became known, a new spasm of fear gripped the population. Support returned to the unionists once more. Gennadios issued another blast against the waverers: that help from the West would lead to the loss of their faith, that its value would be doubtful and that he at least would have nothing to do with it. Gennadios had deeper worries than the loss of the city: he sincerely believed that the end of the world was nigh. He was concerned that the Orthodox should face the apocalypse with spotless souls. There was further disorder in the streets. Monks, nuns and lay people ranged about shouting: 'We don't want Latin help or Latin union; let us be rid of the worship of the unleavened.' Despite Gennadios, it seems that a begrudging decision was taken by the frightened populace to accept the Council of Florence, at least temporarily. (With true sophistry, the Byzantines had a time-honoured let-out clause for such an action: the Doctrine of Economy, which permitted the temporary acceptance of an unorthodox theological position to ensure survival – it was an approach to spiritual matters that had repeatedly infuriated the Catholic Church.) Cardinal Isidore for his part judged that the moment was ripe to enforce the act of union – and to save the imperilled souls of the Greeks.

In this supercharged atmosphere of fear and religious hysteria, a liturgy to celebrate the union was performed on 12 December 1452 in the dead days of winter. It took place in St Sophia 'with the greatest solemnity on the part of the clergy, and also the reverend cardinal of Russia was there, who was sent by the Pope, and also the most serene Emperor with all his lords and the whole population of Constantinople'. The decrees of the union were read out and the Pope was commemorated in the prayers, along with the absent patriarch Gregory, but the details of the service were alien to many of the watching Greeks: the language and ritual of the service were Catholic rather than Orthodox, the consecrated Host consisted of unleavened bread, a heresy to the Orthodox, and cold water was poured into the cup and mixed with the wine. Isidore wrote to the Pope announcing the success of his mission:

> the whole of the city of Constantinople was united with the Catholic church; your Holiness was remembered in the liturgy, and the most reverend patriarch Gregory, who during his stay in Constantinople was not remembered in any church, not even his own monastery, after the union was remembered in the whole city. They were all from the least to the greatest, together with the emperor, thanks be to God, united and catholic.

Only Gennadios and eight other monks had refused to participate, according to Isidore. It was probably wishful thinking. One Italian eyewitness recorded that the day was marked by great lamentations in the city. There was evidently no rioting during the service. More likely the Orthodox faithful participated through clenched teeth, then marched off to the monastery of the Pantocrator to consult Gennadios, who had become de facto the spiritual father of Orthodoxy and the patriarch in waiting. He however had retreated to his cell in silence and would not come out.

Henceforth the Orthodox shunned St Sophia as 'nothing better than a Jewish synagogue or a heathen temple'; they worshipped only in the securely Orthodox churches of the city. Without patriarch or congregation, the great church fell dark and silent. The continuous round of prayer died away, and the thousands of oil lamps that illuminated its dome, 'like the whole heaven, scattered with glittering stars', sputtered and went out. The sparsely attended services of the unionists huddled before the sanctuary. Birds fluttered mournfully round the nave. The Orthodox felt that the fulminations of Gennadios had proved justified: no mighty fleet sailed up the Marmara in defence of Christendom. From now on the split between unionist and Orthodox, between Greek and Latin was deeper than ever and it was reflected, henceforward, in all the Christian accounts of the siege. Schism was to cast a long shadow over Constantine's attempts to defend the city.

On 1 November 1452, shortly before he retreated into self-imposed isolation, Gennadios had posted a manifesto on the monastery door of the Pantocrator. It read like the blast of prophecy, full of apocalyptic doom and self-justification:

> Wretched Romans, how you have been led astray! You have departed from hope, which rests in God, by trusting in the power of the Franks. As well as the City itself, which will soon be destroyed, you have lost the true religion. O Lord, be merciful to me. I give witness in Your presence that I am pure and innocent from blame in this matter. Be aware, miserable citizens, what you are doing today. With slavery, which is hanging over your heads, you have denied the true faith handed down to you by your forefathers. You have confessed your impiety. Woe to you when you are judged!

A hundred and fifty miles away in Edirne Mehmet followed these developments with more than passing interest. Fear of Christian unity had always been one of the guiding principles of Ottoman foreign policy; to Halil Pasha it justified the continuation of a peace policy: any attempt on the city might finally unite Christendom and turn Constantinople into the cause of a new crusade. However to Mehmet the intelligence from the city seemed promising. It encouraged him to be bold.

The sultan spent the short winter days and long nights brooding over his dreams of conquest. He was obsessed but uncertain. He tried on the trappings of imperial power in his new palace at Edirne, continuing to reform his household troops and tampering with the silver content of the currency to pay for it all. Mehmet gathered about him a group of Italian advisers, from whom he gleaned intelligence about the events in the West and military technology. He spent his days poring over illustrated treatises on fortifications and siege warfare. He was restless, febrile, irresolute. He consulted astrologers and turned over in his mind a method for unlocking the city's defences, struggling with the conservative wisdom of the old viziers who declared that it could not be done. At the same time he studied Ottoman history and the accounts of previous sieges of the city, forensically examining the causes for their failure. Unable to sleep, his nights were spent drawing sketches of the fortifications that he had scrutinized in the summer and designing strategies for storming them.

The chronicler Doukas has left a vivid account of these dark obsessive days. The picture he paints of the secretive, mistrustful sultan, eaten up by ambition, has a ring of truth about it, though probably intensified for his Christian audience. According to Doukas, Mehmet took to wandering about the streets at dusk disguised as a common soldier, listening to the gossip about him in the markets and caravanserais. If anyone were unwise enough to recognize and hail their sultan with the customary acclamation, Mehmet would stab the man to death. It was the kind of story, repeated with endless variants, that fully satisfied the Western image of the bloodthirsty tyrant. One night, towards the small hours, he sent his palace guards to fetch Halil, whom he perhaps saw as the main hindrance to his plans. The old vizier trembled at the summons; to be called to appear before 'God's shadow on earth' at such an hour did not bode well. He embraced his wife and children as if for the last time, and followed the soldiers, carrying a golden salver loaded with coins. Doukas suggests that his fear was justified: that he had taken many bribes from the Greeks to dissuade Mehmet from war, though the truth of this remains forever unclear – Halil had been rich enough in his own right to lend money to the old sultan, Mehmet's father. When Halil reached the royal bedchamber, he found Mehmet up and dressed. The old man prostrated himself on the ground and proffered the dish. 'What is this?' Mehmet asked. 'Lord,' Halil replied, 'it is customary when a noble is summoned before his master at an unusual hour not to appear empty handed.' 'I do not need gifts,' Mehmet said, 'just give me the City.' Thoroughly frightened, as he was intended to be, at the strangeness of the summons and the feverish demeanour of the sultan, Halil gave his wholehearted support to the project. Mehmet concluded: 'by placing our trust in the assent of God and in the prayer of the Prophet, we will take the city', and dismissed the chastened vizier back into the night.

Whatever the exact truth of this episode, some time around January 1453 Mehmet called his ministers together and made the case for war in a speech recorded by the Greek chronicler Kritovoulos. It set the matter of Constantinople within the whole story of the rise of the Ottomans. Mehmet clearly understood the damage that the city had inflicted on the fledgling state during the ruinous civil war fifty years earlier, how it 'has not stopped marching against us, constantly arming our people against each other, promoting disorder and civil war and damaging our realm'. He feared its potential to furnish a cause for endless war with Christian powers in the future. Captured, it would provide the centrepiece of the empire, 'without it, or while it is as at present, nothing we have is safe, and we can hope for nothing additional'. Constantine's recent initiative to exploit Orhan must have been clearly in the mind of his listeners. He also attempted to overturn a deep-seated belief in the Islamic mindset dating all the way back to the Arab sieges: that the city was simply not conquerable. He was well informed on recent events in the city; he knew that as he spoke the inhabitants 'are fighting as enemies over their differing religious beliefs, and their internal organisation is full of sedition and disturbance on this very account', and that, unlike in the past, the Christians no longer controlled the sea lanes. There was also an appeal to the *gazi* tradition – like their forefathers, it was the duty of Muslims to wage holy war. Mehmet was particularly keen to emphasize the need for speed; all available resources must be concentrated to deliver a knock-out blow: 'We must spare nothing for the war, neither human resources nor money nor weapons nor anything else, nor must we consider anything else as important until we take or destroy it.' It was the rallying cry for a massive strike and it seemed to have carried the day. Preparations for war started to gather pace.

Winters on the Bosphorus can be surprisingly severe, as the Arabs had discovered during the siege of 717. The site of the city, jutting out into the straits, leaves it exposed to fierce squalls hurtling down from the Black Sea on the north wind. A particularly dank and sub-zero cold penetrates to the marrow of the bones; weeks of cheerless rain can churn the streets into mud and prompt flash floods down the steep lanes; sudden snowstorms arise as if from nowhere to obliterate the Asian shore half a mile away then vanish as quickly as they have come; there are long still days of muffling fog when an eerie silence seems to hold the city in an iron grasp, choking the clappers in church bells and deadening the sound of hooves in the public squares, as if the horses were shod in boots of felt. The winter of 1452–53 seems to have afflicted the citizens with particularly desolate and unstable weather. People observed 'unusual and strange earthquakes and shakings of the earth, and from the heavens thunder and lightning and awful thunderbolts and flashing in the sky, mighty winds, floods, pelting rain and torrential downpours'. It did not improve the overall mood. No flotillas of Christian ships came to fulfil the promises of union. The city gates remained firmly closed and the supply of food from the Black Sea dried up under the sultan's throttle. The common people spent their days listening to the words of their Orthodox priests, drinking unwatered wine in the taverns and praying to the icon of the Virgin to protect the city, as it had in the Arab sieges. A hysterical concern for the purity of their souls seized the people, doubtless influenced by the fulminations of Gennadios. It was considered sinful to have attended a liturgy celebrated by a unionist or to have received communion from a priest who was present at the service of union, even if he were simply a bystander to the rites. Constantine was jeered as he rode in the streets.

Seal depicting the protecting Virgin

Despite this unpromising atmosphere, the emperor made what plans he could for the city's defence. He dispatched envoys to buy food from the Aegean islands and beyond: 'wheat, wine, olive oil, dried figs, chick peas, barley and other pulses'. Work was put in hand to repair neglected sections of the defences – both the land and sea walls. There was a shortage of good stone and no possibility of obtaining more from quarries outside the city. Materials were scrounged from ruined buildings and abandoned churches; even old tombstones were pressed into service. The ditch was cleared out in front of the land wall and it appears that despite their reservations, Constantine was successful in persuading the populace to participate in this work. Money was raised by public collection from individuals and from the churches and monasteries to pay for food and arms. All the available weapons in the city – of which there were far too few – were called in and redistributed. Armed garrisons were dispatched to the few fortified strongholds still held by Byzantium beyond its own walls: at Selymbria and Epibatos on the north shore of the Marmara, Therapia on the Bosphorus beyond the Throat Cutter, and to the largest of the Princes' Islands. In a final gesture of impotent defiance, Constantine sent galleys to raid Ottoman coastal villages on the Sea of Marmara. Captives were taken and sold in the city as slaves. 'And from this the Turks were roused to great anger against the Greeks, and swore that they would bring misfortune on them.'

The only other bright spot for Constantine during this period was the arrival of a straggle of Italian ships that he was able to persuade – or forcibly detain – to take part in the city's defence. On 2 December a large Venetian transport galley from Kaffa on the Black Sea, under the command of one Giacomo Coco, managed to trick its way past the guns at the Throat Cutter by pretending that it had already paid its customs dues further upstream. As it approached the castle the men on board began to salute the Ottoman gunners 'as friends, greeting them and sounding the trumpets and making cheerful sounds. And by the third salute that our men made, they had got away from the castle, and the water took them on towards Constantinople.' At the same time news of the true state of affairs had reached the Venetians and Genoese from their representatives in the city and the Republics stirred themselves into tardy activity. After the sinking of Rizzo's ship, the Venetian Senate ordered its Vice-captain of the Gulf, Gabriel Trevisano, to Constantinople to accompany its merchant convoys back from the Black Sea. Among the Venetians who came at this time was one Nicolo Barbaro, a ship's doctor, who was to write the most lucid diary of the months ahead.

Within the Venetian colony in the city, concern was growing. The Venetian bailey, Minotto, an enterprising and resolute man, was desperate to keep three great merchant galleys and Trevisano's two light

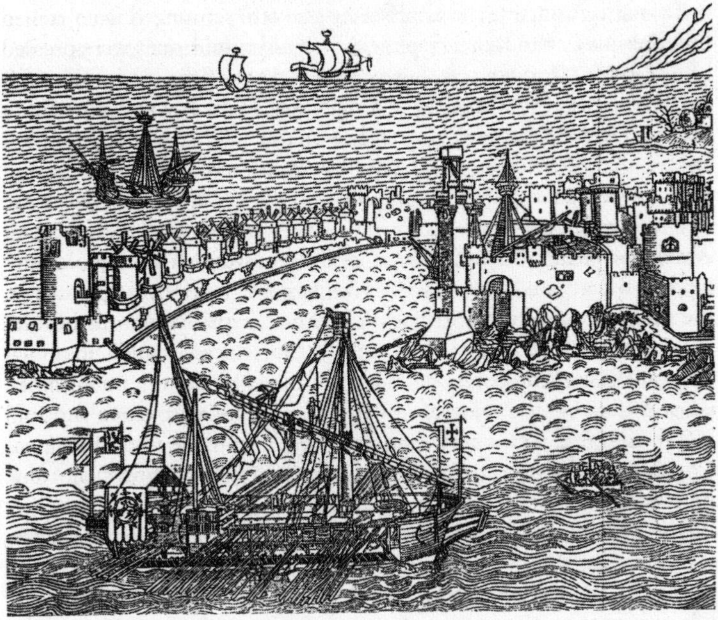

A Venetian great galley, the bulk carriers of the Mediterranean

galleys for the defence of the city. At a meeting with the emperor, Trevisano and the other captains on 14 December he begged them to stay 'firstly for the love of God, then for the honour of Christianity and the honour of our Signoria of Venice'. After lengthy negotiations the ships' masters, to their credit, agreed to remain, though not without considerable wrangling over whether they could have their cargo on board or should keep it in the city as surety of their good faith. Constantine was suspicious that once the cargo was loaded, the masters would depart; it was only after swearing to the emperor personally that they were allowed to load their bales of silk, copper, wax and other stuffs. Constantine's fears were not unfounded: on the night of 26 February one of the Venetian ships and six from the city of Candia on Crete slipped their anchors and fled before a stiff north-easterly wind. 'With these ships there escaped many persons of substance, about 700 in all, and these ships got safely away to Tenedos, without being captured by the Turkish armada.'

This dispiriting event was offset by one other positive contribution. The appeals of the Genoese podesta at Galata had elicited a concrete offer of help. On about 26 January two large galleons arrived loaded 'with many excellent devices and machines for war, and outstanding soldiers, who were both brave and confident'. The spectacle of these ships entering the imperial harbour with 'four hundred men in full armour' on deck made an immediate impression on both the populace and the emperor. Their leader was a professional soldier connected to one of the great families of the republic, Giovanni Giustiniani Longo, a highly experienced commander who had prepared this expedition at his own initiative and cost. He brought 700 well-armed men in all, 400 recruited from Genoa, another 300 from Rhodes and the Genoese island of Chios, the power base of the Giustiniani family. Constantine was quick to realize the value of this man and offered him the island of Lemnos if the Ottoman menace should be repulsed. Giustiniani was to play a fateful role in the defence of the city in the weeks ahead. A straggle of other soldiers came. Three Genoese brothers, Antonio, Paolo and Troilo Bocchiardo brought a small band of men. The Catalans supplied a contingent and a Castilian nobleman, Don Francisco of Toledo, answered the call. Otherwise the appeal to Christendom had brought nothing but disharmony. A sense of betrayal ran through the city. 'We had received as much aid from Rome as had been sent to us by the sultan of Cairo,' George Sphrantzes recalled bitterly.

6 The Wall and the Gun

JANUARY–FEBRUARY 1453

From the flaming and flashing of certain igneous mixtures and the terror inspired by their noise, wonderful consequences ensue which no-one can guard against or endure . . . when a quantity of this powder, no bigger than a man's finger, be wrapped up in a piece of parchment and ignited, it explodes with a blinding flash and a stunning noise. If a larger quantity were used, or the case were made of some more solid material, the explosion would be much more violent and the flash and noise altogether unbearable.

Roger Bacon, thirteenth-century English monk, on the effects of gunpowder

With the arrival of the Genoese contingent the preparations for a siege were carried forward with greater urgency. Giustiniani, who was 'an expert in the art of wall fighting', appraised the city's defences with a cool eye and took appropriate measures. Under his direction, during February and March they 'dredged the fosse and repaired and built up the walls, restoring the battlements, refortifying inner and outer towers and strengthening the whole wall – both the landward and seaward sectors'.

Despite their dilapidated condition, the city still possessed formidable fortifications. Among all the many explanations for the longevity of Byzantium, the impregnable defences of its capital city remain a cardinal factor. No city in the world owed as much to its site as Constantinople. Of the twelve miles of its perimeter, eight were ringed by sea. On the south side, the city was fringed by the Sea of Marmara, whose swift currents and unexpected storms made any sea-borne landing a risky undertaking. In a thousand years no aggressor ever seriously

Inscription on the walls: 'The Tower of St Nicholas was restored from the foundations, under Romanus, the Christ-loving Sovereign' attempted an attack at this point. The seashore was guarded by a single unbroken wall at least fifty feet above the shoreline interspersed with a chain of 188 towers and a number of small defended harbours. The threat to this wall came not from ships but from the ceaseless action of the waves undermining its foundations. At times nature was more brutal still: in the bitter winter of 764 the sea walls were crushed by ice floes that rode up over the parapets. The whole length of the Marmara wall was studded with marble inscriptions commemorating the repairs of successive emperors. The sea ran strongly round this shoreline as far as the tip of the Acropolis point, before turning north into the calmer waters of the Golden Horn. The Horn itself provided an excellent sheltered anchorage for the imperial fleet; 110 towers commanded a single wall along this stretch with numerous water gates and two substantial harbours, but the defences were always considered vulnerable. It was here that the Venetians had driven their ships up on the foreshore during the Fourth Crusade, overtopping the ramparts and storming the city. In order to block the mouth of the Horn in times of war, the defenders had been in the habit, since the Arab siege of 717, of drawing a boom across the entrance of the Horn. This took the form of a 300-yard chain, consisting of massive cast-iron links each twenty inches long that were supported on sturdy wooden floats. With the good will of the Genoese, the chain could then be secured to a tower on the sea wall of Galata on the far side. During the winter months both chain and floats were prepared against the possibility of a naval attack.

The base of the triangle of the city's site on the westward side was protected by the four-mile land wall, the so-called wall of Theodosius, which ran across the grain of the land from the Sea of Marmara to the Golden Horn and sealed off Constantinople from any conventional land-borne assault. Many of the most significant events in the history of the city had been played out along this extraordinary structure. It almost matched the city itself in longevity, and projected a sense of legendary immutability within the Mediterranean world. For many approaching Constantinople across the flat Thracian plains as a trader or pilgrim, an ambassador from a Balkan court or a plundering army with pretensions to conquest, the first sight of Constantinople at its apogee would be the ominous prospect of the land walls riding the gentle undulations of the landscape from horizon to horizon in a regular unbroken succession of ramparts and towers. In the sunlight the limestone walls create a facade of brilliant white, banded with

The walls in cross-section showing the three defensive layers:
inner and outer walls and moat

horizontal running seams of ruby red Roman brick, and arrow slits similarly arched; the towers – square, hexagonal, octagonal, occasionally circular – are so close together that, as one crusader put it, 'a seven-year-old boy could toss an apple from one turret to the next'. They rise up in successive tiers to the summit of the inner wall where the eagle banners of the emperor flutter proudly in the wind. At intervals the eye can pick out the darkness of a heavily guarded entrance to the city through which men and animals vanish in times of peace, and at the western end, close to the Sea of Marmara, a gateway panelled with flat plates of gold and decorated with statues of marble and bronze shines in the sun. This is the Golden Gate, the great ceremonial archway flanked by two massive towers of polished marble through which, in the heyday of Byzantium, emperors returned in triumph with the visible tokens of their victories: conquered kings walking in chains, recaptured sacred relics, elephants, outlandishly dressed barbarian slaves, carts piled high with booty and the whole might of the imperial army. By 1453 the gold and many of the decorations had gone but the structure was still an impressive monument to Roman glory.

The man responsible for the land wall, built to define the mature limits of the city, was not the boy Emperor Theodosius after whom it is named, but a leading statesman of the early fifth century, Anthemius, 'one of the wisest men of the age', for whose far-sightedness the city would owe a limitless debt of gratitude. The first line of the walls built in 413 deterred Attila the Hun, 'the scourge of God', from making an attack on the city in 447. When it collapsed under a severe earthquake the same year with Attila ravaging Thrace not far away, the whole population responded to the crisis. Sixteen thousand citizens totally rebuilt the wall in an astonishing two months, not just restoring Athemius's original structure, but adding an outer wall with a further string of interspaced towers, a protecting breastwork and a brick-lined moat – the fosse – to create a formidable barrier of extraordinary complexity. The city was now protected on this side by a chain of 192 towers in a defensive system that comprised five separate zones, 200 feet wide and 100 feet high from the bed of the moat to the top of the tower. The achievement was recorded with a suitably boastful inscription: 'In less than two months, Constantine triumphantly set up these strong walls. Scarcely could Pallas have built so quickly so strong a citadel.'

In its mature form, the Theodosian wall summarized all the accumulated wisdom of Graeco-Roman military engineering about defending a city before the age of gunpowder. The heart of the system remained the inner wall constructed by Anthemius: a core of concrete faced on both sides by limestone blocks quarried nearby, with brick courses inserted to bind the structure more firmly. Its fighting ramparts were protected by battlements and reached by flights of steps. In line with Roman practice, the towers were not bound to the walls, ensuring that the two structures could each settle at their own rate without breaking apart. The towers themselves rose to a height of sixty feet and consisted of two chambers with a flat roof on which engines to hurl rocks and Greek fire could be placed. Here the sentinels scanned the horizon unceasingly, keeping themselves awake at night by calling out to each other down the line. The inner wall was forty feet high; the outer one was lower, about twenty-seven feet high, and had correspondingly lower towers that interspaced those on the inner wall. The two walls were separated by a terrace sixty feet wide, where the troops defending the outer wall massed, ready to engage the enemy at close quarters. Below the outer wall another terrace sixty feet wide provided a clear killing field for any aggressor who made it over the moat. The brick-lined moat itself was another sixty-feet-wide obstacle, surmounted by a wall on the inner side; it remains unclear whether it was in parts flooded in 1453 or simply comprised a dry ditch. The depth and complexity of the system, the stoutness of its walls and the height from which it commanded its field of fire rendered the Theodosian wall virtually impregnable to an army equipped with the conventional resources of siege warfare in the Middle Ages.

Along its length the land wall was pierced by a succession of gates. Some gave access to the surrounding countryside via bridges over the moat, which would be destroyed in the run-up to a siege; others, the military gates, allowed connection between the different layers of the walls and were used to move troops about within the system. The wall also contained a number of posterns – small subsidiary doorways – but the Byzantines were always aware of the danger these sally ports posed for the security of their city and managed them rigorously. In general the two sets of gates alternated along the length of the wall, with the military gates being referred to by number while the public gates were named. There was the Gate of the Spring, named after a holy spring outside the city, the Gate of the Wooden Circus, the Gate of the Military Boot Makers, the Gate of the Silver Lake. Some spawned multiple names as associations were forgotten and new ones created. The Third Military Gate was also referred to as the Gate of the Reds, after a circus faction in the early city, while the Gate of Charisius, a leader of the blue faction, was also called the Cemetery Gate. And into the structure were built some remarkable monuments that expressed the contradictions of Byzantium. Towards the Golden Horn the imperial palace of Blachernae nestled behind the wall, a building said once to be of such beauty that foreign visitors could find no words to describe it; adjoining it, the dank and dismal prison of Anemas, a dungeon of sinister reputation, scene of some of the most ghastly moments in Byzantine history. Here John V blinded both his son and his three-year-old grandson, and from here one of Byzantium's most notorious emperors, Andronikos the Terrible, already horribly mutilated, was led out on a mangy camel amongst taunting crowds to the Hippodrome, where he was strung upside down between two columns and mockingly slaughtered.

The continuous life of the wall was so long that a deep accretion of history, myth and half-forgotten association attached to the various sectors. There was hardly a place that had not witnessed some dramatic moment in the city's history – scenes of terrible treachery, miraculous deliverance and death. Through the Golden Gate Heraclius brought the True Cross in 628; the Gate of the Spring saw the stoning of the unpopular Emperor Nicephorus Phocas by an enraged mob in 967 and the restoration of the Orthodox emperors after Latin rule in 1261 when the gate was opened from within by sympathizers. The dying Emperor Theodosius II was carried through the Fifth Military Gate in 450 following a fall from his horse in the valley outside, while the Gate of the Wooden Circus was blocked up in the twelfth century after a prophecy that the Emperor Frederick Barbarossa would use it to capture the city.

Next to St Sophia itself no structure expressed the psychic life of the city's people as powerfully as the walls. If the church was their vision of heaven, the wall was their shield against the battering of hostile forces, under the personal protection of the Virgin herself. During sieges the constant prayers and the procession of her sacred relics along the ramparts were considered by the faithful to be generally more crucial than mere military preparations. A powerful spiritual force-field surrounded such actions. Her robe, housed at the nearby church at Blachernae, was accorded more credit for seeing off the Avars in 626 and the Russians in 860 than military engineering. People saw visions of guardian angels on the ramparts and emperors inserted marble crosses and prayers into the outward facing walls. Near the centre point of the wall there is a simple talisman that expresses Constantinople's deepest fear. It says: 'O Christ God, preserve your city undisturbed and free from war. Conquer the fury of the enemies.'

At the same time, the practical maintenance of the walls was the one essential public work for the city, in which every citizen was required to help, without exemption. Whatever the state of the Byzantine economy money was always found to patch up the wall. It was sufficiently important to have its own special officials under the overall authority of the impressively named 'Count of the Walls'. As time and earthquakes shattered towers and crumbled masonry, running repairs were marked by a wealth of commemorative marble inscriptions set into the stonework. They span the centuries from the first reconstruction in 447 to a total renovation of the outer wall in 1433. One of the last dated repairs before the siege expresses the co-operation of divine and human agencies in the maintenance of the city's shield. It reads: 'This God-protected gate of the life-giving spring was restored with the co-operation and at the expense of Manuel Bryennius Leontari, in the reign of the most pious sovereigns John and Maria Palaeologi in the month of May 1438.'

Perhaps no defensive structure summarizes the truth of siege warfare in the ancient and medieval world as clearly as the walls of Constantinople. The city lived under siege for almost all its life; its defences reflected the deepest character and history of the place, its mixture of confidence and fatalism, divine inspiration and practical skill, longevity and conservatism. Like the city itself, the walls were always there, and for anyone in the eastern Mediterranean, it was assumed they always would be. The structure of the defences was mature in the fifth century and changed little thereafter; the building techniques were conservative, harking back to practices of the Greeks and Romans. They had no particular reason to evolve because siege warfare itself remained static. The basic techniques and equipment – blockade, mining and escalade, the use of battering rams, catapults, towers, tunnels and ladders – these were largely unchanging for longer than anyone could recall. The advantage always lay with the defender; in the case of Constantinople its coastal position increased that weighting. None of the armies camped before the land walls had ever succeeded in effecting an entry through the multiple defensive layers, while the city always took prudent measures as a matter of state policy to keep its cisterns brimming and its granaries full. The Avars came with an impressive array of stone-throwing machinery but their looping trajectory made them far too puny to breach the walls. The Arabs froze to death in the cold. The Bulgar Khan Krum tried magic – he performed human sacrifices and sprinkled his troops with seawater. Even its enemies came to believe that Constantinople was under divine protection. Only the Byzantines themselves were ever successful in taking their own city from the land, and always by treachery: the messy final centuries of civil war produced a handful of instances where gates were flung open at night, usually with inside help.

There were just two places where the land wall could be considered potentially weak. In the central section the ground sloped down a long valley to the Lycus River and then up the other side. As the wall followed the downward slope, its towers no longer commanded the high ground and were effectively below the level occupied by a besieging army on the hill beyond. Furthermore the river itself, which was ducted into the city through a culvert, made it impossible to dig a deep moat at this point. Nearly all besieging armies had identified this area as vulnerable, and though none had succeeded, it provided attackers with a vestige of hope. A second anomaly in the defences existed at the northern end. The regular procession of the triple wall was suddenly interrupted as it approached the Golden Horn. The line took an abrupt right-angle turn outwards to include an extra bulge of land; for 400 yards, until it reached the water, the wall became a patchwork structure of different-shaped bastions and sectors, which, though stoutly built on a rocky outcrop, was largely only one line deep and for much of its length unmoated. This was a later addition undertaken to include the sacred shrine of the Virgin at Blachernae. Originally the church had been outside the walls. With a typical Byzantine logic it had been held initially that the protection of the Virgin was sufficient to safeguard the church. After the Avars nearly burned it in 626 – the shrine was saved by the Virgin herself – the line of the wall was altered to include the church, and the palace of Blachernae was also built in this small bight of land. Both these perceived weak spots had been keenly appraised by Mehmet when he reconnoitred in the summer of 1452. The right-angle turn where the two walls joined was to receive particular attention.

As they patched up their walls under Giustiniani's direction and paraded the sacred icons on the ramparts, the people of the city could be pardoned for expressing confidence in their protective powers. Immutable, forbidding and indestructible, they had proved time and again that a small force could keep a huge army at bay until its willpower collapsed under the logistical burden of siege, or dysentery or the disaffection of the men. If the walls were decayed in places, they were still basically sound. Brocquière found even the vulnerable right angle to be protected by 'a good and high wall' when he came in the 1430s. The defenders however were unaware that they were preparing for conflict on the cusp of a technological revolution that would profoundly change the rules of siege warfare.

No one knows exactly when the Ottomans acquired guns. Gunpowder weapons probably made their way into the empire through the Balkans some time around 1400. By medieval standards this was a technology travelling at lightning speed – the first written mention of a gun does not occur until 1313, the first pictorial representation dates from 1326 – but by the end of the fourteenth century, cannon were being widely manufactured across Europe. Small-scale workshops for the production of iron and bronze guns mushroomed in France, Germany and Italy and secondary industries developed around them. Saltpetre 'factories' sprang up; middlemen imported copper and tin; technical mercenaries sold their skills in metal casting to the highest bidder. In practical terms the benefits of early gunpowder weapons were dubious: field artillery present at the battle of Agincourt beside the longbow made little material difference. The weapons themselves were cumbersome, tedious to prepare, impossible to aim with any accuracy and as dangerous to their crews as to the enemy. However, cannon fire undoubtedly had a psychological effect. King Edward III at Creçy 'struck terror into the French Army with five or six pieces of cannon, it being the first time they had seen such thundering machines' and the giant Dutch gun of Philip van Artevelde in 1382 'made such a noise in the going as though all the devils of hell had been in the way'. Metaphors of the inferno are common to these early accounts. There was something infernal about the thunderous roar of 'the devilish instrument of war': it upturned the natural order of things and stripped the chivalry out of combat. The church placed a ban on the use of fiery compositions for military purposes as early as 1137 and anathematized the crossbow for good measure, but it made little difference. The genie had exploded out of the bottle.

With the exception of sieges, the contribution of artillery to the conduct of warfare was still minimal by 1420, the moment when the Ottomans started to show a serious interest. Pushing into the Balkans, they captured the resources and the craftsmen to begin manufacturing guns of their own. These included foundries and skilled foundry men, copper mines, cutters of stone balls, makers of saltpetre and gunpowder factories. The Ottomans learned fast. They were hugely receptive to new techniques and adept at integrating skilled Christians into their armies and training their own soldiers too. Murat, Mehmet's father, created the infrastructure for an artillery force, forming a gunnery corps and corps of gun-carriage drivers in the palace army. At the same time, despite a papal edict that outlawed gunrunning to the infidel, Venetian and Genoese merchants shipped weapons across the eastern Mediterranean, and technical mercenaries, keen to sell their skills to the rising sultanate, made their way to the Ottoman court.

Constantinople experienced its first taste of this new capability in the summer of 1422 when Murat laid siege to the city. The Greeks record that he brought huge 'bombards' to the walls under the direction of

Germans – and that they were largely ineffective: seventy balls struck one tower without inflicting significant damage. When Murat brought guns to another wall twenty-four years later, the story was completely different. In the 1440s Constantine was attempting to protect one of the city's few remaining provinces, the Peloponnese, from Ottoman incursions and rebuilt a six-mile wall, the Hexamilion, across the Isthmus of Corinth from sea to sea to fence it off. It was a substantial piece of military engineering thought capable of withstanding prolonged assault. Early in December 1446 Murat attacked the wall with long cannon and breached it in five days. Constantine barely escaped with his life.

In between the two events the Ottomans had deepened their knowledge of artillery, and they had done so at a critical moment in the evolution of cannon construction and explosives. Some time in the 1420s a development took place throughout Europe in the manufacture of gunpowder that substantially increased its potency and stability. Up till then it had been the practice to carry the constituent ingredients – sulphur, saltpetre and charcoal – in different barrels and to mix them on site. The resulting powder was slow burning, susceptible to damp and had a tendency to separate out. In the early fifteenth century experimentation revealed that mixing the ingredients into a paste and drying it into preformed cakes that could be broken down into granules as required produced better results. The so-called 'corned' powder was faster burning, 30 per cent more powerful and more resistant to atmospheric moisture. A heavy shot could now be projected at a city wall with impressive momentum. By then giant siege guns, up to sixteen feet long and capable of hurling balls well over 750 pounds, had also begun to appear. Dulle Griete, the Great Bombard of Ghent, roared with a noise 'made by the furies of Hell' and shattered the walls of

Packing a cannon with gunpowder

Bourges in 1412. At the same time the new powder increased the danger to gunners and affected cannon founding: barrels were built stronger and longer, and there was a move to guns made in one piece, which had to be cast of bronze – and at a huge price differential. A bronze cannon cost three times as much as a forged iron one, but the exponential benefits evidently justified the expense. For the first time since trumpets flattened the walls of Jericho, a significant advantage was handed back to the side besieging a stoutly fortified castle. Fifteenth-century Europe rang to the roar of great siege guns, the shattering of stone balls against stone walls and the sudden collapse of hitherto impregnable bastions.

The Ottomans were uniquely placed to take advantage of these developments. The expanding empire was self-sufficient in copper and naturally occurring saltpetre; it acquired the expertise by conquest or purchase and then set up the structures to disseminate it amongst its own army corps. It quickly became proficient in manufacturing, transporting and firing its artillery – and was second to none in the deep logistical requirements of gunpowder warfare. To put an effective cannon battery in the field at a given moment made exceptional demands on medieval supply chains: adequate quantities of stone balls matched in calibre to the barrels and serviceable gunpowder had to coincide with the arrival of the slow-moving guns. The Ottomans sourced men and materials from across the empire – cannon balls from the Black Sea, saltpetre from Belgrade, sulphur from Van, copper from Kastamonu, tin from overseas trade, scrap bronze from the church bells of the Balkans – and distributed them through an overland transport network by cart and camel that was unmatched in its efficiency. Deep planning was a hallmark of the Ottoman military machine and it transferred these talents naturally to the special requirements of the gunpowder age.

So rapid was the Ottoman assimilation of cannon technology that by the 1440s they had evidently acquired the unique ability, widely commented on by eyewitnesses, to cast medium-sized barrels on the battlefield in makeshift foundries. Murat transported gunmetal to the Hexamilion and cast many of his long guns on the spot. This allowed extraordinary flexibility during siege warfare: rather than hauling the finished weapon to the siege, it could be transported more quickly in bits and could be broken up again afterwards if need be. Guns that ruptured in use, as they frequently did, could be repaired and pressed back into service, and in an age when the match between gun calibre and available cannon balls could be uncertain, barrels could be tailor-made to the ammunition available. (This facility reached its logical conclusion during the epic siege of the Venetian city of Candia on Crete in the seventeenth century. After twenty-one years of fighting, the Ottomans had collected 30,000 Venetian cannon balls unusable in their own guns. They cast three new barrels matched to the enemy calibres and fired them back.)

For the Ottomans, the siege gun seemed to answer something particularly deep in the tribal soul: it fed their rooted opposition to defended settlements. The descendants of the steppe nomads had proved their continuous superiority in open battle; it was only when confronted with the city walls of sedentary peoples that military matters became intractable. Artillery offered the possibility of a quick solution to the dangers of long-drawn-out sieges. It immediately attracted Mehmet's scientific interest as he considered the impregnable walls of the city. Early in his reign he began to experiment with casting large guns.

The Byzantines were also aware of the potential of gunpowder weapons. Within the city they had some medium-sized cannon and handguns, for which Constantine made strenuous attempts to stockpile resources. He was successful in obtaining supplies of gunpowder from the Venetians but the empire was too poor to invest heavily in expensive new weapons. Some time, probably earlier than 1452, there arrived in the city a Hungarian cannon founder called Orban, seeking his fortune at the imperial court. He was one of the growing band of technical mercenaries who plied their trade across the Balkans; he offered the Byzantines his skill in casting large, single-piece bronze guns. The cash-strapped emperor was interested in the man but had few resources to use his skill; he authorized a tiny stipend to detain Orban in the city, but even this was not paid regularly. The luckless master craftsman became increasingly destitute; some time during 1452 he left the city and made his way to Edirne to seek an audience with Mehmet. The sultan welcomed the Hungarian, provided him with food and clothes, and questioned him closely. The ensuing interview was vividly recreated by the Greek chronicler, Doukas. Mehmet asked if he could cast a cannon suitable to project a stone large enough to smash the city walls, and gestured the size of the stone he had in mind. Orban's reply was emphatic: 'If you want, I can cast a cannon of bronze with the capacity of the stone you want. I have examined the walls of the city in great detail. I can shatter to dust not only these walls with the stones from my gun but the very walls of Babylon itself. The work required to make the gun, I can fully carry out, but', he added, keen to limit his guarantee, 'I don't know how to fire it and I cannot guarantee to do so.' Mehmet ordered him to cast the cannon, and declared that he would see to its firing afterwards.

Whatever the details of the actual interview it seems that Orban set to work to create his first great gun some time during the building of the Throat Cutter in the summer of 1452. At about this time, Mehmet must have started to stockpile substantial quantities of materials for guns and gunpowder: copper and tin, saltpetre, sulphur and charcoal. He also seems to have sent out the order for masons to produce granite balls in quarries on the Black Sea. Within three months Orban had cast his first great gun, which was lugged to the Throat Cutter to guard the Bosphorus. It was this weapon that shattered Rizzo's galley in November 1452 and first sent news of Ottoman artillery power rippling through the city. Satisfied with the results, Mehmet now ordered Orban to produce a truly monstrous cannon, double its size – the archetype of a supergun.

The Ottomans were probably already casting guns at Edirne by this time; what Orban brought was the skill to construct the moulds and control the critical variables on a far greater scale. During the winter of 1452, he set to on the task of casting what was probably the largest cannon ever built. This painstaking and extraordinary process was described in detail by the Greek chronicler, Kritovoulos. Initially, a barrel-shaped mould some twenty-seven feet long was constructed of clay mixed with finely chopped linen and hemp. The mould was of two widths: the front compartment for the stone ball had a diameter of thirty inches, with a smaller after-chamber to take the powder. An enormous casting pit had to be excavated and the fired clay core was placed in it with the muzzle face down. An outer cylindrical clay casing 'like a scabbard' was fashioned to fit over this and held in position, leaving space between the two clay moulds to receive the molten metal. The whole thing was packed about tightly with 'iron and timbers, earth and stones, built up from outside' to support the huge weight of the bronze. At the last moment wet sand would be drizzled around the mould and the whole thing covered over again, leaving just a hole through which the molten metal could be poured. Meanwhile Orban constructed two brick-lined furnaces faced with fired clay inside and out and reinforced with large stones – sufficient to withstand a temperature of 1,000 degrees centigrade – and surrounded on the outside by a mountain of charcoal 'so deep that it hid the furnaces, apart from their mouths'.

The operation of a medieval foundry was fraught with danger. A visit by the later Ottoman traveller, Evliya Chelebi, to a gun factory catches the note of fear and risk surrounding the process:

On the day when cannon are to be cast, the masters, foremen and founders, together with the Grand Master of the Artillery, the Chief Overseer, Imam, Muezzin and timekeeper, all assemble and to the cries of 'Allah! Allah!', the wood is thrown into the furnaces. After these have been heated for twenty-four hours, the founders and stokers strip naked, wearing nothing but their slippers, an odd kind of cap which leaves nothing but their eyes visible, and thick sleeves to protect the arms; for, after the fire has been alight in the furnaces twenty-four hours, no person can approach on account of the heat, save he be attired in the above manner. Whoever wishes to see a good picture of the fires of Hell should witness this sight.

When the furnace was judged to have reached the correct temperature the foundry workers started to throw copper into the crucible along with scrap bronze probably salvaged, by a bitter irony for Christians, from church bells. The work was incredibly dangerous – the difficulty of hurling the metal piece by piece into the bubbling cauldron and of skimming dross off the surface with metal ladles, the noxious fumes given off by the tin alloys, the risk that if the scrap metal were wet, the water would vaporize, rupturing the furnace and wiping out all close by – these hazards hedged the operation about with superstitious dread. According to Evliya, when the time came to throw in the tin:

the Vezirs, the Mufti and Sheikhs are summoned; only forty persons, besides the personnel of the foundry, are admitted all told. The rest of the attendants are shut out, because the metal, when in fusion, will not suffer to be looked at by evil eyes. The masters then desire the Vezirs and sheikhs who are seated on sofas at a great distance to repeat unceasingly the words 'There is no power and strength save in Allah!' Thereupon the master-workmen with wooden shovels throw several hundredweight of tin into the sea of molten brass, and the head-founder says to the Grand Vizier, Vezirs and Sheikhs: 'Throw some gold and silver coins into the brazen sea as alms, in the name of the True Faith!' Poles as long as the yard of ships are used for mixing the gold and silver with the metal and are replaced as fast as consumed.

For three days and nights the lit charcoal was superheated by the action of bellows continuously operated by teams of foundry workers until the keen eye of the master founder judged the metal to be the right tone of molten red. It was another critical moment, the culmination

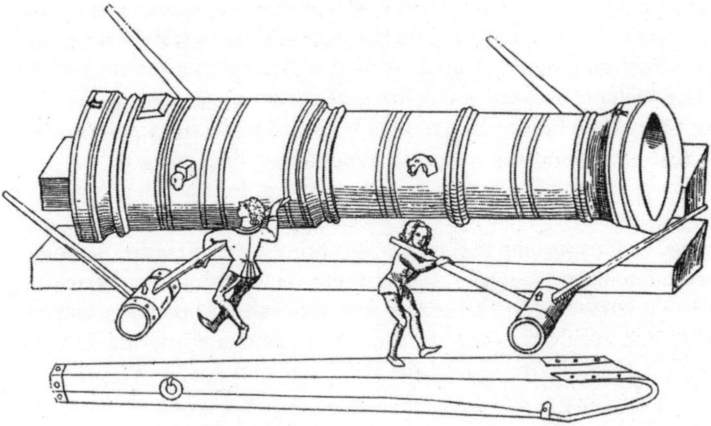

Fifteenth-century cast cannon

of weeks of work, involving fine judgement: 'The time limit having expired . . . the head-founder and master-workmen, attired in their clumsy felt dresses, open the mouth of the furnace with iron hooks exclaiming "Allah! Allah!" The metal, as it begins to flow, casts a glare on the men's faces at a hundred paces' distance.' The molten metal flowed down the clay channel like a slow river of red-hot lava and into the mouth of the gun mould. Sweating workers prodded the viscous mass with immensely long wooden poles to tease out air bubbles that might otherwise rupture the gunmetal under fire. 'The bronze flowed out through the channel into the mould until it was completely full and the mould totally covered, and it overflowed it by a cubit above. And in this way the cannon was finished.' The wet sand packed round the mould would hopefully slow the rate of cooling and prevent the bronze cracking in the process. Once the metal was cold, the barrel was laboriously excavated from the ground like an immense grub in its cocoon of clay and hauled out by teams of oxen. It was a powerful alchemy.

What finally emerged from Orban's foundry after the moulds had been knocked out and the metal scraped and polished was 'a horrifying and extraordinary monster'. The primitive tube shone dully in the winter light. It was twenty-seven feet long. The barrel itself, walled with eight inches of solid bronze to take the force of the blast, had a diameter of thirty inches, big enough for a man to enter on his hands and knees and designed to accommodate a monstrous stone shot eight feet in circumference weighing something over half a ton. In January 1453 Mehmet ordered a test firing of the great gun outside his new royal palace at Edirne. The mighty bombard was hauled into position near the gate and the city was warned that the following day 'the explosion and roar would be like thunder, lest anyone should be struck dumb by the unexpected shock or pregnant women might miscarry'. In the morning the cannon was primed with powder. A team of workmen lugged a giant stone ball into the mouth of the barrel and rolled it back down to sit snugly in front of the gunpowder chamber. A lighted taper was put to the touch hole. With a shattering roar and a cloud of smoke that hazed the sky, the mighty bullet was propelled across the open countryside for a mile before burying itself six feet down in the soft earth. The explosion could be heard ten miles off: 'so powerful is this gunpowder', recorded Doukas, who probably witnessed this test firing personally. Mehmet himself ensured that ominous reports of the gun filtered back to Constantinople: it was to be a psychological weapon as well as a practical one. Back in Edirne Orban's foundry continued to turn out more guns of different sizes; none were quite as large as the first supergun, but a number measured more than fourteen feet.

During early February, consideration turned to the great practical difficulties of transporting Orban's gun the 140 miles from Edirne to Constantinople. A large detachment of men and animals was detailed for the task. Laboriously the immense tube was loaded onto a number of wagons chained together and yoked to a team of sixty oxen. Two hundred men were deployed to support the barrel as it creaked and lurched over the rolling Thracian countryside while another team of carpenters and labourers worked ahead, levelling the track and building wooden bridges over rivers and gullies. The great gun rumbled towards the city walls at a speed of two and a half miles a day.

7 Numerous as the Stars
MARCH–APRIL 1453

When it marched, the air seemed like a forest because of its lances and when it stopped, the earth could not be seen for tents.
Mehmet's chronicler, Tursun Bey, on the Ottoman army

Mehmet needed both artillery and numerical superiority to fulfil his plans. By bringing sudden and overwhelming force to bear on Constantinople, he intended to deliver a knockout blow before Christendom had time to respond. The Ottomans always knew that speed was the key to storming fortresses. It was a principle clearly understood by foreign observers such as Michael the Janissary, a prisoner of war who fought for the Ottomans at this time: 'The Turkish Emperor storms and captures cities and also fortresses at great expense in order not to remain there long with the army.' Success depended on the ability to mobilize men and equipment quickly and on an impressive scale.

Accordingly, Mehmet issued the traditional call to arms at the start of the year. By ancient tribal ritual, the sultan set up his horsetail banner in the palace courtyard to announce the campaign. This triggered the dispatch of 'heralds to all the provinces, ordering everyone to come for the campaign against the City'. The command structure of the two Ottoman armies – the European and the Anatolian – ensured a prompt response. An elaborate set of contractual obligations and levies enlisted men from across the empire. The provincial cavalry, the *sipahis*, who provided the bulk of the troops, were bound by their ties as land-

Ottoman tents and guns

holders from the sultan to come, each man with his own helmet, chain mail and horse armour, together with the number of retainers relative to the size of his holding. Alongside these, a seasonal Muslim infantry force, the *azaps*, were levied 'from among craftsmen and peasants' and paid for by the citizens on a pro-rata basis. These troops were the cannon fodder of the campaign: 'When it comes to an engagement,' one cynical Italian commented, 'they are sent ahead like pigs, without any mercy, and they die in great numbers.' Mehmet also requisitioned Christian auxiliaries from the Balkans, largely Slavs and Vlachs, obligated under the laws of vassalage, and he prepared his elite professional household regiments: the infantry – the famous Janissaries – the cavalry regiments and all the other attendant corps of gunners, armourers, bodyguards and military police. These crack troops, paid regularly every three months and armed at the sultan's expense, were all Christians largely from the Balkans, taken as children and converted to Islam. They owed their total loyalty to the sultan. Although few in number – probably no more than 5,000 infantry – they comprised the durable core of the Ottoman army.

Horsetail banner: symbol of Ottoman authority

The mobilization for the season's campaign was extraordinarily efficient. Within the Muslim heartlands it was not a press gang. Men came at the call to arms with a willingness that amazed European eyewitnesses such as George of Hungary, another prisoner in the empire at this time:

> When recruiting for the army is begun, they gather with such readiness and speed you might think they are invited to a wedding not a war. They gather within a month in the order they are summoned, the infantrymen separately from the cavalrymen, all of them with their appointed chiefs, in the same order which they use for encampments and when preparing for battle . . . with such enthusiasm that men put themselves forward in the place of their neighbours, and those left at home feel an injustice has been done to them. They claim they will be happier if they die on the battlefield among the spears and arrows of the enemy than at home . . . Those who die in war like this are not mourned but are hailed as saints and victors, to be set as an example and given high respect.

'Everyone who heard that the attack was to be against the City came running', added Doukas, 'both boys too young to march and old men bent double with age.' They were fired by the prospect of booty and personal advancement and holy war, themes that were woven together in the Koran: by Islamic holy law, a city taken by force could be legitimately subjected to three days of plunder. Enthusiasm was made all the keener by knowledge of the objective: the Red Apple of Constantinople was popularly, but perhaps mistakenly, held to possess fabulous hoards of gold and gems. Many came who had not been summoned: volunteers and freelance raiders, hangers-on, dervishes and holy men inspired by the old prophecies who stirred the populace with words of the Prophet and the glories of martyrdom. Anatolia was on fire with excitement and remembered that 'the promise of the Prophet foretold that that vast city . . . would become the abode of the people of the Faith'. Men flocked from the four corners of Anatolia – 'from Tokat, Sivas, Kemach, Erzurum, Ganga, Bayburt and Trabzon' – to the collecting points at Bursa; in Europe they came to Edirne. A huge force was gathering: 'cavalry and foot soldiers, heavy infantry and archers and slingers and lancers'. At the same time, the Ottoman logistical machine swung into action, collecting, repairing and manufacturing armour, siege equipment, cannons, tents, ships, tools, weapons and food. Camel trains criss-crossed the long plateau. Ships were patched up at Gallipoli. Troops were ferried across the Bosphorus at the Throat Cutter. Intelligence was gathered from Venetian spies. No army in the world could match the Ottomans in the organization of a military campaign.

In February, troops of the European army under its leader, Karaja Bey, started to clear the hinterland of the city. Constantinople still had some fortified outposts on the Black Sea, the north shore of the Marmara and the Bosphorus. Greeks from the surrounding countryside retreated into the strongholds. Each was systematically encircled. Those that surrendered were allowed to go unharmed; others, such as those at a tower near Epibatos on the Marmara, resisted. It was stormed and the garrison slaughtered. Some could not be quickly taken; they were bypassed but kept under guard. News of these events filtered back to Constantinople and intensified the woe of the population, now riven by religious feuding. The city itself was already under careful observation by three regiments from Anatolia lest Constantine should sally out and disrupt preparations. Meanwhile the sapper corps was at work strengthening bridges and levelling roads for the convoys of guns and heavy equipment that started to roll across the Thracian landscape in February. By March a detachment of ships from Gallipoli sailed up past the city and proceeded to ferry the bulk of the Anatolian forces into Europe. A great force was starting to converge.

Finally on 23 March Mehmet set out from Edirne in great pomp 'with all his army, cavalry and infantry, travelling across the landscape, devastating and disturbing everything, creating fear and agony and the utmost horror wherever he went'. It was a Friday, the most holy day of the Muslim week, and carefully chosen to emphasize the sacred dimension of the campaign. He was accompanied by a notable religious presence: 'the ulema, the sheikhs and the descendants of the Prophet . . . repeating prayers . . . moved forward with the army, and rode by the rein of the Sultan'. The cavalcade also probably included a state functionary called Tursun Bey, who was to write a rare first-hand Ottoman account of the siege. At the start of April, this formidable force converged on the city. The first of April was Easter Sunday, the most holy day in the Orthodox calendar, and it was celebrated throughout the city with a mixture of piety and apprehension. At midnight candlelight and incense proclaimed the mystery of the risen Christ in the city's churches. The haunting and simple line of the Easter litany rose and fell over the dark city in mysterious quarter-tones. Bells were rung. Only St Sophia itself remained silent and unvisited by the Orthodox population. In the preceding weeks people had 'begged God not to let the City be attacked during Holy Week' and sought spiritual strength from their icons. The most revered of these, the Hodegetria, the miracle-working image of the Mother of God, was carried to the imperial palace at Blachernae for Easter week according to custom and tradition.

The next day Ottoman outriders were sighted beyond the walls. Constantine dispatched a sortie to confront them and in the ensuing skirmish some of the raiders were killed. As the day wore on however, ever increasing numbers of Ottoman troops appeared over the horizon and Constantine took the decision to withdraw his men into the city. All the bridges over the fosse were systematically destroyed and the gates closed. The city was sealed against whatever was to come. The sultan's army began to form up in a sequence of well-rehearsed manoeuvres that combined caution with deep planning. On 2 April, the main force came to a halt five miles out. It was organized into constituent units and each

A Janissary

regiment was assigned its position. Over the next few days it moved forward in a series of staged advances that reminded watchers of the remorseless advance of 'a river that transforms itself into a huge sea' – a recurrent image in the chroniclers' accounts of the incredible power and ceaseless motion of the army.

The preparatory work progressed with great speed. Sappers began cutting down the orchards and vineyards outside the walls to create a clean field of fire for the guns. A ditch was dug the length of the land wall and 250 yards from it, with an earth rampart in front as a protection for the guns. Latticework wooden screens were placed on top as a further shield. Behind this protective line, Mehmet moved the main army into its final position about a quarter of a mile from the land walls: 'According to custom, the day that camp was to be made near Istanbul the army was ordered by regiment into rows. He ranged at the centre of the army around his person the white-capped Janissary archers, the Turkish and European crossbowmen, and the musketeers and cannonneers. The red-capped *azaps* were placed on his right and left, joined at the rear by the cavalry. Thus organised, the army marched in formation on Istanbul.' Each regiment had its allotted place: the Anatolian troops on the right, in the position of honour, under their Turkish commander Ishak Pasha, assisted by Mahmut Pasha, another Christian renegade; the Christian, Balkan troops on the left under Karaja Pasha. A further large detachment under the Greek convert Zaganos Pasha were sent to build a roadway over the marshy ground at the top of the Horn and to cover the hills down to the Bosphorus, watching the activities of the Genoese settlement at Galata in the process. On the evening of 6 April, another Friday, Mehmet arrived to take up his carefully chosen position on the prominent hillock of Maltepe at the centre of his troops and opposite the portion of the walls that he considered to be the most vulnerable to attack. It was from here that his father Murat had conducted the siege of 1422.

Before the appalled gaze of the defenders on the wall, a tented city sprang up in the plain. According to one writer 'his army seemed as numberless as grains of sand, spread . . . across the land from shore to shore'. Everything in an Ottoman campaign was conducted with a sense of order and hushed purpose that was all the more threatening for its quietness. 'There is no prince', conceded the Byzantine chronicler Chalcocondylas, 'who has his armies and camps in better order, both in abundance of victuals and in the beautiful order they use in encamping without any confusion or embarrassment.' Conical tents were ranged in ordered clusters, each unit with its officer's tent at its centre and a distinctive banner flying from its principal pole. In the heart of the encampment, Mehmet's richly embroidered red and gold pavilion had been erected with due ritual. The tent of the sultan was the visual symbol of his majesty – the image of his power and an echo of the khanate origins of the sultans as nomadic leaders. Each sultan had a ceremonial tent made at his accession; it expressed his particular kingship. Mehmet's was sited beyond the outer reach of crossbow fire, and was by custom protected by a palisade, ditch and shields and surrounded in carefully formed concentric circles 'as the halo encircles the moon' by the protecting corps of his most loyal troops: 'the best of the infantry, archers and support troops and the rest of his personal corps, which were the finest in the army'. Their injunction, on which the safety of the empire depended, was to guard the sultan like the apple of their eye.

The encampment was carefully organized. Standards and ensigns fluttered from the sea of tents: the *ak sancak*, the supreme white and gold banner of the sultan, the red banner of his household cavalry, the banners of the Janissary infantry – green and red, red and gold – the structural emblems of power and order in a medieval army. Elsewhere the watchers on the walls could make out the brightly coloured tents of the viziers and leading commanders, and the signifying hats and clothes of the different corps: the Janissaries in the distinctive white headdresses of the Bektashi order, the *azaps* in red turbans, cavalrymen in pointed turban helmets and chain-mail coats, Slavs in Balkan costumes. Watching Europeans commented on the array of men and equipment. 'A quarter of them', declared the Florentine merchant Giacomo Tetaldi, 'were equipped with mail coats or leather tunics, of the others many were armed in the French manner, others in the Hungarian and others still had iron helmets, Turkish bows and crossbows. The rest of the soldiers were without equipment apart from the fact that they had shields and scimitars – a type of Turkish sword.' What further astonished the watchers on the walls were the vast numbers of animals. 'Whilst conceding that these are found in greater numbers than men in military encampments, to carry supplies and food,' noted Chalcocondylas, 'only these people . . . not only take enough camels and mules with them to meet their needs, but also use them as a source of enjoyment, each one of them being eager to show the finest mules or horses or camels.'

The defenders could only survey this purposeful sea of activity with trepidation. As sunset approached the call to prayer would rise in a sinuous thread of sound above the tents from dozens of points as the muezzins called the men to prayer. Camp fires would be lit for the one meal of the day – for the Ottoman army campaigned frugally – and smoke drifted in the wind. A bare 250 yards from their citadel, they could catch the purposeful sounds of camp activity: the low murmuring of voices, the hammering of mallets, the sharpening of swords, the snorting and braying of horses, mules and camels. And far worse, they could probably make out the fainter sound of Christian worship from the European wing of the army. For an empire intent on holy war, the Ottomans ruled their vassals with remarkable tolerance: 'although they were subjects of the Sultan, he had not compelled them to resign their Christian faith, and they could worship and pray as they wished', Tetaldi noted. The help the Ottomans received from Christian subjects, mercenaries, converts and technical experts was a theme of repeated lament for the European chroniclers. 'I can testify', howled Archbishop Leonard, 'that Greeks, Latins, Germans, Hungarians, Bohemians and men from all the Christian countries were on the side of the Turks . . . Oh, the wickedness of denying Christ like this!' The vituperation was not wholly justified; many of the Christian soldiers came under duress as vassals of the sultan. 'We had to ride forward to Stambol and help the Turks,' remembered Michael the Janissary, recording that the alternative was death. Among those brought unwillingly to the siege was a young Orthodox Russian, Nestor-Iskander. He had been captured by an Ottoman detachment near Moldavia on the fringes of southern Russia and circumcised for conversion to Islam. When his troop reached the siege he evidently escaped into the city and wrote a lively account of the events that ensued.

No one knows exactly how many men Mehmet brought to the siege. The Ottoman genius for mobilizing both regular troops and volunteers on a grand scale repeatedly stunned their opponents into the wildest projections. To the eulogizing Ottoman chroniclers they were simply 'a river of steel' 'as numerous as the stars'. The European eyewitnesses were more mathematical but given to very large round numbers. Their calculations ranged from 160,000 men to upwards of 400,000. It took Michael the Janissary, who had seen Ottoman armies up close, to impose some sense of realism on such 'facts': 'Know therefore that the Turkish emperor cannot assemble such a large army for pitched battle as people tell of his great might. For some relate that they are innumerable, but it is an impossible thing, that an army could be without number, for every ruler wants to know the number of his army and to have it organised.' The most realistic numerical guess seems to be that of Tetaldi, who soberly calculated that 'at the siege there were altogether two hundred thousand men, of whom perhaps sixty thousand were soldiers, thirty to forty thousand of these being cavalry'. In the fifteenth century, when the French and English fought the Battle of Agincourt with a combined total of 35,000 men, this was a huge force. If Tetaldi's estimate was anywhere close, even the number of horses that must have come to the siege was impressive. The rest of the Ottoman host were auxiliaries or hangers-on: supply teams, carpenters, gun-founders, blacksmiths, ordnance corps as well as 'tailors, pastry-cooks, artisans, petty traders, and other men who followed the army in the hope of profit or plunder'.

Constantine had no such difficulty estimating his army. He simply counted it. At the end of March he ordered a census of districts to record 'how many able-bodied men there were including monks, and whatever weapons each possessed for defence'. Having collected the returns he entrusted the adding up to his faithful chancellor and lifelong friend, George Sphrantzes. As Sphrantzes recalled, 'The Emperor summoned me and said, "This task belongs to your sphere of duties and to no-one else, because you are competent to make the necessary calculations and to observe that the proper measures are taken for the defence and that full secrecy is observed. Take these lists and study them at home. Make an accurate assessment of how many hand weapons, shields, bows and cannon we have."' Sphrantzes duly did the totting up. 'I carried out the Emperor's orders and presented to him a detailed estimate of our resources with considerable gloom.'

The reason for his mood was clear: 'In spite of the great size of our city, our defenders amounted to 4,773 Greeks, as well as just 200 foreigners.' In addition there were the genuine outsiders, the 'Genoese, Venetians and those who came secretly from Galata to help the defence', who numbered 'hardly as many as three thousand', amounting to something under 8,000 men in total to defend a perimeter wall of twelve miles. Even of these, 'the greater part of the Greeks were not skilled in warfare, and fought with shields, swords, lances and bows by natural instinct rather than with any skill'. Desperately lacking were those 'skilled in the use of the bow and cross-bow'. Nor was it certain what help the disaffected Orthodox population would give to the cause. Constantine was appalled by the possible effects of this information on morale, and determined to suppress it. 'The true figure remained a secret known only to the emperor and myself,' Sphrantzes recalled. It was clear that the siege was to be a conflict between the few and many.

Constantine kept this knowledge to himself and set about making final preparations. On 2 April, the day that the gates were closed for the last time, he ordered the boom to be hauled across the Golden Horn by ship, from Eugenius the gate near to the Acropolis Point in the city, to a tower within the sea walls of Galata. The work was undertaken by a Genoese engineer, Bartolamio Soligo, chosen probably for his ability to persuade his fellow Genoese at Galata to let the chain be fixed to their walls. This was a contentious matter. By permitting it, the citizens could be said to be compromising their strict neutrality. It was certain to invoke Mehmet's ire if the siege went badly, but they agreed. For Constantine it meant that the four-mile stretch of shoreline along the Horn could be left virtually unguarded as long as sufficient naval resources were deployed to protect the boom itself.

As Mehmet spread his army out around the city, Constantine called a council of war with Giustiniani and his other commanders to deploy his small force along the twelve-mile front. He knew that the Horn was secure as long as the boom was held; the other sea walls were also not cause for major concern. The Bosphorus currents were too strong to permit an easy assault by landing craft round the point of the city; the Marmara walls were similarly unpromising for concerted attack because of currents and the pattern of shoals off the shore. It was the land walls, despite their apparent strength, that needed the most detailed attention.

Both sides were well aware of the two weak spots. The first was the central section of wall, called by the Greeks the *Mesoteichion*, the 'middle wall' that lay between two strategic gates, the St Romanus and the Charisian, on ridges either side. Between the gates the land sloped down about a hundred feet to the Lycus valley, where the small stream was culverted under the wall and into the city. This section had been the focus of the Ottoman siege of 1422 and Mehmet set up his headquarters on the hill of Maltepe opposite as a clear signal of intent. The second vulnerable zone was the short length of single wall near the Golden Horn that was unmoated, particularly the point where the two walls met at right angles. In late March Constantine had persuaded the Venetian galley crews hurriedly to dig out a ditch along part of this stretch, but it remained a cause for concern.

Constantine set about organizing his forces accordingly. He divided the fourteen zones of the city into twelve military divisions and allocated his resources. He decided to establish his headquarters in the Lycus valley, so that emperor and sultan almost confronted each other across the walls. Here he stationed the bulk of his best troops, about 2,000 in all. Giustiniani was originally positioned at the Charisian Gate on the ridge above, but subsequently moved his Genoese soldiers to join the emperor in the central section and to take effective day-to-day command of this critical sector.

Sections of the land wall were then parcelled out for defence under the command of 'the principal persons of Constantinople'. On the emperor's right the Charisian Gate was probably commanded by Theodore of Karystes, 'an old but sturdy Greek, highly skilful with the bow'. The next section of the wall north, up to the right-angle turn, was entrusted to the Genoese Bocchiardi brothers who had come 'at their own expense and providing their own equipment', which included handguns and powerful frame-mounted crossbows, and the vulnerable section of single wall that ran round the Blachernae Palace was also largely entrusted to Italians. The Venetian bailey, Minotto, took up residence in the palace itself; the flag of St Mark flew from its tower beside that of the emperor. One of its gates, the Caligaria, was commanded by 'John from Germany', a professional soldier and 'an able military engineer' who was actually Scottish. He was also given the task of managing the city's supply of Greek fire.

Constantine's force was truly multi-national but was similarly divided along the fault lines of religion, nationality and commercial rivalry. In order to minimize potential friction between Genoese and Venetian, Orthodox and Catholic, Greek and Italian, he seems to have made it a deliberate policy to intermix the forces in the hope of increasing their interdependence. On his immediate left a section of wall was commanded by his kinsman, 'the Greek Theophilus, a noble from the house of Palaiologos, highly erudite in Greek literature and an expert geometrician' – a man who probably knew more about the *Iliad* than actually defending Troy's walls. Towards the Golden Gate, the wall was supervised by a succession of Greek, Venetian and Genoese soldiers, with a noble of the great Byzantine family of Cantacuzenos, Demetrios, at the corner point where the land wall meets the sea wall at the Marmara shore.

The defences along the Marmara shore were even more mixed. Another Venetian – Jacopo Contarini – was stationed at the village of Studion, while Orthodox monks watched an adjacent section where little attack was expected. Constantine had then placed his renegade Turkish contingent under the pretender Prince Orhan at the harbour of Eleutherii – well away from the land walls, though their loyalty was hardly to be questioned given their certain fate should the city fall. Towards the apex of the city, the seashore was manned by a Catalan contingent and the Acropolis point itself was entrusted to Cardinal Isidore and a force of 200. It says much about the fighting skills of the men on these sections, that despite the natural protection afforded by the sea Constantine decided to supply each tower with two skilled marksmen – one archer plus a crossbowman or handgunner. The Golden Horn itself was guarded by Genoese and Venetian sailors under the command of the Venetian sea captain Trevisano, while the crews of two Cretan ships in the harbour manned a gate near the boom, the Horaia. Protection of the boom itself and the ships in the harbour was in the charge of Aluvixe Diedo.

In order to provide further support for his overstretched 'army', Constantine decided to keep a rapid-reaction force in reserve. Two troops were kept in readiness back from the walls. One, under the Grand Duke Lucas Notaras, a skilled soldier and 'the most important man in Constantinople apart from the emperor', was stationed in the Petra quarter with a hundred horses and some mobile guns; another under Nicephorus Palaiologos was placed on the central ridge near the ruined church of the Holy Apostles. These reserves comprised about a thousand men.

Constantine brought a lifetime's experience of warfare and troop management to these arrangements, but he probably had little idea how well this democracy of competing contingents would function together in days ahead. Many of the crucial positions had been given to foreigners because he was uncertain where his own position on church union placed him with the Orthodox faithful of the city. He entrusted keys to four of the principal city gates to leading Venetians and ensured that the Greek commanders on the walls were unionist in their religious leanings. Lucas Notaras, who was probably against union, had been pointedly kept away from having to co-operate with Catholics at the defence of the walls.

As Constantine sought to match his scanty resources to the four-mile extent of the land wall, there was one further crucial decision to take. The triple wall had been designed for defence by a far larger contingent, which could man it in depth – at both the high inner wall and the lower outer one. He lacked the resources adequately to defend both layers, so he was forced to choose where to make a stand. The wall had been bombarded in the 1422 siege, and whereas the outer one had been substantially repaired, the inner had not. Defenders at the previous siege had faced the same choice and had opted – successfully – for a defence of the outer wall. Constantine and his siege expert, Giustiniani, adopted the same strategy. In some quarters it was a controversial decision. 'This was always against my advice', wrote the ever-critical Archbishop Leonard, 'I urged us not to desert the protection of our high inner walls', but this was probably the counsel of perfection.

The emperor resolved to do all he could for the morale of his troops, and knowing that Mehmet feared the possibility of Catholic aid arriving for the Orthodox city, decided on his own small show of force. At his request on 6 April the men of the Venetian galleys disembarked and paraded the length of the land walls in their distinctive European armour 'with their banners in front . . . to give great comfort to the people of the city', as a highly visible statement that there were Franks at the siege. On the same day the galleys themselves were put on a war footing.

Mehmet for his part sent a small detachment of cavalry up to the city gates, pennants fluttering in the wind, indicating that they had come to parley. They brought with them the traditional invitation to surrender required under Koranic law: 'Nor do We punish', says the Koran, 'until We have sent forth a messenger. When We resolve to raise a city, We first give warning to those its people who live in comfort. If they persist in sin, judgement is irrevocably passed, and We destroy it utterly.' Under this formula the Christian defenders could convert to Islam, surrender and pay the poll tax, or hold out and anticipate three days of plunder, should their city be stormed. The Byzantines had first heard this formula as long ago as 674, and several times since. The response had always been the same: 'We accept neither the tax, nor Islam, nor the capitulation of our fortress.' With this denial, the Ottomans could feel that the siege had been sanctioned by Holy Law and heralds moved among the camp formally proclaiming the start of the siege. Mehmet proceeded to wheel up his guns.

Constantine decided on a policy of maximum visibility. His headquarters was a large tent behind the St Romanus gate, from which he rode out on his small Arab mare each day with George Sphrantzes and the Spaniard Don Francisco of Toledo, 'encouraging the soldiers, inspecting the watches, and searching for those missing from their posts'. He heard Mass in whatever church was closest at the time and ensured that a group of monks and priests was attached to each body of men to hear confession and deliver the last rites in battle. Orders were also issued to conduct services day and night for the salvation of the city, and morning liturgies were concluded by procession of the icons through the streets and along the walls to cheer the troops. The watching Muslims could make out the long beards of the Christians and catch the sound of hymns in the spring air.

The morale of the defenders was not improved by the weather. There was a series of minor earthquakes and torrential rain. In the heightened atmosphere, portents were seen and old prophecies remembered. 'Icons sweated in the churches, and the pillars and statues of saints,' recalled the chronicler Kritovoulos. 'Men and women were possessed and inspired by visions that did not bode well, and soothsayers foretold many misfortunes.' Constantine himself was probably more perturbed by the arrival of the guns. He must have known what to expect from his previous experience of Ottoman artillery fire at the Hexamilion in 1446 when his carefully built wall collapsed in five days and a massacre ensued.

With his logistical skill in co-ordinating equipment, materials and huge numbers of men, Mehmet was now ready to act. His supplies of cannonballs and saltpetre, mining equipment, siege engines and food were collected, counted and ordered; weapons were cleaned, cannon were hauled into position, and the men – cavalry and infantry, archers and lancers, armourers, gunners, raiders and miners – had been assembled and brought to a pitch of expectation. The Ottoman sultans were close enough to a shared tribal past to understand the motivations of men and how to work their enthusiasm into a common purpose. Mehmet knew well how to whip up fervour for holy war. The ulema went among the corps, reciting the old prophecies from the Hadith about the city's fall and its meaning to Islam. Daily Mehmet prayed in public on a carpet in front of the red and gold tent turned east towards Mecca – and also towards St Sophia. This went hand in hand with the promise of limitless booty if the city had to be taken by force. The lure of the Red Apple was dangled before the expectant gaze of the faithful. It was on these dual promises, so attractive to the tribal raider, of taking plunder whilst fulfilling the will of God, that Mehmet prepared his strike.

He knew, and his old vizier Halil Pasha knew even better, that speed was now essential. Capturing cities required human sacrifice. The enthusiasm and expectation whipped up for the assault – and the willingness to fill up ditches with trampled corpses – had a limited time frame. Unexpected setbacks could quickly tip morale; among such a condensed body of men, rumour, dissent and disaffection could ripple through the tents like wind over the grasslands, and even the well-organized camps of the Ottomans were prey to typhus if they tarried too late in the summer. There was clearly danger for Mehmet in this venture. He was aware, through his network of Venetian spies, that help from the West would eventually come by land or sea no matter how quarrelsome and divided the Christian powers might be. As he gazed up from the hill at Maltepe at the rise and fall of the land walls with their close-packed towers, their triple defensive system and their history of stubborn resistance, he might have expressed public faith in the valour of his troops, but his ultimate confidence was probably in the potential of the guns.

Time was the prime co-ordinate for Constantine too. The calculation for the defenders was depressingly simple. There was no possibility of lifting the siege by counter-attack. Their only hope lay in holding on long enough for some relieving force from the West to muscle its way through the blockade. They had resisted the Arabs in 678. They must hold out now.

If Constantine possessed one trump card it lay in the person of Giovanni Giustiniani. The Genoese had come to the city with a reputation that preceded him as a 'man experienced in war'. He understood how to appraise and rectify obvious weaknesses in the fortifications, the best use of defensive weapons such as catapults and handguns, and deployment of the limited numbers of men to greatest advantage. He drilled the defenders in effective techniques of siege fighting and contemplated the opportunities for counter-attack from the city's sally ports. The vicious wars amongst Italian city-states bred generations of such talented specialists, technical mercenaries who studied city defence as both a science and an art. However Giustiniani could never have encountered massive artillery bombardment before. The events about to unfold would test his skill to the limit.

8 The Awful Resurrection Blast

6–19 APRIL 1453

Which tongue can profess or speak of these misfortunes and fears?
Nestor-Iskander

The big guns took a long time to arrive, lurching along the muddy tracks from Edirne on their solid-wheeled carts through the spring rain. They could be heard far ahead. The ox teams floundered and bellowed; the men shouted; the grating axles emitted a continuous, single-note music like an eerie transmission from the stars.

When they did reach the front line, each cannon took an age to unload on hoists, site and aim. By 6 April only some of the light guns were probably in place. They fired their first shots at the walls with apparently little effect. Soon after the start of the siege an enthusiastic but ragged assault by irregular troops was made against the weak section of the wall in the Lycus valley. Giustiniani's men sallied out from the ramparts and put the intruders to flight, 'killing some and wounding a few'. Order in the Ottoman camp was only restored by a substantial counter-attack that forced the defenders back behind the walls. The initial failure probably convinced the sultan to await a full deployment of artillery, rather than risk further damage to morale.

In the interim he instigated the other set procedures of an Ottoman siege. Hidden in bunkers behind the earth ramparts sappers commenced discreet mining operations in the central sector; their aim was to tunnel the 250 yards to the wall, which could then be collapsed

Firing a cannon

from underneath. Orders were also given to start trying to fill in the great fosse at suitable points by 'bringing up stones and timbers and mounds of earth and amassing every other kind of material', against the day when a concerted assault of the walls should be undertaken. This was dangerous, even deadly, work for the troops. The fosse was only forty yards from the defended wall and provided an unprotected sector that could be raked from the ramparts unless deterred by heavy counter-fire. Each sphere of operation where a toehold could be established or a line moved forward was to be bitterly contested. Giustiniani studied the terrain and set about disrupting their efforts. Sorties were made and ambushes laid in the dark when defenders would 'burst out of the city gates to attack those outside the walls. Leaping out of the fosse, they would sometimes be beaten back; at other times they would take Turkish captives' who could then be tortured for intelligence. These fierce skirmishes for the ditch were effective, but it quickly became clear to the defenders that the ratio of losses was unacceptable. The death of each skilled fighter was significant, no matter how many Turks were killed in the process, so the decision was taken early on to fight mainly from the ramparts, 'some firing crossbow bolts, others plain arrows'. The war for the fosse was to be one of the bitter inner struggles of the siege.

In the days after 7 April while he awaited the arrival of his heavy guns, the impatient sultan turned his attention to other matters. As the Ottoman army had swept up through Thrace it had taken the Greek villages in its path, but a few isolated strongholds still held out. These Mehmet had bypassed, leaving detachments to watch them. Probably on 8 April he set out with a sizeable force and some guns to eradicate the fortress of Therapia, which stood on a hilltop overlooking the Bosphorus beyond the Throat Cutter. It resisted for two days until the cannons destroyed its fortifications and killed most of the defenders. The rest 'when they could not hold out any longer, surrendered and said he could do with them as he wanted. And he impaled these forty men.' A similar castle at Studius on the Sea of Marmara was quickly demolished by gunfire. This time the thirty-six unfortunate survivors were impaled outside the city walls.

A few days later Baltaoglu, Mehmet's admiral, took a portion of the fleet to seize the Princes' Islands in the Sea of Marmara, the traditional retreat of the imperial family in times of trouble. On the largest island, Prinkipo, there was a solid fortress, manned by 'thirty heavily-armed men and some of the local people', that refused to surrender. When gunfire failed to reduce them to submission, Baltaoglu's men piled huge quantities of brushwood against the walls and set fire to it. With the help of pitch and brimstone and a stiff wind the flames licked the turrets so that the castle itself was soon alight. Those who were not burned alive surrendered unconditionally. The soldiers were killed on the spot and the villagers sold into slavery.

By 11 April Mehmet was back at his red and gold tent and the full complement of guns had been assembled. Mehmet grouped them into fourteen or fifteen batteries along the walls at key points considered to be vulnerable. One of Orban's great guns, 'a terrible cannon', was stationed at the single Blachernae wall near the Horn, 'which was protected by neither a ditch nor an outer wall'. Another was positioned near the right-angle join between the two walls, and a third at the Gate of the Spring further south. Others were trained on critical points along the vulnerable Lycus valley. Orban's supergun, which the Greeks called the Basilica – 'the royal gun' – was positioned in front of the sultan's tent, from where he could critically appraise its performance, to threaten the St Romanus Gate, 'the weakest gate in all the city'. Each large cannon was supported by a posse of smaller ones in a battery that the Ottoman gunners affectionately named 'the bear with its cubs'. They fired stone balls that ranged from 200 pounds up to a colossal 1,500 pounds, in the case of Orban's monster gun. In the estimate of one observer, the two largest cannons fired 'a shot that reached the knee and a shot that reached the girdle' respectively. Another declared the largest shot to measure 'eleven of my palms in circumference'. Though eyewitnesses spoke of 'innumerable engines of war', Mehmet probably had about sixty-nine cannon in total, a huge artillery force by the standards of the day, that were supported at various points by other, more antique technologies for hurling stones, such as the trebuchet, a counterweighted traction catapult. The trebuchet had been enormously influential in the Muslim capture of crusader castles three hundred years earlier. Now it looked merely like a device from another age.

Installing and readying the cannon for action was a laborious process. The barrels were freestanding and did not have integral gun carriages. They were simply strapped to sturdy wagons for transportation. On arrival a massive block and tackle system had to be erected to lower the barrel into position on a sloping wooden platform constructed on the protected side of the Ottoman front line and guarded from enemy fire by a wooden palisade and a hinged door which could be swung open at the moment of firing.

The logistical support behind this operation was immense. Great quantities of black stone balls had been mined and shaped on the northern coast of the Black Sea and transported by merchant ships. On 12 April such a consignment arrived at the Double Columns with 'stone balls for cannon, hurdles and timber, and other munitions for their camp.' Substantial quantities of saltpetre also had to be requisitioned if the guns were to fire for any length of time. The roadway that Mehmet had ordered his general Zaganos Pasha to build round the top of the Horn to the harbour was presumably to facilitate the movement of such supplies. Transporting the guns themselves required large wooden carts and substantial teams of men and oxen. The founders who worked with Orban at Edirne were also their gun crews. They moved, positioned, loaded and fired their handmade charges – and repaired them on site. For although Orban's superguns had been manufactured 150 miles away, the Ottomans brought sufficient resources to the siege to remake existing cannons in the camp, and even to forge and cast new ones, creating a whole secondary sphere of activity. Quantities of iron, copper and tin would have to be brought to the siege, domed charcoal pits dug and brick-lined foundries constructed. A separate zone of the military encampment must have been transformed into an ad hoc industrial workshop, from whence smoke billowed and blacksmiths' hammers rang in the spring air.

Preparing the big cannon needed time and attention to detail. Gunpowder was loaded into the barrel of the gun, backed by a wooden wad that was pounded tight by iron bars, or a sheepskin one, to ensure that 'whatever happened, it could not be forced out by any means except by the explosion of the gunpowder'. The stone ball was then manhandled round to the front of the cannon and eased down the barrel. It was designed to be a good fit in the chamber but an exact match of ball to calibre was frequently not achieved. Aim was reckoned by 'certain techniques and calculations about the target'– in practice this meant trial and error – and the angle of the cannon adjusted accordingly by chocking its platform up with wooden wedges. The guns were further wedged into place with great beams of timber weighted down with stones that acted as shock absorbers, 'lest by the force of its charge and by the violent recoil in its position, it should be displaced and shoot wide of the target'. Priming powder was poured into the touchhole and all was ready. On 12 April lighted tapers were put to the touchholes of the sultan's guns along a four-mile sector and the world's first concerted artillery bombardment exploded into life.

If there is any single moment in the history of warfare at which an authentic sense of awe at the exponential power of gunpowder could be palpably felt, it is here in the accounts of the firing of the great guns in the spring of 1453. The taper ignited the powder:

> And when it had caught fire, faster than you can say it, there was first a terrifying roar and a violent shaking of the ground beneath and for a great distance around, and a din such as has never been heard. Then with a monstrous thundering and an awful explosion and a flame that illuminated everything round about and scorched it, the wooden wad was forced out by the hot blast of dry air and propelled the stone ball powerfully out. Projected with incredible force and power, the stone struck the wall, which it immediately shook and demolished, and it was itself shattered into many fragments and the pieces were hurled everywhere, dealing death to those standing nearby.

When the giant stone balls struck the walls at an advantageous spot, the effects were devastating: 'Sometimes it destroyed a complete portion of wall, sometimes half a portion, sometimes a greater or smaller part of a tower, or a turret, or a parapet, and nowhere was the wall strong enough or sturdy enough or thick enough to withstand it, or to hold out totally against such a force or the velocity of the stone ball.' At first it seemed to the defenders that the whole history of siege warfare was unravelling in front of their eyes; the Theodosian land wall, the product of two thousand years of defensive evolution, a miracle of engineering devised by human ingenuity and protected by divine blessing, started to collapse wherever it was hit by a volley of well-aimed balls. Archbishop Leonard watched the effects on the single wall near the palace: 'They pulverized the wall with it, and although it was extremely thick and strong, it collapsed under the bombardment of this appalling device.'

Balls from the superguns that cleared the walls could be propelled a mile into the heart of Constantinople, shattering with devastating force against houses or churches, mowing down civilians or more likely burying themselves in the orchards and fields of the shrunken city. One eyewitness was astonished to see a ball strike a church wall and fall apart like dust. According to others, the ground was shaken for two miles around and even the galleys tied up safely in the harbours within the Golden Horn felt the explosions transmitted through their stout wooden hulls. The sound of gunfire was heard in Asia, five miles away across the Bosphorus. At the same time the trebuchets, with their more looping arc of fire, hurled rocks onto the roofs of houses behind the walls and onto parts of the Imperial Palace.

The psychological effects of artillery bombardment on the defenders were initially even more severe than its material consequences. The noise and vibration of the massed guns, the clouds of smoke, the shattering impact of stone on stone dismayed seasoned defenders. To the civilian population it was a glimpse of the coming apocalypse and a retribution for sin. It sounded, according to one Ottoman chronicler, 'like the awful resurrection blast'. People ran out of their houses beating their chests, crossing themselves and shouting 'Kyrie Eleison! What is going to happen now?' Women fainted in the streets. The churches were thronged with people 'voicing petitions and prayers, wailing and exclaiming: "Lord, Lord! We moved far away from You. All that fell upon us and Your holy City was accomplished through righteous and true judgements for our sins." By the flickering light of their most sacred icons their lips moved in the same unceasing prayer: "Do not betray us in the end to Your enemies; do not destroy Your worthy people; and do not take away Your loving kindness from us and render us weak at this time."'

Constantine worked unstintingly to maintain the morale of the city on both a practical and religious level. He toured the walls hourly, stiffening the morale of the commanders and their soldiers. Church bells were rung unceasingly and he exhorted 'all of the people so that they would not renounce hope nor slacken their resistance against the enemy but place their trust in the Almighty Lord'.

The defenders tried different strategies to mitigate the shock of the stone balls. A mortar of chalk and brick dust was poured down the wall's outer face as a toughened coating; in other places bales of wool attached to wooden beams, sheets of leather and precious tapestries were suspended to muffle the velocity of the projectiles. These measures made little difference to the extraordinary force of gunpowder propulsion. The defenders did their best to try to knock out the big guns with their own few cannon, but they were short of saltpetre and the Ottoman guns were screened by their palisades. Worse still it was found that the walls and towers were chronically unsuitable as gun platforms. They were neither wide enough to accommodate the recoil of large explosive charges nor strong enough to withstand the vibrations, which 'shook the walls, and did more damage to them than to the enemy'. Their largest cannon quickly exploded, enraging the harassed defenders so much that they wanted to put the gun master to death for being in the pay of the sultan, 'but since there was no clear proof that he deserved this fate, they set him free'. Underneath it all, it was quickly clear that in a new age of warfare the Theodosian walls were structurally inadequate.

The Greek chroniclers struggled to convey what they saw, or even to find a vocabulary to describe the guns. 'No ancient name exists for this device', declared the classically minded Kritovoulos, 'unless someone refers to it as a battering ram or a propeller. But in common speech everyone now calls it an apparatus.' Other names proliferated: bombards, skeves, helepoles – 'takers of cities' – torments and teleboles. In the pressure of the moment, language was being shaped by a terrifying new reality – the infernal experience of artillery bombardment.

Mehmet's strategy was attritional – and impatient. He decided to batter the walls day and night with artillery fire and to launch unpredictable skirmishes to wear down the defenders and to make a major breach for a final assault. 'The assault continued night and day with no relief from the clashes and explosions, crashing of stones and cannon-balls on the walls,' reported Melissenos, 'for the Sultan hoped in this way to take the city easily, since we were few against many, by pounding us to death and exhaustion, and so he allowed us no rest from attack.' The bombardment, and the struggle for the fosse, continued unabated from 12 to 18 April.

Despite their initial psychological impact, managing the great cannon was difficult work. Loading and aiming were such laborious operations that the Basilica could only be fired seven times a day, with a preliminary shot before dawn to warn of the day's firing. The guns could be unpredictable, bad-tempered and deadly to their teams. In the spring rain they proved hard to keep in position, recoiling with the slam of a charging rhino so that they frequently slipped from their cradles into the mud. The possibility of being crushed to death was only exceeded by the risk of being blown to pieces by the shrapnel of disintegrating gun barrels. The Basilica quickly became a cause for concern to Orban; the intense heat of the explosions had started to exploit hairline fractures in the impure metal – evidently casting on this scale was extremely demanding. The Greek chronicler Doukas, who had a keen technical interest in the problem, recalled how, in order to control the problem, the barrel was soaked in warm oil as soon as the ball had been shot to try to prevent cold air penetrating and enlarging the fissures.

However, the possibility that the barrel would shatter like glass continued to trouble Orban, and according to legend nemesis soon overtook the Christian mercenary. Close examination had revealed that the cracks were indeed serious. Orban wished to withdraw the gun and recast it. Mehmet, ever present to watch the performance of his great guns and impatient for success, ordered the firing to continue. Weighing up the risks of a faulty gun against the sultan's displeasure, Orban reloaded and asked Mehmet to stand back. On lighting the powder charge, the Basilica 'cracked as it was being fired and split into many pieces, killing and wounding many nearby' – including Orban. There is however strong evidence to suggest that his demise – devoutly wished for by the Christian chroniclers – never happened in this way, though it seems clear that the great gun ruptured early in the siege. It was quickly strengthened with iron hoops and pressed back into service but soon cracked again – to the intense anger of Mehmet. The supergun was evidently working beyond the tolerances of contemporary metallurgy. Its chief effect had been psychological; it was left to the slightly smaller but still formidable posse of other bombards to do the damage.

Mehmet's need to take the city quickly was soon underlined by the arrival of a deputation from the Hungarian, John Hunyadi. Mehmet's policy had been to ensure that his enemies were divided; to this end he had signed a three-year peace treaty with Hunyadi, then regent of Hungary, to ensure that no land attack from the west should take place during his attempt on Constantinople. Hunyadi's embassy had now come to the Ottoman court to announce that, since their master had resigned his regency and surrendered power back to his ward King Vladislas, the treaty was no longer binding. In consequence he wished to return the truce document and receive his own back. It was conceived by the wily Hungarian as a threat to pressurize the Ottoman cause and had probably been instigated by agents from the Vatican. It raised the spectre of a Hungarian army crossing the Danube to lift the siege and it caused a ripple of uncertainty throughout the camp; the news must have correspondingly strengthened the will of the defenders.

Unfortunately the visit also gave way to unsubstantiated rumours that the visiting Hungarians had provided valuable assistance to the Ottoman cause. One of the ambassadors at the camp watched the firing of the great cannons with interest. When he saw a shot strike the wall at a certain point and the gunners prepare a second shot at the same point, professional interest overcame him and he openly laughed at their naivety. He advised them to aim their second shot 'about thirty to thirty-six feet from the first shot, but at the same height' and to position a third shot between the two 'so that the shots form a triangular shape. Then you will see that portion of wall collapse'. The immediate effect of this firing strategy was to accelerate the speed at which sections of the wall could be brought down. Very soon the 'bear and cubs' were working as co-ordinated teams. Smaller guns would make two outer hits, then one of Orban's great guns completed the triangle in the now weakened central section: 'the shot being carried by such devilish force and irresistible impetus that it caused irreparable damage'. The chroniclers attached a weird explanation for this helpful piece of advice: a Serbian prophet had declared that the misfortunes of the Christians would not come to an end until Constantinople fell to the Turks. The story of the Hungarian visit neatly wrapped up repeated preoccupations of the Christians in one narrative: the belief that the Ottomans could only prosper with the superior technological knowledge of Europeans, that the decline of Christendom was responsible for the fall, and the role of religious prophecy.

Despite the difficulties of aiming and the slow rate of fire, the bombardment continued unabated from 12 April for six days. Now the heaviest fire was concentrated on the Lycus valley and the Romanus Gate. About 120 shots a day could be launched at the city. Inexorably the wall began to crumble. Within the week a section of the outer wall had fallen and two towers and a turret on the inner wall behind. However, after their initial terror at the bombardment, the defenders regained heart under fire: 'by experiencing the force of the sultan's war engines daily our soldiers became accustomed to them and displayed neither fear nor cowardice'. Giustiniani worked unceasingly to repair the damage, and quickly devised an effective ad hoc solution to the collapsing outer wall. A makeshift replacement was constructed of stakes, and on this foundation the defenders dumped any material that came to hand. Stones, timber, brushwood, bushes and large quantities of earth were moved into the breach. Screens of skin and hide were stretched over the outer wooden stockade as protection against incendiary arrows, and when the new defensive mound was of sufficient height, barrels filled with earth were placed on top at regular intervals to act as crenellated fighting positions to protect the defenders against volleys of arrows and bullets with which the Ottomans attempted to sweep clean the ramparts. Immense human labour was thrown into this effort; after dark men and women came from the city to work all night, carrying timber, stones and earth to rebuild the defences wherever they had been smashed during the day. This incessant nocturnal labour took its toll on the energy of the increasingly exhausted population, but the resulting earthworks provided a surprisingly effective solution to the devastating impact of the stone balls. Like throwing stones into mud, the balls were smothered and neutralized: they were 'buried in the soft and yielding earth, and did not make a breach by striking against hard and unyielding materials'.

At the same time the bitter struggle continued for control of the moat. By day Ottoman troops attempted to fill it in with any material to hand: soil, timber, rubble, even – according to one account – their own tents, were dragged up into no man's land under a protecting volley of fire, and tipped into the trench. At night the defenders mounted counter-offensives from their sally ports to clear the fosse out again and restore it to its original depth. The skirmishing in front of the walls was bitter, and at close range. Sometimes the attackers used nets to try to retrieve precious cannon balls that had rolled back into the fosse; at others soldiers would advance to test weakened sections of the wall and to ensure the overstretched defenders could never relax. With hooked sticks they attempted to drag down the earth barrels from the top.

At close range these encounters favoured the better-armoured and protected defenders, but even the Greek and Italian eyewitnesses were impressed by their enemy's courage under fire. 'The Turks fought bravely at close quarters,' remembered Leonard, 'so they all died.' Raked by fire from the walls from longbows, crossbows and arquebuses, the carnage was terrible. Having found their cannon unusable for firing heavy balls, the defenders had reinvented their artillery pieces as huge shotguns. A cannon would be packed with five or ten lead balls, the size of walnuts. Fired at close range the effect of these bullets was appalling: they had 'immense power in penetrating and perforating, so that if one hit a soldier in armour, it went straight through both his shield and body, then through another behind who was in the line of fire, and then another, until the force of the powder was dissipated. With one shot two or three men could be killed at the same time.'

Hit by this withering fire, the Ottoman casualties were terrible and their desire to retrieve their dead provided the defenders with another shooting gallery. The Venetian surgeon Nicolo Barbaro was startled by what he saw:

> And when one or two of them were killed, at once other Turks came and carried off the dead ones, hoisting them over their shoulders as one would a pig, without caring how near they came to the city walls. But our men who were on the ramparts shot at them with guns and crossbows, aiming at the Turk who was carrying away his dead comrade, and both of them would fall to the ground dead, and then other Turks came and took them away, not fearing death in the slightest, but preferring to let ten of themselves be killed rather than suffer the shame of leaving a single Turkish corpse in front of the city walls.

Despite the defenders' best efforts, remorseless bombardment provided sufficient cover for a section of the fosse in the Lycus valley to be filled in. On April 18 Mehmet judged that the damage to the wall and attritional skirmishing had been sufficient to launch a concerted attack. It had been a fine spring day; as evening fell, the call to prayer rose with peaceful certainty over the Ottoman camp and within the walls the Orthodox retired to the churches to hold vigils, light candles and to pray to the Mother of God. Two hours after sunset, under a soft spring moon, Mehmet ordered forward a substantial detachment of his crack troops. To the rhythmic thudding of camel-skin drums, the braying of pipes and the clashing of cymbals – all the psychological warfare of the Ottoman military band – amplified by flares, shouts and battle cries, Mehmet started to roll forward 'the heavy infantry and the bowmen and the javelin-men and all the imperial foot-guards'. He directed them at a vulnerable spot in the Lycus valley where a section of wall had collapsed. The citizens were panic-stricken, experiencing the hair-raising sound of a full-throated Ottoman assault for the first time. 'I cannot describe the cries with which they came at the walls,' Barbaro later recalled with a shudder.

Constantine was deeply alarmed. He feared a general assault along the whole line and knew that his men were unprepared. He ordered the church bells to be rung; terrified people ran into the streets and soldiers scrambled back to their stations. Under a heavy covering fire of cannon, guns and bows the Ottomans crossed the fosse. Withering volleys made it impossible to stand on the improvised earth ramparts so that the Janissaries were able to reach the walls with ladders and battering rams. They worked to strip the ramparts of their protective crenellations and further expose the defenders to blanket fire. At the same time attempts were made to burn the wooden stockade, but these failed and the narrowness of the gap in the wall and the sloping terrain hampered the onrush of the attackers. In the darkness pandemonium broke out, a confused hubbub of sounds, according to Nestor-Iskander:

> the clatter of cannons and arquebuses, the roar of the bells, the cracking of arms – like lightning flashing from both weapons – as the crying and sobbing of the people (the women and children of the city) made one believe that the sky and the earth had joined the earth and they both trembled; one could not hear another man's words. Weeping and screaming, the cries and sobs of the people, the roar of the cannons, and the pealing of bells combined into one din resembling great thunder. Again, rising from many fires and the explosions of cannons and arquebuses, the smoke thickened on both sides and covered the city. The armies were unable to see one another and did not know against whom they fought.

Slashing and hacking at each other in the narrow spaces of the defile under the bright moon, advantage rested with the defenders who were well armoured and stoutly marshalled by Giustiniani. Slowly the momentum of the attackers died: 'slashed to pieces, they exhausted themselves on the walls'. After four hours an abrupt quietness descended on the ramparts, broken only by the moans of men dying in the ditch. The Ottomans retreated to camp, 'without even thought for their dead', and the defenders, after six days of continuous defence, 'collapsed from the struggle as if dead'.

In the cool light of morning Constantine and his retinue came to inspect the aftermath. The ditch and the banks were lined with 'completely broken corpses'. Battering rams lay abandoned before the walls and fires smouldered in the morning air. Constantine could rouse neither the army nor the exhausted citizenry to bury the Christian dead, and this work had to be assigned to the monks. As always, casualty figures varied wildly: Nestor-Iskander gave the number of Ottoman dead at 18,000; Barbaro a more realistic 200. Constantine ordered that no attempt should be made to hinder the enemy from collecting their corpses, but the battering rams were burned. Then he proceeded to St Sophia with the clergy and nobles to give thanks to 'the all-powerful God and to the most pure Mother of God, hoping that now the godless would retreat, having seen so many of their own fall'. It was a moment of respite for the city. Mehmet's response was to intensify the bombardment.

9 A Wind from God

1–20 APRIL 1453

Battles on the sea are more dangerous and fierce than the battles by land, for on the sea there is no recoiling nor fleeing, there is no remedy but to fight and to abide fortune, and every man show his prowess.
Jean Froissart, fourteenth-century French chronicler

In early April, while the big guns were busy pounding the land walls, Mehmet began to deploy the fleet, his other new weapon, for the first time. He had been quick to grasp a fact obvious to all potential besiegers from the time of the Arabs onwards – that without firm control of the sea an attempt on the city was likely to fail. His father Murat had come to the siege of 1422 with no ability to strangle Byzantine sea-lanes – the Ottoman fleet had been caught and destroyed at Gallipoli by the Venetians six years earlier. Without a blockade of the Bosphorus and the Dardanelles the city could be easily resupplied by the Greek cities of the Black Sea or by Christian sympathizers from the Mediterranean basin. It was with this in mind that the Throat Cutter had been built and equipped with heavy guns in the summer of 1452. No ship could henceforth pass up or down the Bosphorus into the Black Sea unexamined.

At the same time he had set to work repairing and strengthening the navy. During the winter of 1452 an ambitious programme of shipbuilding work was undertaken at the Ottoman naval base at Gallipoli and probably at Sinop on the Black Sea and other shipyards on the

Sailing ship off the sea walls

Aegean coast. According to Kritovoulos, Mehmet 'thought that the fleet would be more influential in the siege and the fighting ahead than the army', and gave great personal attention to this work. The empire had acquired an experienced resource of shipwrights, sailors and pilots, both of Greek and Italian origin, as it rolled up the coasts of the Black Sea and Mediterranean, and this skilled manpower could be brought into play in naval reconstruction. Mehmet also had access to the substantial natural resources essential to naval endeavour: timber and hemp, cloth for sails, cast iron for anchors and nails, pitch and tallow for caulking and greasing hulls. These materials were sourced widely from within the empire and beyond. It was the logistical skill of Mehmet to bring together all these resources for war.

As with cannon, the Ottomans were swift to adopt the ships of their Christian enemies. The key fighting vessel of the Mediterranean Middle Ages was the oared galley, the natural successor of the Roman and Greek galleys of classical antiquity, a vessel that dominated the Mediterranean in evolving forms from the start of the Bronze Age until the seventeenth century, and whose basic shape, echoed on Minoan seals, Egyptian papyri and the pottery of classical Greece, was to be as central to the sea's history as the vine and the olive tree. By the late Middle Ages the prototype war galley was long, fast and very lean, typically perhaps 100 feet in length, under twelve feet in width with a raised prow or spur at the front to act as a fighting platform or boarding bridge onto enemy ships. The tactics of naval warfare were hardly distinguishable from those on land. The galleys would be packed with a complement of fighting men who, after an initial discharge of missiles, would attempt to storm the opposing vessel in vicious hand-to-hand combat.

The galley itself was startlingly low in the water. To maximize the mechanical advantage of the oars, a laden war galley might have clearance above the water of two feet. It could be powered by sail, but it was the oars that gave the galley its punch and flex in battle. The rowers were arranged in a single tier, above deck – which left them horribly exposed in battle – and usually two or three to a side on a single bench; each man worked an individual oar whose length was determined by his place on the bench. Conditions were cramped; galley rowing meant operating an oar in the seat space of a modern passenger plane so that the basic rowing motion, where sideways space was at a premium, involved the oarsman pushing the oar straight forward with his elbows kept in and rising up out of his seat in the process, then dropping back into it. Not surprisingly galley rowing required skilled crews able to row in perfect time – and considerable muscle power to work an oar up to thirty feet long weighing some 100 pounds. The war galley was bred for speed and manoeuvrability in battle; a galley with a well-greased keel could maintain a dash speed of seven and a half knots for twenty minutes under human power. The demand to row for longer than an hour quickly tired the crew.

For all its pace on a calm sea, the galley suffered from extraordinary disadvantages. The low freeboard rendered it surprisingly unseaworthy, even in the short choppy seas of the Mediterranean, so that galley sailing tended to be confined to the summer months and dictated a preference for hugging the coast to making long journeys over open water. Galley fleets were not infrequently swamped by unseasonal storms. The sails were only useful with the wind full astern, and the oars themselves were useless against any strong headwind. In addition the requirement for speed had created a hull that was fragile and so low in the water as to be at a serious disadvantage when attacking a high-sided vessel, such as a merchant sailing ship or one of the taller Venetian great galleys. The galley's strengths and weaknesses were to be severely tested in the struggle for the city.

Mehmet had assembled a substantial fleet. He repaired and recaulked older vessels and built a number of new triremes – galleys with oars grouped in threes – as well as smaller scaled-down raiding galleys, 'long ships, fast and fully decked, with thirty to fifty rowers', which Europeans called *fustae*. He appears to have supervised much of this work himself, choosing 'skilled seamen from all the Asian and European coasts – oarsmen with particular skills, deckhands, helmsmen, commanders of triremes, captains and admirals, and the other ships' crews'. Some of this fleet was already in the Bosphorus in March, ferrying troops across the straits, but it was not until the start of April that the main force could be assembled at Gallipoli under his appointed admiral Baltaoglu, 'a great man, a skilful admiral experienced in sea warfare'. It was the first time in seven sieges that the Ottomans had brought a fleet to the city. It was a crucial development.

Gallipoli, 'homeland of defenders of the faith', was a talismanic city for the Ottomans and an auspicious point of departure. It was here that they had gained their first foothold in Europe in 1354 after a fortuitous earthquake. The fleet, fired with zeal for holy war and the enterprise of conquest, started out from the Dardanelles and began to work its way up the Sea of Marmara. The crews apparently set out 'with cries and cheering and the singing of rowing chants, encouraging each other with shouts'. In practice the enthusiasm may have been more muted: a substantial portion of the rowing force were in all likelihood Christians working under compulsion. According to a later chronicler 'the wind of divine help pushed them forward', but the reality must have been different. By now the prevailing wind was blowing from the north so the passage up the Marmara had to made against wind and current. The 120 miles to Constantinople presented a hard slog for the galleys. News of their progress preceded them up the sea-lane with a mixture of astonishment and panic. As with his army Mehmet understood the psychological value of superior numbers. It was the impression of a sea covered with oars and masts that appalled the watching Greek villages along the coast. The most reliable estimates of the Ottoman navy were made by experienced Christian seafarers, such Giacomo Tetaldi and Nicolo Barbaro, rather than by more impressionable landlubbers. Between them they estimated a fleet of something between twelve and eighteen full war galleys composed of a mixture of triremes and biremes, then seventy to eighty smaller *fustae*, about twenty-five *parandaria* – heavy transport barges – and a number of light brigantines and other small message boats, a force of about 140 boats in all. It was an awesome sight to glimpse over the curve of the western horizon.

Word of Mehmet's impressive naval preparations reached the city long before his ships, so that the defenders had time to draw up their naval plans with care. On 2 April they closed the Golden Horn with the great chain to create a secure anchorage for their ships and to seal off the puny sea walls from attack. It was a practice embedded deep in the history of the city. As early as 717 a chain had been strung across the strait to hamper besieging Muslim navies. On 6 April, according to Barbaro, 'we put ready for battle the three galleys from Tana and the two narrow galleys', and their crews then progressed the length of the land wall in a show of military strength. On the 9th all the naval resources available to the defenders in the harbour were organized and made ready. It was a mixed collection of craft, brought together for a range of motives. There were ships from the Italian city-states and their colonies – Venice, Genoa, Ancona and Crete – as well as a Catalan ship, one from Provence, and ten Byzantine craft. There were galleys of various sizes including the three 'great galleys', the bulk carriers of Italian maritime trade, slower than conventional war galleys but stoutly built with higher sides, and two 'narrow galleys', slender hulled and low in the water. The majority of the vessels at anchor in the Golden Horn in early April 1453 were merchant sailing ships – high-sided, sail-driven 'round ships' – carracks with high poops and sterns, stoutly timbered and masted. In theory none of these were fighting ships, but in the dangerous, pirate-threatened waters of the Mediterranean, the distinction was a fine one. Their height and the vantage points of their decks and crow's nests gave them natural advantages over low-slung war galleys if supplied with weapons and skilled troops. At this snapshot moment in the history of naval warfare the sailing ship could often hold its own against the most determined attack. Galley-mounted guns were in their infancy; they were too small and mounted too low to threaten a carrack. It was to be another fifty years before the Venetians devised an effective ship-killing gun that could be mounted on a galley. Furthermore, the sailors from Venice and Genoa in particular, who depended totally on their prowess at sea for survival and prosperity, approached all maritime matters with supreme confidence. They made their plans accordingly.

On 9 April therefore, they drew their ten largest merchantmen up in front of the boom 'in close array and with bows forward'. Barbaro faithfully recorded their captains and the size of each one, ranging from that of Zorzi Doria of Genoa, '2,500 botte', to one of '600 botte'; three he named: the *Filomati* and *Guro* of Candia, the *Gataloxa* of Genoa. Alongside these were stationed the stoutest of the galleys. The ships, which were 'well armed and in excellent order, as if they wanted to join battle, and all equally good', spanned the length of the boom from the city to Galata on the other side. In the inner harbour a further seventeen square-rigged merchantmen were kept in reserve, together with more galleys, including five of the emperor's which were probably disarmed to provide a concentration of equipment at the boom. A few surplus ships were scuttled to lessen the risk of being hit by cannon and spreading fire, the waking nightmare of mariners in a closely packed fleet. Secure in both their defences and their nautical skill, with cannon positioned on the foreshore as an extra assurance, the captains sat to await the arrival of the Ottoman fleet. They had perhaps thirty-seven ships in total against an armada of 140, on paper a huge discrepancy, but the Italian seafarers understood the critical issues in sea warfare. Ship handling was a craft skill dependent on well-trained crews, so that the outcome of naval encounters rested less on numbers than on experience, determination and the random luck of winds and currents. 'Seeing that we had such an impressive fleet, we felt ourselves confidently secure against the fleet of the infidel Turks,' recorded Barbaro smugly, betraying a consistent Venetian tendency to underestimate Ottoman maritime skills.

The Ottoman fleet was finally sighted on 12 April at about one o'clock in the afternoon, battling up against the north wind. Doubtless the sea walls were crowded with watching citizens as the horizon slowly filled with masts. The fleet came rowing on 'with determination', but seeing the Christian ships drawn up at the boom in line of battle, it went over to the other side of the strait, lining the opposite shore. It made a strong impression on those watching and deepened the city's gloom, hearing the 'eager cries and the sound of castanets and tambourines, with which they filled our fleet and those in the city with fear'. Later in the afternoon, the whole fleet moved two miles further up the Bosphorus to a small harbour on the European shore called by the Greeks the Double Columns, now the site of the Dolmabache Palace. The size and power of the warlike fleet had undoubtedly dented the confidence of even the Italians, because the ships at the boom stood to arms all that day and into the night 'waiting hour after hour in case they came to attack our fleet', but nothing happened. It was to be the start of an attritional game of cat and mouse. To minimize the risk of being surprised, two men were stationed permanently on the town walls of neutral Galata from which vantage point the fleet at the Double Columns further up the Bosphorus could be closely watched. At any sign of movement along the straits by even a single ship, a man hurried back down the streets of Galata to the Horn to alert Aluvixe Diedo the harbour commander. The battle trumpet was sounded and those on the ships stood immediately to arms. In this state of nervy apprehension they waited day and night, rocking gently at anchor in the calm waters of the Horn.

Mehmet had three clear objectives for his new fleet: to blockade the city, to attempt to force a way into the Horn, and to oppose any relieving fleet that might sail up the Marmara. Initially Baltaoglu did nothing more than send out patrols round the waters of the city specifically to prevent ships entering or leaving the two small harbours on the Marmara side of the city. At about the same time a further detachment of ships came from the Black Sea laden with cannon balls and other munitions for the army. The arrival of these supplies seemed to precipitate a new cycle of activity in the Ottoman camp.

Impatient to tighten his stranglehold on the city, Mehmet ordered Baltaoglu to make an attempt on the boom. If the Ottomans could force their way into the Horn, Constantine would be compelled to strip the land wall of much-needed defenders to guard the shoreline. Both sides had made careful preparations for this moment. Doubtless at the instigation of Mehmet, whose appetite for artillery innovations was boundless, the Ottomans loaded small cannon onto their galleys. They packed the fighting beaks with heavy infantry and provisioned the vessels with stocks of weapons: stone cannon balls, arrows, javelins and inflammable material. The lookouts on the Galata walls closely observed these preparations, so that Lucas Notaras, the commander of the Byzantine ships, had ample time to prepare the big merchant carracks and galleys with men and ammunition.

Probably on 18 April, at the same time as the first major assault on the land walls at the St Romanus Gate, Baltaoglu launched the new navy's first attack. Putting out in force from the Double Columns, the fleet rounded the point and advanced at speed towards the boom. They rowed hard at the steady line of tall ships anchored in front of the chain, with the crews encouraging each other with shouts and battle cries. They came on to within a bowshot, then slowed and released a volley of fire from bows and cannon; stone balls, metal bolts and flaming arrows whistled across the water and swept the enemy decks. After the initial salvoes, they came on again towards the anchored ships. As they clashed, the Ottomans attempted the standard boarding procedures of close engagement. Grappling hooks and ladders were thrown up as they tried to scale the sides of the taller ships; attempts were made to slash the merchantmen's anchor cables. A hail of javelins, pikes and spears was hurled at the defenders. The ferocity of the assault was unquestionable but the advantage of battle lay with the higher and more stoutly built carracks. Stone balls from the ship-mounted cannon of the Ottoman galleys were too small to inflict damage on the sturdy wooden hulls, and the sea-borne soldiers were attacking from below, like troops trying to storm the land walls from the bottom of a ditch. The sailors and marines on board the Christian ships could hurl down missiles from the bow and stern platforms and from higher up in the crow's nests. Volleys of gads – iron javelins with stabilizing fins – arrows and stones were rained down on the undefended attackers scrabbling at the sides of the ships, 'wounding many, and killing a considerable number too'. The merchantmen were practised and equipped for close combat at sea; jars of water were at hand to extinguish incendiary devices and simple rope hoists extending from their masts allowed them to swing out heavy stones clear from the sides of the ships and drop them onto the fragile shells of the swarming long boats, 'and inflicted considerable damage in this way'. The struggle to capture and to protect the chain was intense, but eventually the Christians started to prevail. They manage to turn the flank of the galley fleet. Fearing humiliation Baltaoglu withdrew his ships and sailed back to the Double Columns.

The first round of naval warfare had gone to the defenders. They understood their ships well and a basic fact of naval warfare: that a well-prepared merchantman could hold its own against a swarm of low-lying galleys if the crew were disciplined and well equipped. Mehmet's hopes for artillery power had not been met at sea. The guns that could be mounted on light-framed galleys were too small to be effective against the stout sides of sailing ships, and the conditions of operation – the difficulty both of preventing the powder absorbing atmospheric moisture at sea and of aiming effectively on a pitching deck – further decreased the chances of success. By the morning of 19 April, Mehmet's troops had been repulsed by both land and sea, while the spirits of the defenders remained undaunted. The lengthening timeframe of the siege increased Mehmet's impatience day by day – and the possibility of aid from the West.

For Constantine a successful defence of the city depended on relief from Christian Europe. The endless round of diplomatic missions that preceded the siege had all been undertaken to beg or borrow men and resources for the cause of Christendom. Daily the population looked in the direction of the setting sun for another fleet – a squadron of Venetian or Genoese war galleys, their beaked prows surging up the Marmara to the beating of drums, the rallying of war trumpets, the lion flags of St Marks or the gonfalons of Genoa cracking in the salt wind. But the sea remained ominously empty.

In effect the fate of the city hung on the complex internal politics of the Italian city-states. As early as the end of 1451 Constantine had sent messengers to Venice to report that the city would fall without help. The matter had been debated by the Venetian Senate at length; it was the subject of prevarication in Genoa; in Rome the Pope was concerned but required evidence that the union of the churches had been fully implemented. In any case he lacked practical resources to intervene without the Venetians. Genoa and Venice eyed each other in cold commercial rivalry and did nothing.

Constantine's appeal to the West rested on notions that were religious and medieval but they were directed at states whose motivations were economic – and surprisingly modern. The Venetians were largely indifferent to whether the Byzantines were unionists or not and had little appetite for the role of defenders of the faith. They were hard-nosed traders, preoccupied with commercial agreements, the security of their sea routes and the calculation of interest. They worried about pirates more than theology, about commodities rather than creeds. Their merchants studied the price of what could be bought and sold – wheat, fur, slaves, wine and gold – the supply of manpower for the galley fleets and the pattern of Mediterranean winds. They lived by trade and the sea, by discount, profit margins and ready coin. The doge was on excellent terms with the sultan and trade with Edirne was profitable; furthermore Constantine had considerably damaged Venetian interests in the Peloponnese in the previous twenty years.

It was in this spirit that in August 1452 a minority of senators actually voted to abandon Constantinople to its fate. The lack of concern was modified the following spring as reports trickled in of the throttling of trade routes to the Black Sea and the sinking of Venetian ships. On 19 February the Senate decided to prepare a fleet of two armed transports and fifteen galleys to sail on 8 April. The organization of the expedition was entrusted to Alviso Longo with cautious instructions that included a helpful diktat to avoid confrontation with the Ottomans in the straits. He finally departed on 19 April, one day after the first major assault on the walls. Others made similarly uncoordinated efforts. On 13 April the government of the Republic of Genoa invited its citizens, merchants and officials 'in the East, in the Black Sea and in Syria' to help with all means the Emperor of Constantinople and Demetrios, despot of the Morea. Five days earlier it had been authorizing loans to arm ships against the Venetians. At about the same time the Pope had written to the Venetian Senate informing them of his desire to get up five galleys, on loan from the Venetians, for the relief of the city. The Venetians, ever sticklers for a debt, accepted the commission in principle but wrote back reminding the papacy that the cost of galleys for the failed crusade of Varna in 1444 was still outstanding.

Pope Nicholas had however already undertaken one prompt initiative at his own expense. Fearful of the fate of Constantinople, in March he hired three Genoese merchant ships, provisioned them with food, men and weapons, and dispatched them to the city. By the start of April they had reached the Genoese island of Chios off the Anatolian coast but could proceed no further. The north wind that impeded the Ottoman fleet held the Genoese at Chios for a fortnight. On 15 April the wind shifted to the south and the ships set sail. By the 19th they had reached the Dardanelles where they fell in with a heavy imperial transport, laden with a cargo of corn the emperor had purchased from Sicily and commanded by an Italian, Francesco Lecanella. They swept up the Dardanelles and passed the Ottoman naval base at Gallipoli unopposed – the entire fleet had decamped to the Double Columns. The ships were in all likelihood similar to those that had seen off the Ottomans at the boom a few days previously: high-sided sail-powered vessels, probably carracks, described by the Ottoman chronicler Tursun Bey as 'cogs'. On the swell of the south wind they made rapid time up the Marmara so that by the morning of 20 April the crews could make out the great dome of St Sophia forming on their eastern horizon.

The look-out for a relieving fleet was a constant obsession in the city. The ships were seen at about ten in the morning and the Genoese flags – a red cross on a white background – identified. The news caused an instant stir among the people. Almost simultaneously the ships were also sighted by Ottoman naval patrols and word was sent to Mehmet in his camp at Maltepe. He galloped down to the Double Columns to deliver clear and peremptory orders to Baltaoglu. Doubtless stung by the failure of his fleet at the boom and the reversal at the land walls, Mehmet's message to commander and fleet was unequivocal; 'either to take the sailing ships and bring them to him or never to come back alive'. The galley fleet was hurriedly made ready with a full complement of rowers and crammed with crack troops – heavy infantry, bowmen and Janissaries from his personal bodyguard. Light cannon were again loaded on board, as well as incendiary materials and 'many other weapons: round and rectangular shields, helmets, breast plates, missiles and javelins and long spears, and other things useful for this kind of battle'. The fleet set out down the Bosphorus to confront the intruders.

Success was imperative for morale, but this second naval battle was to be fought further out in the straits where the vagaries of the Bosphorus's extraordinary winds and local currents were less predictable and the demands on ships could be exacting. The Genoese merchantmen were battering up the straits with the wind astern. The Ottoman fleet, unable to use their sails against the wind, lowered them as they rowed downstream against a choppy sea.

By early afternoon the four ships were off the south-east of the city, keeping a steady course for the tower of Demetrios the Great, a prominent landmark on the city's Acropolis, and well out from the shore, ready to make the turning manoeuvre into the mouth of the Horn. The huge disparity in numbers filled Baltaoglu's men 'with ambition and hope of success'. They came on steadily, 'with a great sounding of castanets and cries towards the four ships, rowing fast, like men wanting victory'. The sound of beating drums and the braying of *zornas* spread across the water as the galley fleet closed in. With the masts and oars of a hundred ships converging on the four merchantmen, the outcome seemed inevitable. The population of the city crowded to the walls, onto the roofs of houses or to the Sphendone of the Hippodrome, anywhere that had a wide view of the Marmara and the entrance of the Bosphorus. On the other side of the Horn, beyond the walls of Galata, Mehmet and his retinue watched from the vantage point of an opposing hill. Each side looked on with a mixture of hope and anxiety as Baltaoglu's trireme drew near to the lead ship. From the poop he peremptorily ordered them to lower their sails. The Genoese kept their course and Baltaoglu commanded his fleet to lie to and rake the carracks with fire. Stone shot whistled through the air; bolts, javelins and incendiary arrows were poured up at the ships from all directions but the Genoese did not waver. Again the advantage was with the taller ships: 'they fought from high up, and indeed from the yardarms and the wooden turrets they hurled down arrows, javelins and stones'. The weight of the sea made it hard for the galleys to steady their aim or to manoeuvre accurately around the carracks still surging forward with the south wind in their sails. The fight developed into a running skirmish, with the Ottoman troops struggling to get close enough in the choppy sea to board or to fire the sails, the Genoese flinging a hail of missiles from their castellated poops.

The small convoy of tall ships reached the point of the Acropolis unscathed and was ready to make the turn into the safety of the Horn when disaster struck. The wind suddenly dropped. The sails hung lifeless from the masts, and the ships, almost within touching distance of the city walls, lost all headway and started to drift helplessly on a perverse counter-current across the open mouth of the Horn and towards Mehmet and his watching army on the Galata shore. At once the balance shifted from the ships with sails to the galleys with oars. Baltaoglu gathered his larger vessels around the merchantmen at a slight distance and again pelted them with missiles, but with no greater effect than before. The cannon were too light and too low in the water to damage the hulls or disable the masts. The Christian crews were able to put out any fires with barrels of water. Seeing the failure of raking fire, the admiral 'shouted in a commanding voice' and ordered the fleet to close in and board.

The swarm of galleys and long boats converged on the cumbersome and disabled carracks. The sea congealed into a struggling mass of interlocking masts and hulls that looked, according to the chronicler Doukas, 'like dry land'. Baltaoglu rammed the beak of his trireme into the stern of the imperial galley, the largest and least heavily armed of the Christian ships. Ottoman infantry poured up the boarding bridges trying to get onto the ships with grappling hooks and ladders, to smash their hulls with axes, to set fire to them with flaming torches. Some climbed up anchor cables and ropes; others hurled lances and javelins up at the wooden ramparts. At close quarters the struggle developed into a serious of vicious hand-to-hand encounters. From above, the defenders, protected by good armour, smashed the heads of their assailants with clubs as they emerged over the ships' sides, cut off scrabbling hands with cutlasses, hurled javelins, spears, pikes and stones down on the seething mass below. From higher up in the yardarms and crow's nests 'they threw missiles from their terrible catapults and a rain of stones hurled down on the close-packed Turkish fleet'. Crossbowmen picked off chosen targets with well-aimed bolts and crewmen deployed cranes to hoist and drop weighty stones and barrels of water through the light hulls of the longboats, damaging and sinking many. The air was a confused mass of sounds: shouts and cries, the roaring of cannon, the splash of armoured men falling backwards into the water, the snapping of oars, the shattering of stone on wood, steel on steel, the whistling of arrows falling so fast 'that the oars couldn't be pushed down into the water', the sound of blades on flesh, of crackling fire and human pain. 'There was great shouting and

Ottoman galleys attacking Christian sailing ships

confusion on all sides as they encouraged each other', recorded Kritovoulos, 'hitting and being hit, slaughtering and being slaughtered, pushing and being pushed, swearing, cursing, threatening, moaning – it was a terrible din.'

For two hours the Ottoman fleet grappled with its intractable foe in the heat of battle. Its soldiers and sailors fought bravely and with extraordinary passion, 'like demons', recorded Archbishop Leonard begrudgingly. Gradually, and despite heavy losses, the weight of numbers started to tell. One ship was surrounded by five triremes, another by thirty long boats, a third by forty barges filled with soldiers, like swarms of ants trying to down a huge beetle. When one long boat fell back exhausted or was sunk, leaving its armoured soldiers to be swept off in the current or clinging to spars, fresh boats rowed forward to tear at their prey. Baltaoglu's trireme clung tenaciously to the heavier and less well-armed imperial transport, which 'defended itself brilliantly, with its captain Francesco Lecanella rushing to help'. In time, however it became apparent to the captains of the Genoese ships that the transport would be taken without swift intervention. Somehow they managed to bring their ships up alongside in a practised manoeuvre and lash the four vessels together, so that they seemed to move, according to an observer, like four towers rising up among the swarming seething confusion of the grappling Ottoman fleet from a surface of wood so dense that 'the water could hardly be seen'.

The spectators thronging the city walls and the ships within the boom watched helplessly as the matted raft of ships drifted slowly under the point of the Acropolis and towards the Galata shore. As the battle drew closer, Mehmet galloped down onto the foreshore, shouting excited instructions, threats and encouragement to his valiantly struggling men, then urging his horse into the shallow water in his desire to command the engagement. Baltaoglu was close enough now to hear and ignore his sultan's bellowed instructions. The sun was setting. The battle had been raging for three hours. It seemed certain that Ottomans must win 'for they took it in turns to fight, relieving each other, fresh men taking the places of the wounded or killed'. Sooner or later the supply of Christian missiles must give out and their energy would falter. And then something happened to shift the balance back again so suddenly that the watching Christians saw in it only the hand of God. The south wind picked up. Slowly the great square sails of the four towered carracks stirred and swelled and the ships started to moved forward again in a block, impelled by the irresistible momentum of the wind. Gathering speed, they crashed through the surrounding wall of frail galleys and surged towards the mouth of the Horn. Mehmet shouted curses at his commander and ships 'and tore his garments in his fury' but by now night was falling and it was too late to pursue the ships further. Beside himself with rage at the humiliation of the spectacle, Mehmet ordered the fleet to withdraw to the Double Columns.

In the moonless dark, two Venetian galleys were dispatched from behind the boom, sounding two or three trumpets on each galley and with the men shouting wildly to convince their enemies that a force of 'at least twenty galleys' was putting to sea and to discourage any further pursuit. The galleys towed the sailing ships into the harbour to the ringing of church bells and the cheering of the citizens. Mehmet was 'stunned. In silence, he whipped up his horse and rode away.'

10 Spirals of Blood
20–28 APRIL 1453

Warfare is deception.
A saying attributed to the Prophet

The immediate consequences of the naval engagement in the Bosphorus were profound. A few short hours had tipped the psychological balance of the siege sharply and unexpectedly back to the defenders. The spring sea had provided a huge auditorium for the public humiliation of the Ottoman fleet, watched both by the Greek population thronging the walls and the right wing of the army with Mehmet on the shore opposite.

It was obvious to both sides that the massive new fleet, which had so stunned the Christians when it first appeared in the Straits, could not match the experience of Western seamanship. It had been thwarted by superior skill and equipment, the innate limitations of war galleys – and not a little luck. Without secure control of the sea, the struggle to subdue the city would be hard fought, whatever the sultan's guns might achieve at the land walls.

Within the city, spirits were suddenly high again: 'the ambitions of the sultan were thrown into confusion and his reputed power diminished, because so many of his triremes couldn't by any means capture just one ship'. The ships not only brought much needed grain, arms and manpower, they had given the defenders precious hope. This small flotilla might be merely the precursor of a larger rescue fleet. And if

Medieval catapult

four ships were able to defy the Ottoman navy, what might a dozen well-armed galleys of the Italian republics not do to decide the final outcome? 'This unhoped-for result revived their hopes and brought encouragement, and filled them with very favourable hopes, not only about what had happened, but also about their expectations for the future.' In the fevered religious atmosphere of the conflict, such events were never just the practical contest of men and materials or the play of winds, they were clear evidence of the hand of God. 'They prayed to their prophet Muhammad in vain,' wrote the surgeon Nicolo Barbaro, 'while our Eternal God heard the prayers of us Christians, so that we were victorious in this battle.'

Some time about now, it seems that Constantine, buoyed by this victory or the failure of the earlier Ottoman land attack, sensed that the moment was right to make a peace offer. He probably proposed a face-saving payment that would allow Mehmet to withdraw with honour, and he may have delivered it via Halil Pasha. Siege warfare involves a complex symbiosis between besieger and besieged and he was fully aware that outside the walls the Muslim camp was plunged into a corresponding mood of crisis. For the first time since the siege began, serious doubts were voiced. Constantinople remained obdurate – a 'bone in the throat of Allah' – like the crusader castles. The city was a psychological as much as a military problem for the warriors of the Faith. The technological and cultural self-confidence needed to defeat the infidel and to overturn the deep pattern of history was suddenly fragile again and the death of the Prophet's standard-bearer Ayyub at the walls eight centuries before would have been keenly in mind. 'This event', wrote the Ottoman chronicler Tursun Bey, 'caused despair and disorder in the ranks of the Muslims . . . the army was split into groups.'

It was a defining moment for the self-belief of the cause. In practical terms, the possibility of a long-drawn-out siege, with all its problems for logistics and morale, the likelihood of disease – the scourge of medieval besieging armies – and the chance that men might slip away, must have loomed larger on the evening of 20 April. It spelled clear personal danger for Mehmet's authority. An open revolt by the Janissaries became an idea on the fringe of possibility. Mehmet never commanded the love of his standing army as his father Murat had done. It had revolted against the petulant young sultan twice before and this was remembered, particularly by Halil Pasha, the chief vizier.

These feelings were brought into sharp focus that evening when Mehmet received a letter from Sheikh Akshemsettin, his spiritual adviser and a leading religious figure in the Ottoman camp. It presented the mood of the army and brought a warning:

> This event . . . has caused us great pain and low morale. Not having taken this opportunity has meant that certain adverse developments have taken place: one . . . is that the infidels have rejoiced and held a tumultuous demonstration; a second is the assertion that your noble majesty has shown little good judgement and ability in having your orders carried out . . . severe punishments will be required . . . if this punishment is not carried out now . . . the troops will not give their full support when the trenches must be levelled and the order is given for the final attack.

The sheikh also pointed out that the defeat threatened to undermine the religious faith of the men. 'I have been accused of having failed in my prayers', he went on, 'and that my prophecies have been shown to be unfounded . . . you must take care of this so that in the end we shall not be obliged to withdraw in shame and disappointment.'

Spurred by this, Mehmet set out early next morning, 21 April, with 'about ten thousand horse' and rode from his camp at Maltepe to the harbour at the Double Columns where the fleet was anchored. Baltaoglu was summoned ashore to answer for the naval debacle. The unfortunate admiral had been badly wounded in one eye from a stone hurled by one of his own men in the heat of battle; he must have presented a ghastly spectacle as he prostrated himself before his sultan. In the colourful words of a Christian chronicler, Mehmet 'groaned from the depths of his heart and breathed smoke from his mouth in his rage'. Furiously he demanded to know why he had failed to take the ships when the sea was flat calm: 'if you could not take them, how do you hope to take the fleet which is in the harbour at Constantinople?' The admiral replied that he had done everything in his power to seize the Christian ships: 'You know,' he pleaded, 'it was visible to all, that with the ram of my galley I never let go of the poop of the Emperor's ship – I fought fiercely all the time – the events were plainly visible, that my men are dead and there are many dead on the other galleys too.' Mehmet was so upset and angry that he ordered his admiral to be impaled. Appalled, the council and courtiers threw themselves before Mehmet to plead for his life, arguing that he had fought bravely to the end and that the loss of his eye was visible proof of his efforts. Mehmet relented. The death sentence was commuted. In front of his fleet and the watching circle of cavalry, Baltaoglu received a hundred lashes. He was stripped of his rank and property, which was distributed among the Janissaries. Mehmet understood the negative and positive propaganda value of such actions. Baltaoglu vanished into the obscurity of history and the poisoned chalice of naval command passed back to Hamza Bey, who had been admiral under Mehmet's father. The lessons of this episode would not have been wasted on either the watching soldiers and sailors or on the inner circle of viziers and advisers. It was a chance to observe the perils of the sultan's displeasure at first hand.

There is another version of this episode told by the Greek chronicler Doukas, whose tale of the siege is vivid but often implausible. In this account Mehmet had Baltaoglu stretched on the ground and delivered the hundred strokes himself 'with a golden rod weighing five pounds, which the tyrant had ordered to be made so that he might thrash people'. Then one of the Janissaries, keen to gain further credit from the sultan, smashed him on the head with a stone and gouged out his eye. The story is colourful and almost certainly untrue but it reflected the popular Western view of Mehmet the Eastern tyrant, barbaric in his opulence, sadistic in his pleasures, unquestioningly served by a slave army.

Having made an example of his admiral, Mehmet called an immediate meeting of his inner council to discuss Constantine's peace offer of the preceding day. In the speed of events, initiatives were starting to overlap each other out of any sequence. Confronted by a significant setback and the first stirrings of dissent, the question was simply whether to continue with the siege or to seek favourable terms.

There were two factions in the Ottoman high command that were engaged in their own long-running struggle for survival and power under the sultan's volatile rule. On the one side was the chief vizier, Halil Pasha, an ethnic Turk of the old Ottoman ruling class who had been vizier under Murat, Mehmet's father, and who had steered the young sultan through his turbulent early years. He had witnessed the crisis years of the 1440s and the Janissary revolt against Mehmet at Edirne and he was cautious about the chances of survival for Mehmet in the case of humiliation at the Greek walls. During the whole of the siege Halil's strategy was undermined by the taunts of his opponents, who nicknamed him 'the friend of the infidel', the lover of Greek gold.

In opposition were the new men of Ottoman power: a group of ambitious military leaders who were largely outsiders – converted renegades from the sultan's ever-expanding empire. They had always repudiated any peace policy and encouraged Mehmet's dreams of world conquest. They attached their fortunes to the capture of this city. Foremost amongst them was the second vizier Zaganos Pasha, a Greek convert, 'the one who was most feared and had the most voice and authority', and who was a leading military commander. This faction had a strong backing from religious leaders, proponents of holy war, such as the learned Islamic scholar, Ulema Ahmet Gurani, Mehmet's formidable tutor, and Sheikh Akshemsettin, who represented the long-cherished Islamic fervour to take the Christian city.

Halil argued that the opportunity should be taken to withdraw honourably from the siege on favourable terms: that the failed naval encounter revealed the difficulty of capturing the city and the possibility of a relieving Hungarian army or Italian fleet increased as the campaign dragged on. He voiced his conviction that the apple would one day fall into the sultan's lap, 'as the ripe fruit falls from the tree', but that this golden fruit was not ripe yet. By imposing a punitive peace settlement, that day could be hastened. He proposed the demand of a massive 70,000 ducats as a yearly tribute from the emperor to lift the siege.

The war party strenuously opposed this line. Zaganos replied that the campaign should be pursued with intensified vigour, that the arrival of the Genoese ships only underlined the need for a decisive blow. It was a key moment. The Ottoman command recognized that their fortunes had reached a critical point but the intensity of the debate also reflected awareness amongst the leading viziers that they were arguing for their influence with the sultan, and ultimately their own survival. Mehmet sat on his dais above the debate whilst the rivals jockeyed for position, but by temperament and inclination he was always of the war party. The council decided by a clear majority to continue the campaign. An answer was sent back to Constantine that peace could only result from an immediate surrender of the city. The sultan would cede the Peloponnese to Constantine and compensate his brothers who currently held it. It was an offer designed to be refused and it duly was. Constantine had his own awareness of the obligations of history and stood in the shoes of his father. When the Ottomans were at the gates in 1397 Manuel II had been heard to murmur: 'Lord Jesus Christ, let it not come to pass that the great multitude of Christian people should hear it said that it was in the days of the Emperor Manuel that the City, with all its sacred and venerable monuments of the Faith, was delivered to the infidel.' In this spirit, the emperor would fight to the last. The siege went on, while the war party, feeling the growing pressure of events, resolved to intensify the conflict.

Three miles away the assault on the city continued regardless, propelled by an integrated plan of attack that was secret to all but Mehmet and his generals. A huge bombardment of the land walls, which had commenced the day before, continued without ceasing throughout the night and into the day of the military council. The Ottoman fire was concentrated on the wall near the St Romanus Gate in the Lycus valley, the section of the defences that both sides knew to be most vulnerable.

Under incessant gunfire, a major tower, the Bactatinian, collapsed and several yards of outer wall fell with it. A sizeable breach had been effected and the defenders were suddenly exposed. 'This was the start of fear of those in the city and in the fleet,' recorded Nicolo Barbaro. 'We did not doubt that they wanted to make an all-out attack right away; everyone generally believed that they would soon see Turkish turbans inside the city.' What demoralized the defenders was again the speed with which the Ottoman guns could demolish apparently redoubtable defences when sufficient firepower was concentrated on a single spot. 'For such a big stretch of the wall had been ruined by the bombardment that everyone thought himself lost, considering how in a few days they had destroyed so much of the wall.' It seemed obvious to the defenders looking out from the gaping hole that a concerted attack at this point 'with only ten thousand men' would result in certain loss of the city. They waited for the inevitable assault but Mehmet and all the military command were at the Double Columns debating the future of the campaign and no order was given. In comparison to the fragmented volunteer nature of the Christian defence that relied heavily on individual initiative, it seemed that the Ottoman troops only responded to central directives. Nothing happened to press home the advantage of the guns and the defenders had time to regroup.

Under cover of darkness Giustiniani and his men set about making running repairs to the damaged wall. 'These repairs were made with barrels filled with stones and earth, and behind them there was made a very wide ditch with a dam at the end of it, which was covered with strips of vine and other layers of branches drenched with water to make them solid, so that it was as strong as the wall had been.' This stockade of wood, earth and stones continued to be effective, smothering the force of the giant stone balls. Somehow these ad hoc repairs were undertaken in the face of continuous fire from 'their huge cannon and from their other cannon, and from very many guns, countless bows and many hand guns'. Barbaro's account of the day closes with a final haunting image of the enemy, swarming and alien, a glimpse of horror to the ship's doctor: the ground in front of the wall 'could not be seen, because it was covered by the Turks, particularly Janissaries, who are the bravest soldiers the Great Turk has, and also many of the Sultan's slaves, who could be recognised by their white turbans, while the ordinary Turks wore red turbans'. Still no attack came. It was apparent that good luck – and 'our merciful Lord Jesus Christ, who is full of compassion' – had spared the city that day.

Events on 21 April seem suddenly to speed up and overlap each other, as if both sides recognized a moment of significant intensity. For the defenders it was a process of continuous reaction; without the resources to make sorties, they could only watch from within the triangle of the ancient walls, trust in the firmness of their fortifications and wait, rushing to each particular crisis, plugging gaps – and quarrelling. Blown back and forth by hope and despair, by rumours of attack and relieving armies, they worked ceaselessly to hold the line and they looked west for the smudge of approaching sails.

Mehmet seems to be have been spurred into a frenzy of activity by the events of these days. The failure of his navy, the fear of relief, the pessimism of his troops: these were the problems which occupied him on the 21st. He moved restlessly around the perimeter of the city, from the red and gold tent to the Double Columns to his troops above Galata, analyzing the problem in three dimensions, viewing the 'golden fruit' from different angles, turning it over in his mind. His desire for Constantinople went back to his childhood. From his first distant views of the city as a boy to his nocturnal ramblings through the streets of Adrianople in the winter of 1452 the city was an obsession that had informed his intense preoccupation with Western treatises on siege warfare, the preliminary studies of the terrain, the detailed sketches of the walls. Mehmet was incessant in its pursuit: asking questions, garnering resources and technical skills, interrogating spies, storing information. The obsession was linked to secrecy, learned young in the dangerous world of the Ottoman court, which made him keep plans close to himself until they were ripe. On being asked once about a future campaign, Mehmet is reputed to have refused a direct answer and replied: 'Be certain that if I knew that one of the hairs of my beard had learned my secret, I would pull it out and consign it to the flames.' His next move was to be similarly guarded.

The problem, he reasoned, was the chain that guarded the entrance to the Horn. It barred his navy from pressurizing the city from more than one side and allowed the defenders to concentrate their meagre forces on defending the land walls, diminishing his huge numerical advantage. Ottoman guns had destroyed Constantine's defensive wall across the Isthmus at Corinth in a week, but here, although the great cannon had certainly blasted holes in Theodosius's ancient structure, progress had been slower than he had hoped. Seen from the outside, the defensive system was too complex and many-layered and the ditch too deep for quick results. Furthermore Giustiniani had proved to be a strategist of genius. His marshalling of limited manpower and materials had been highly effective: earth had succeeded where stone had failed and the line had held – just.

Closed, the Horn provided a safe anchorage for any relieving fleet and constituted a base for naval counter-attack. It also lengthened the line of communication between the different parts of Mehmet's army and his navy, as troops were forced to make a long detour around the top of the Horn to pass from the land walls to the Double Columns. The problem of the chain had to be solved.

No one knows for certain where Mehmet came up with the idea, or how long he had been developing it, but on 21 April he accelerated an extraordinary solution to the chain. If it could not be forced, he reasoned, it must be bypassed, and this could only be done by bodily transporting his fleet over land and launching it into the Horn beyond the defensive line. Contemporary Christian chroniclers had their own ideas about the origin of this strategy. Archbishop Leonard was clear: yet again it was the know-how and advice of perfidious Europeans; Mehmet was prompted 'by the recollections of a faithless Christian. I think that the man who revealed this trick to the Turks learned it from a Venetian strategy at Lake Garda.' Certainly the Venetians had carried galleys from the River Adige into Lake Garda as recently as 1439, but medieval campaigns are littered with other precedents, and Mehmet was a keen student of military history. Saladin had transported galleys from the Nile to the Red Sea in the twelfth century; in 1424 the Mamluks had taken galleys from Cairo to Suez. Whatever its origin it is certain that the scheme was already well under way before the 21st; events merely emphasized its urgency.

Mehmet had one further reason for attempting this manoeuvre. He felt it was important to pressurize the Genoese colony on the other side of the Horn at Galata, whose ambiguous neutrality in the conflict was the source of complaints by both sides. Galata traded profitably with both city and besiegers. In the process it acted as a membrane through which materials and intelligence passed to and fro. There were rumours that the citizens of Galata circulated openly in the Ottoman camp by day, supplying oil to cool the great guns and whatever else could be sold, then slipped across the Horn at night to take their place on the walls. The boom was secured within the walls of Galata and could not be tackled directly, as Mehmet was anxious not to seek open warfare with the Genoese. He was aware that direct hostilities could risk the dispatch of a powerful fleet from the mother city. At the same time he recognized that the natural sympathies of the citizens of Galata were with their fellow Christians; Giustiniani himself was Genoese. The arrival of the relieving Genoese ships had also probably tipped the balance of sympathy, as Leonard of Chios recognized: 'The people of Galata had been acting very cautiously . . . but now they were anxious to provide both weapons and men, but only in secret, lest the enemy, who was just feigning peace towards them, should find out.' The double life of the Genoese community meant, however, that information could pass both ways, and this was soon to have tragic consequences.

All the land behind Galata, which had originally been covered with vineyards and rough scrub, was in Ottoman hands under the command of Zaganos Pasha. It is probable that early in the siege a decision was taken to construct a road from the Bosphorus at a point close to the Double Columns up a steep valley to a ridge behind Galata and then down another valley to the Golden Horn beyond the Genoese settlement at a place called the Valley of the Springs, where there was a Genoese graveyard outside the walls. Mehmet decided that this should be the route for the venture. At its greatest height this road rose to about 200 feet above sea level and would have presented a tough challenge for anyone attempting to haul ships overland. However, the one thing that Mehmet never lacked was human labour. With his usual secrecy and forethought, he had gathered the materials for this attempt: timber for making a primitive trackway, rollers and cradles to carry the ships, barrels of lard, teams of oxen and men. The ground was cleared of brushwood and levelled as effectively as possible. On 21 April the work on this project was accelerated. Teams of labourers laid the wooden track up the valley from the Bosphorus, rollers were prepared and greased with animal fat, cradles constructed to lift the ships from the water. To deflect interest from these preparations, Mehmet brought a battery of guns up onto a hill just north of the Galata settlement and ordered Zaganos to bombard the ships defending the Horn.

It is still puzzling to understand how the Christians failed to hear of such a substantial piece of engineering through the intelligence portal of Galata or via Christian soldiers in the Ottoman camp. In the early days, the Genoese probably saw the preparatory groundworks as a straightforward road-building project. Later they were either deterred from watching too closely by the artillery bombardment behind them, or they were guilty of collusion in the project, as the Venetians believed. It is probable too that Mehmet ensured that none of his Christian troops were employed in the project. Whatever the truth, no hint reached the city of what was about to ensue .

Early on the morning of Sunday 22 April while this gunfire continued and the Christians who were able made their way to church, the first cradle was lowered into the water of the Bosphorus. A small *fusta* was floated into it, then eased onto the greased wooden rollers on the trackway by means of pulleys. The ever-present sultan was there to witness and encourage the attempt. 'And having girdled them well with ropes, he attached long cables to the corners and assigned them to the soldiers to drag, some by hand, others with certain winches and capstans.' The ship was pulled up the slope by teams of oxen and men and supported on either side by further gangs of workmen and soldiers. As it moved up the track further rollers were laid in its path; with the huge resources of animals and manpower organized for the attempt, the vessel inched slowly up the steep slope towards the ridge 200 feet above.

A favourable morning breeze was blowing off the sea and in an inspired moment Mehmet ordered a skeleton crew to take their places at the oars. 'Some raised the sails with great shouts as if they were setting sail, and the wind caught the sails and swelled them. Others seated themselves on the rowing benches, took the oars in their hands and moved them back and forward as if they were actually rowing. And the commanders, running about by the mast holders, with whistles and shouts and whips lashing those on the benches, ordered them to row.' The ships were decked out with coloured pennants, drums were beaten and small bands of musicians played trumpets from the prows. It was a surreal moment of improvised carnival: the flags fluttering, the band playing, the oars moving, the sails billowing in the early morning breeze, the oxen straining and bellowing – a brilliant psychological gesture in the middle of war that was to become a potent ingredient in the Conqueror myth for the Turkish people. 'It was an extraordinary sight to behold', recorded Kritovoulos, 'and unbelievable to relate apart from to those who saw it with their own eyes, the ships being carried over the dry land as if sailing on the sea, with their crews and sails and all their equipment.' From the plateau nearby Zaganos Pasha continued to bombard the harbour below and two miles further off the great cannons pummelled the land walls at the St Romanus Gate.

From the ridge the trial ship made its ponderous descent down into the Valley of the Springs. With meticulous attention to detail Mehmet had moved a second battery of guns down to the shoreline to prevent any attack on the boats as they were launched. Well before noon this first ship splashed its way into the still waters of the Horn with its crew ready to repel any surprise attack, to be followed in rapid succession by others. In the course of the day about seventy boats were lowered one by one into the water at the Valley of the Springs. These boats were *fustae* – smaller fast biremes and triremes that were 'of fifteen banks of oars up to twenty and even twenty-two banks' and probably up to about seventy feet in length. The larger Ottoman galleys remained in the outer harbour at the Double Columns.

All the fine details of this operation – the timing, the route, the technology employed – remain deeply mysterious. In practice it is highly unlikely that it could have been completed in twenty-four hours. The ergonomics involved – hauling seventy ships a minimum of one and a quarter miles up an eight degree slope and then managing a controlled descent, even with the aid of large numbers of men and animals and the use of winches – suggest a far longer time span. It is possible that

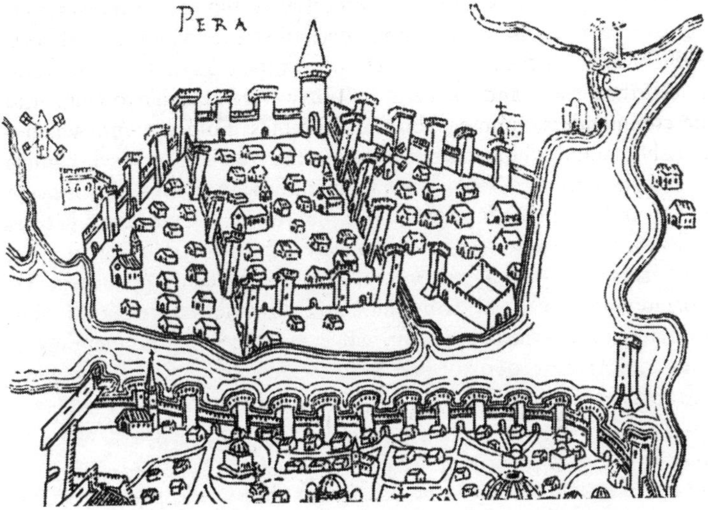

Galata (Pera) and the Golden Horn: the Double Columns are at the top right, the Valley of the Springs is below the windmill on the left

the larger ships had been disassembled and rebuilt close to the Horn shore well before 22 April, and that transportation of others had also been underway for some time. It is typical of Mehmet's secretiveness and deep planning that the truth will never be known, but all the chroniclers are in agreement that suddenly, on the morning of 22 April, the ships rolled one by one into the Galata basin. The whole operation was a strategic and psychological masterstroke, brilliantly conceived and executed. Even later Greek chroniclers gave it begrudging praise. 'It was a marvellous achievement and a superb stratagem of naval tactics,' recorded Melissenos. It was to have appalling consequences for the defenders.

Because of its protected position within the boom and the immense pressure being applied at the land wall, the sea wall along the Horn was barely guarded at all. There would have been few soldiers about to see the first ship breast the brow of the opposing hill and begin its descent into the water. When they did, panic spread quickly. People ran down the steep streets and watched in horror from the ramparts as one after another the Ottoman fleet slipped into the Horn. It was an extraordinary strategic and psychological riposte to the triumph of the fight in the Bosphorus.

Constantine immediately recognized the implications for his hard-pressed troops: 'Now that the wall along the Horn was opened up to warfare, they were compelled to guard it and were forced to strip other defended sectors and to send men there. It was an obvious danger to take front-rank soldiers from the rest of the walls, while those who were left were too few to defend it adequately.' The Venetians, as commanders of naval operations, were also deeply disturbed. The Ottoman fleet was less than a mile away in a closed strait only a few hundred yards wide; the Horn, which had been a sanctuary against attack, was now transformed into a claustrophobic cockpit where there was no room to breathe.

> When those in our fleet saw the *fustae*, they were undoubtedly very frightened, because they were certain that one night they would attack our fleet, together with their fleet which was at the Columns. Our fleet was inside the chain, the Turkish fleet was both inside and outside the chain, and from this description it can be grasped how great the danger was. And we were also very concerned about fire, that they might come to burn the ships lying at the chain, and we were perforce compelled to stand to arms at sea, night and day, with great fear of the Turks.

It was obvious to the defenders that an attempt to destroy the inner fleet was essential and urgent. The following day a council of war gathered in the Venetian church of St Mary, called by the Venetian bailey and the emperor with the express aim 'to burn the enemy fleet'. Only twelve men were present and they met in secret. Apart from Constantine, the majority were the Venetian commanders and sea captains. There was just one outsider to affairs the Venetians considered their own: Giovanni Giustiniani the Genoese, 'a man reliable in all matters', whose opinion commanded universal respect. A long and heated debate followed in which rival ideas were ardently promoted. Some wanted to make a full-scale attack in broad daylight with the whole fleet, involving the co-operation of the Genoese ships. This was rejected on the grounds that negotiations with Galata would be complex and speed was of the essence. Others wanted to deploy a land force to destroy the guns protecting the enemy fleet and then burn the ships; this was considered too risky given the small numbers of soldiers available. Lastly Giacomo Coco, the master of a galley that had come from Trebizond, 'a man of action, not words', spoke strongly in favour of a third option: mount a small naval expedition at night to attempt to catch and burn the Turkish fleet by surprise, prepare it in strict secrecy without consulting the Genoese and execute it without delay – time was everything. He offered to lead the attempt himself. This strategy was put to the vote and won the day.

On 24 April Coco set to work to implement this plan. He chose two sturdy high-sided merchant ships and packed wadded sacks of wool and cotton over the sides to protect them against stone cannon balls from Ottoman guns. Two large galleys were to accompany the merchantmen and repel any counter-attacks, while the actual damage was to be inflicted by a pair of light, fast *fustae* manned by seventy-two oarsmen each. These were filled with Greek fire and other combustible materials to burn the enemy fleet. Each ship was to be accompanied by a smaller boat with further materials. The plan was simple: the 'armoured' sailing vessels would protect the faster boats from gunfire until they were close up to the enemy, then these would dash out from the protective screen and attempt to fire the close-packed Ottoman ships. The vessels were to assemble one hour after sunset and the attack would set off at midnight. Everything was prepared; the commanders gathered on the galley of Aluvixe Diedo, the captain of the harbour, for a final briefing when the plan was unexpectedly stalled. The Genoese in the city had somehow got wind of it and wanted a role in the attack. They pressed hard for a delay to prepare their ships. Reluctantly the Venetians consented. The attack was postponed.

Four days passed while the Genoese readied their ships. Bombardment of the land walls continued unabated. The Venetians kicked their heels. 'From the twenty-fourth to the twenty-eighth of this month we waited,' recorded Barbaro. 'On the twenty-eighth of April, in the name of our Master Jesus Christ, it was decided to make an attempt to burn the fleet of the perfidious Turks.' The attack fleet had been slightly modified to accommodate the touchy sensibilities of the Genoese: the Venetians and the Genoese provided one padded merchantman each; there were two Venetian galleys, commanded by Gabriel Trevisano and Zacaria Grioni, three of the faster *fustae* with the combustible material led by Coco and a number of smaller boats with further supplies of pitch, brushwood and gunpowder.

Two hours before dawn on 28 April the attack force pulled silently out from under the lee of Galata's sea walls on the north-east side of the Horn and round the curve of the darkened shore towards the Valley of the Springs, a distance of less than a mile. The merchantmen, with Giustiniani aboard the Genoese vessel, led the way. The attack ships followed in their lee. Nothing moved on the calm water. The only sign of life was a light flaring briefly from the top of the Genoese Galata Tower. No sounds could be heard as they pulled towards the Ottoman fleet.

The larger sailing ships could only move slowly under oars compared to the swift many-oared *fustae* they were designed to protect, and whether it was the silence and suspense of the slow approach, a pent-up frustration at the delay of the attack, or a desire 'to win honour in the world', is not clear, but Giacomo Coco suddenly abandoned the carefully worked-out plan. On his own initiative he pulled his vessel ahead of the convoy and began to row at full speed at the anchored fleet to launch the attack. For a moment there was silence. Then out of the darkness a volley of cannon fire opened up at the unprotected vessel. A first shot fell near but missed. A second hit the *fusta* amidships and went straight through it. 'And this *fusta* could not have stayed afloat for as long as it took to say ten *Our Fathers*,' recorded Barbaro. In a flash the armoured soldiers and the rowers were pitched into the night sea and vanished.

In the darkness the vessels following were unable to see what had happened and pressed forward. More guns opened up at close range. 'There was so much smoke from the cannon and from the handguns that one could not see anything, and there were furious shouts from one side or the other.' As the ships moved up, Trevisano's larger galley came into the line of fire and was immediately hit by two cannon balls that passed straight through the hull. Water started to pour into the vessel but two wounded men lying below decks acted with great presence of mind to prevent it sinking. Plugging the holes with a store of cloaks they managed to staunch the inrush of water. The crippled galley, though half submerged, somehow stayed afloat and was rowed back to safety with great difficulty. The other ships tried to press home the attack but the intensity of the barrage of rocks, cannonballs and other missiles, and the sight of the damaged galley, induced them to withdraw.

Dawn was starting to break but in the confusion the two large merchant ships remained anchored in a defensive position according to the plan, unaware of the retreat of the remaining force. Seeing these ships unexpectedly isolated, the Ottoman fleet put out from its anchorage to surround and take them. 'A terrible and ferocious battle took place . . . it seemed truly to be like hell itself; there were bullets and arrows without number, and frequent cannon shots and gunfire.' The Muslim sailors shouted out the name of Allah as their seventy smaller ships swarmed forward to grapple with the enemy, but the two padded transports with their higher sides and skilled crews were able to hold them at bay. Fighting at close quarters continued fiercely for an hour and a half without either side being able to gain an advantage, until eventually they disengaged and returned to their anchorages. The Ottomans had lost one *fusta* but it was clear which side had won the day. 'Throughout the Turkish camp there were great celebrations because they had sent the *fusta* of master Giacomo Coco to the bottom', recalled Barbaro, 'and we were weeping with fear, lest the Turks should snatch victory against us with their fleet.' The Italians counted their losses: one *fusta* sunk with her crew and more men besides – some ninety skilled sailors and soldiers in all – one galley seriously damaged, the notion of Italian naval supremacy undermined. The roll call of the individual dead was long and the names well known to their comrades: 'Giacomo Coco, master; Antonio de Corfu, partner; Andrea Steco, mate; Zuan Marangon, crossbowman; Troilo de Grezi, crossbowman . . .' and so it went on. 'All these went down with the *fusta* and were all drowned, may God have mercy on them.'

As the morning of 29 April wore on, however, the nature of the loss was to assume a more ghastly shape. It transpired that not all the missing men had drowned. Some forty had swum free of their sinking craft, and in the darkness and the confusion of battle they made for the enemy shore and were captured. Mehmet now ordered them to be impaled in full view of the city as a punishment and a warning. In horror the survivors watched the preparations from the walls. What they would have seen has been graphically recorded by Jacopo de Campi, a Genoese merchant who spent twenty-five years trading in the Ottoman Empire at this time:

> The Grand Turk [makes] the man he wishes to punish lie down on the ground; a sharp long pole is placed in the rectum; with a big mallet held in both hands the executioner strikes it with all his might, so that the pole, known as a *palo*, enters the human body, and according to its path, the unfortunate lingers on or dies at once; then he raises the pole and plants it in the ground; thus the unfortunate is left in extremis; he does not live long.

So 'the stakes were planted, and they were left to die in full view of the guards on the walls'.

European writers of the time made great play of the barbarity of this method of execution and took it to be particularly Turkish. Impalement, especially as a means of demoralizing besieged cities, was a widely practised shock tactic that the Ottomans had learned in the Christian Balkans. They themselves later suffered one of the most infamous atrocities of history in this manner: reportedly 25,000 of them died on the stakes of Vlad Dracul on the Danubian plains in 1461. Even Mehmet would be appalled and haunted by the accounts brought back by eyewitnesses of 'countless stakes planted in the ground, laden not with fruit but with corpses' and in the centre of this arrangement on a taller stake to mark his status, the body of his one-time admiral Hamza Bey, still wearing his red and purple robes of office.

On the afternoon of 28 April the bodies of the Italian sailors staked in full view of the walls had their desired effect: 'the lamentation in the city for these young men was incalculable,' reported Melissenos, but grief swiftly turned to fury and in an attempt to assuage their loss and their frustration at the failure of the attack they responded with an atrocity of their own. Since the start of the siege the city had been holding about 260 Ottoman prisoners. The following day, presumably on the orders of Constantine, the defenders retaliated in kind. 'Our men were enraged, and savagely slaughtered the Turks they were holding prisoner on the walls, in full view of their comrades.' One by one they were brought up to the ramparts and hung 'in circles' in front of the watching Ottoman army. 'In this way', lamented Archbishop Leonard, 'by a combination of impiety and cruelty, the war became more brutal.'

The dangling prisoners and the staked sailors mocked each other over the front line, but in the aftermath of this cycle of violence it was clear that the initiative had shifted back to the besieging force. The inner Ottoman fleet still floated and it was obvious to the defenders that crucial control of the Horn had been lost. The bungled night attack had severely tipped the scales against the city. As they reflected on this, reasons for failure were sought and blame was attributed, particularly amongst the Italians themselves. It was clear that the delay in Coco's attack had proved fatal. Somehow the enemy had got to know of their plans and were lying in wait: Mehmet had moved more guns up to the inner harbour ready for the raiding party, the light from the Galata Tower had been a signal from someone within the Genoese colony. The recriminations between the Italian factions were about to develop a logic of their own.

11 Terrible Engines
28 APRIL–25 MAY 1453

There is a need for machines for conducting a siege: different types and forms of tortoises . . . portable wooden towers . . . different forms of ladders . . . different tools for digging through different types of walls . . . machines for mounting walls without ladders.

Tenth-century manual on siege craft

'Alas, most blessed Father, what a terrible disaster, that Neptune's fury should drown them in one blow!' Recriminations for the failure of the night attack were bitter and immediate. The Venetians had lost eighty or ninety of their close companions in the disaster and they knew whom they held responsible: 'This betrayal was committed by the cursed Genoese of Pera, rebels against the Christian faith,' declared Nicolo Barbaro, 'to show themselves friendly to the Turkish Sultan.' The Venetians claimed that someone from Galata had gone to the sultan's camp with news of the plan. They named names: it was the podesta himself who had sent men to the sultan, or it was a man called Faiuzo. The Genoese replied that the Venetians had been entirely responsible for the debacle; Coco was 'so greedy for honour and glory' that he had ignored instructions and brought disaster on the whole expedition. Furthermore they accused the Venetian sailors of secretly loading their ships and making ready to escape from the city.

A furious row broke out, 'each side accusing the other of intending to escape'. All the deeper enmities between the Italians bubbled to the sur-

A siege tower attacks a castle

face. The Venetians declared that they had unloaded their ships again at the command of the emperor and suggested that the Genoese should likewise 'put the rudders and sails from your ships in a safe place in Constantinople'. The Genoese retorted that they had no intention of abandoning the city; unlike the Venetians, they had wives, families and property in Galata 'which we are preparing to defend to the last drop of our blood' and refused to put 'our noble city, an ornament to Genoa, into your power'. The deep ambiguity of the position of the Genoese at Galata laid them open to charges of deception and treachery from every direction. They traded with both sides yet their natural sympathies lay with their fellow Christians and they had compromised their overt neutrality by allowing the chain to be fixed within their walls.

It is probable that Constantine had to intervene personally in the quarrel between the suspicious Italians, but the Horn itself remained a zone of unresolved tension. Haunted by the fear of night attacks or a pincer movement between the two arms of the Ottoman fleet, the one inside the Horn at the Springs and the other outside at the Columns, it was impossible for the Christian fleet to relax. Day and night they stood to arms, straining their senses for the sound of approaching fire ships. At the Springs the Ottoman guns remained primed against a second assault but their ships did not move. The Venetians reorganized themselves after the loss of Coco. A new commander, Dolfin Dolfin, was appointed to his galley and consideration was given to other strategies for destroying the Ottoman ships in the Horn. Evidently another ship-borne assault was considered too risky after the failure of 28 April so the decision was taken to use long-range means to discomfort the enemy.

On 3 May two fairly large cannon were placed by one of the water gates onto the Horn directly opposite the Ottoman fleet at a distance of about 700 yards across the water and proceeded to bombard the ships. Initial results were promising. Some of the *fustae* were sunk and 'many of their men were being killed by our bombardment', according to Barbaro, but the Ottomans took swift measures to counter this threat. They moved their ships back out of range and replied with three large cannon of their own 'and caused considerable damage'. The two sets of guns blasted away at each other day and night for ten days across the strait but neither could knock the other out, 'because our cannon were behind the walls, and theirs were protected by good embankments, and the bombardment was carried out across a distance of half a mile'. In this way the contest petered away into a stalemate, but the pressure in the Horn remained and on 5 May Mehmet responded with an artillery initiative of his own.

His restless mind had evidently been considering for some time how to bombard the ships at the boom, given that the walls of Galata lay within the line of fire. The solution was to create a cannon with a more looping trajectory that could fire from behind the Genoese town. He accordingly put his gun founders to work devising a primitive mortar, 'that could fire the stone very high, so that when it came down it would hit the ships right in the middle and sink them'. The new cannon had duly been made and was now ready. From a hill behind Galata it opened fire on the ships at the boom. The trajectory was complicated by the walls of the town within the line of fire but this was probably a positive advantage to Mehmet: it also allowed him to put psychological pressure on the suspect Genoese. As the first shots from the mortar hurtled over their roofs, the townspeople must have felt the Ottoman noose tightening on their enclave. The third shot of the day 'came from the top of the hill with a crash' and hit not an enemy vessel but the deck of a neutral Genoese merchant ship 'of three hundred botte, which was loaded with silk, wax and other merchandise worth twelve thousand ducats, and immediately it went straight to the bottom, so that neither the masthead nor the hull of the ship were visible, and a number of men on the ship were drowned'. At once all the vessels guarding the boom moved into the lee of Galata's city walls. The bombardment went on, the range was shortened slightly and balls started to hit the walls and houses of the town itself. Men on the galleys and ships continued to be killed by the stone bullets, 'some shots killing four men', but the walls afforded sufficient protection to prevent any more ships being sunk. For the first time the Genoese found themselves under direct bombardment and although only one person was killed, 'a woman of excellent reputation, who was standing in the middle of a group of thirty people', the declaration of intent was clear.

A deputation from the city made its way to the sultan's camp to complain about this attack. The vizier protested with a straight face that they thought the ship belonged to the enemy and blandly assured them that 'whatever they were owed they would be repaid' when the city was finally captured. 'With this act of aggression did the Turks repay the friendship which the people of Galata had shown them,'

Doukas proclaimed sarcastically, referring to the intelligence that had undone Coco's attack. Meanwhile stone balls continued to loop down over the Horn in an arced trajectory. By 14 May, according to Barbaro, the Ottomans had fired 'two hundred and twelve stone balls, and they all weighed at least two hundred pounds each'. The Christian fleet remained pinned down and useless. Well before that date it was clear that the Christians had surrendered effective control of the Horn, and the pressing need to provide more men and materials on the land walls further deepened the divisions amongst the sailors. With the pressure easing, Mehmet ordered a pontoon bridge to be constructed across the Horn just above the city walls to shorten his lines of communication and to allow men and guns to be moved about at will.

At the land walls Mehmet also set about tightening the screw. His tactics became attritional and increasingly psychological. Now that the defenders had to be spread even more thinly, he decided to wear them down with incessant gunfire. In late April he moved some of the big guns to the central section of wall near the St Romanus Gate, 'because in that place the wall was lower and weaker', though attention was still also being directed to the single wall in the palace area. Day and night the guns blasted away; occasional skirmishes were mounted at irregular moments to test the resolve of the defence, then suspended for days at a time to lull the defenders into a false sense of security.

Towards the end of April a substantial bombardment brought down about thirty feet from the top of the wall. After dark Giustiniani's men set to once again, walling up the breach with an earth bank, but the following morning the cannon renewed their attack. However, towards mid-day the chamber of one of the big guns cracked, probably because of flaws in the barrel, although the Russian Nestor-Iskander claims that it had been hit by one of the defenders' own cannon. Infuriated by this setback, Mehmet called for an impromptu attack. A charge was made at the wall that took the defenders by surprise. A huge firefight ensued. Bells were rung in the city and people rushed to the ramparts. With the 'clatter and flashing of weapons, it seemed to all that the city had been uprooted from its foundation'. The charging Ottoman troops were mown down and trampled underfoot by those coming up behind in their frenzy to reach the walls. To the Russian Nestor-Iskander it was a ghoulish prospect: 'as if on the steppes, the Turks walked over the broken human corpses crammed to the top and fought on, for their dead resembled a bridge or a stairway to the city'. With huge difficulty the attack was eventually repulsed, although it took until nightfall. Corpses were left piled in the ditches; 'from near the breach to the valleys they were filled with blood'. Exhausted by the effort, soldiers and townspeople retired to sleep, leaving the wounded groaning outside the walls. The following day the monks again started their lugubrious task of burying the Christian dead and counting the number of their fallen enemy. Constantine, now strained by the attritional fighting, was visibly upset by the casualties.

In effect exhaustion, hunger and despair were beginning to take their toll on the defenders. By early May food supplies were running short; it was now more difficult to trade with the Genoese at Galata and dangerous to row out into the Horn to fish. During quiet spells soldiers at the wall took to deserting their posts in search of food for their families. The Ottomans became aware of this and made surprise raids to drag down the barrels of earth on the ramparts with hooked sticks; they could even openly approach the walls and retrieve cannon balls with nets. Recriminations mounted. The Genoese archbishop, Leonard, accused the Greeks who had left their posts of being afraid. They replied, 'What is the defence to me, if my family's in need?' Others, he considered, 'were full of hatred for the Latins'. There were complaints of hoarding, cowardice, profiteering and obstruction. Rifts started to open up across the fault lines of nationality, language and creed. Giustiniani and Notaras competed for military resources. Leonard railed against 'what certain people did – drinkers of human blood – who hoarded food or raised its price'. Under the stress of the siege, the fragile Christian coalition was falling apart. Leonard blamed Constantine for failing to control the situation: 'The Emperor lacked severity, and those who did not obey were neither punished with words nor the sword'. These rifts probably made their way back to Mehmet outside the wall. 'The forces defending the city fell into disunity,' recorded the Ottoman chronicler, Tursun Bey, of these days.

To ensure that the walls were not neglected in the search for food, Constantine ordered that supplies should be evenly distributed among the dependants of the soldiers. So serious was the situation that with the advice of his ministers he began to requisition church plate and had it melted down for coin to pay the men so that whatever food was available might be purchased. It was probably a controversial move,

A late-fifteenth-century map of the triangular city, showing St Sophia and the ruined hippodrome on the right, with the main roads leading from the land walls on the left. The Imperial Palace is in the tip of the triangle top left. Above the Golden Horn is the Genoese town of Pera or Galata. Anatolia, marked Turquia, is beyond the straits on the far right.

Mehmet the aesthete and scholar: a semi-stylised Ottoman miniature of the sultan in his later years

'We knew not whether we were in heaven or on earth': the great nave of St Sophia, the most miraculous building of late antiquity

A nineteenth-century photograph of the Imperial Palace of Blachernae, Constantine's headquarters during the siege, which is set into the single-layered land wall near the Golden Horn

A section of the triple land wall showing first the line of inner towers, then the lower outer towers shattered by cannon fire. In the centre is the moat, now largely filled in but once bricklined and ten feet deep, that cost the Ottomans so much trouble during the siege. Having crossed it, would-be attackers had to rush the open terrace under heavy fire before they could tackle the outer wall.

The great chain with its massive eighteen-inch links that was stretched across the Golden Horn. This nineteenth-century photograph shows that substantial lengths of it were still lying around in the city four hundred years after the siege.

Orban's great siege gun has long since disappeared but several slightly smaller cannon still survive in Istanbul. This massive bronze piece is fourteen feet long, weighs fifteen tons and fired a five-hundred-pound stone ball.

A contemporary drawing by Bellini of a Janissary in his distinctive white headdress with arrow quiver, bow and sword. Mehmet is said to have been fascinated but also superstitiously frightened by the Italian master's ability to conjure apparently living, three-dimensional figures out of the flat paper in defiance of Islamic law.

A fascinating European version of the siege painted in 1455 that compresses many of the key events into one image. Constantinople has been transformed into a scene from chivalry but the picture has been created by someone who knew many details of the story.

A French reworking of one of the great images of Turkish history: Fatih the Conqueror, enters the city through the Edirne gate, accompanied by the warriors of Islam. Dead Christians lie strewn in the foreground.

A sixteenth-century picture of St Sophia, converted into the Aya Sofya mosque with the addition of minarets by the famous Ottoman architect Sinan

Mehmet in Bellini's famous late portrait, framed within an imperial arch bearing the legend 'Conqueror of the World' but looking somewhat gaunt and ill

Constantine's palace at Mistra in the Peloponnese, 'little Constantinople', perched high above the Spartan plain – a poignant memorial to the Byzantine spirit

unlikely to win the favour of the pious Orthodox who saw the sufferings of the city as a consequence of sin and error.

Deliberations amongst the commanders intensified. The presence of the enemy fleet in the Horn had greatly confused the defence and they were forced to reallocate their troops and commands accordingly. The sea was watched from the walls twenty-four hours a day but nothing stirred on the western horizon. Probably on 3 May a major council was called, involving the commanders, civic dignitaries and churchmen, to discuss the situation. The guns were still pummelling the walls, morale was weakening and there was a feeling that all-out assault was imminent. In an atmosphere charged with foreboding, a move was made to persuade Constantine to leave the city for the Peloponnese where he could regroup, gather new forces and strike again. Giustiniani offered his galleys for the emperor's escape. The chroniclers give an emotional account of Constantine's response. He 'fell silent for a long time and shed tears. He spoke to them as follows: "I praise and thank your counsel and all of you, as all of this is in my interest; it can only be so. But how can I do this and leave the clergy, the churches of God, the empire and all of the people? What will the world think of me, I pray, tell me? No, my lords, no: I will die here with you." Falling, he bowed to them and cried in grief. The patriarch and all of the people present started to weep in silence.'

Recovering from this moment, Constantine made a practical suggestion that the Venetians should send out a ship at once to search the eastern Aegean for signs of a rescue fleet. Twelve men volunteered for the hazardous duty of running the Ottoman blockade and a brigantine was accordingly prepared for the task. Towards midnight on 3 May the crew, dressed as Turks, stepped aboard the small boat, which was towed to the boom. Sporting the Ottoman flag, it unfurled its sail and slipped unnoticed through the enemy patrol and headed west down the Marmara under cover of darkness.

Mehmet continued to bombard the walls despite technical difficulties with the big guns. On 6 May he decided that the time was right for a knock-out blow: 'he ordered all of the army to march once more on the city and to make war for all day'. News from within the city probably convinced him that morale was collapsing; other reports may have warned him of the slowly gathering momentum of an Italian relief force. He sensed that the weakness of the central section of wall was now at a critical point. He decided to attempt another major attack.

The big guns opened up on 6 May, supported by smaller cannon in the now familiar pattern of firing, accompanied by 'cries and the banging of castanets to frighten the people of the city'. Soon another portion of wall fell in. The defenders waited for nightfall to make their repairs but on this occasion the guns continued firing in the dark. It became impossible to repair the gap. The following morning the cannon again plugged away at the base of the wall and brought down a further substantial section. All day the Ottomans kept firing. At about 7 o'clock at night, with the customary din, a massive assault was launched at the breach. Away in the harbour the Christian sailors heard the wild cries and stood to arms, fearing a matching attack by the Ottoman fleet. Thousands of men crossed the ditch and ran for the breach, but numbers were not an advantage in the limited space and they trampled one another in their attempt to force their way in. Giustiniani rushed to meet the intruders and a desperate hand-to-hand struggle took place in the gap.

In the first wave, a Janissary called Murat led the assault, slashing fiercely at Giustiniani, who was only saved from death by a Greek jumping down from the wall and cutting off his assailant's legs with an axe. A second wave was led by one Omar Bey, the standard bearer of the European army – and was met by a substantial contingent of Greeks commanded by their officer Rhangabes. In the slashing, hacking confusion, the two leaders squared up to each other in single combat in front of their men. Omar 'bared his sword, he attacked him and with fury did they slash at each other. Rhangabes stepped on a rock, grasped his sword with two hands, struck him on the shoulder, and cut him into two, for he had great strength in his arms.' Infuriated at the death of their commander, the Ottoman troops encircled Rhangabes and cut him down. Like a scene from the *Iliad*, the two sides surged forward to try to seize the body. The Greeks were desperate to gain control of the corpse and piled out of the gates, 'but they were unable and suffered many losses'. The Ottomans cut the mutilated body to pieces and drove the Greek soldiers back into the city. For three hours the battle raged on but the defenders successfully held the line. As the fighting died down, the cannon started to open up again to prevent the breach being filled and the Ottomans launched a second diversionary raid, trying to set fire to the gate near the palace. This was again defeated. In the darkness Giustiniani and the exhausted defenders worked to rebuild the makeshift defences. Because of the firing at the wall, they were forced to build their protective barrier of earth and timber slightly inside its original line. The wall was holding – but only just. And inside the city 'there was great mourning and dread among the Greeks over Rhangabes, because he was a great warrior, was courageous, and was beloved of the Emperor'.

For the defenders the continuous cycles of bombardment, attack and repair began to blur. Like diaries of trench warfare, the chroniclers' accounts become repetitive and monotonous. 'On the eleventh of May', records Barbaro, 'on this day nothing happened either on land or at sea except a considerable bombardment of the walls from the landward side, and nothing else worth mentioning happened . . . on the thirteenth of May there came some Turks to the walls, skirmishing, but nothing significant happened during the whole day and night, except for continuous bombardment of the unfortunate walls.' Nestor-Iskander starts to lose track of time; events jump out of sequence, converge and repeat. Both soldiers and civilians were growing weary of fighting, repairing, burying corpses and counting the enemy dead. The Ottomans, with their scrupulous concern for the hygiene of their camp, carried their casualties away and burned the bodies daily but the ditches were still choked with rotting corpses. The slaughter risked contaminating water supplies: 'the blood remained in the rivers and putrefied in the streams, giving off a great stench'. Within the city the people turned increasingly to the churches and the miracle-working power of their icons, preoccupied by sin and the theological explanation for events. 'Thus one could see throughout the entire city all the people and the women who came in miraculous procession to the churches of God with tears, praising and giving thanks to God and to the most pure Mother of God.' In the Ottoman camp the hours of the day were marked out by the call to prayer; dervishes went among the troops enjoining the faithful to hold fast and remember the prophecies of the Hadith: 'In the jihad against Constantinople, one third of Muslims will allow themselves to be defeated, which Allah cannot forgive; one third will be killed in battle, making them wondrous martyrs; and one third will be victorious.'

As losses continued to mount, Constantine and his commanders hunted anxiously for resources to fill the gaps, but the difficulty of getting all the defenders to co-operate continued to frustrate their best efforts. The Grand Duke Lucas Notaras quarrelled with Giustiniani, while the Venetians largely operated as an independent force. The only supply of untapped manpower and weapons remained on the galleys, and an appeal was made to the Venetian community accordingly. On 8 May the Venetian Council of the Twelve met and voted to unload the arms stored on the three Venetian great galleys, to transfer the men to the walls and then sink the galleys in the arsenal. It was a desperate measure designed to ensure the full-hearted involvement of the sailors in the fate of the city but it provoked another furious backlash. As the unloading was about to begin, the crews leaped to bar the gangways with drawn swords, declaring: 'Let us see who will take the cargoes from these galleys! . . . we know that once we have unloaded these galleys and sunk them in the arsenal, at once the Greeks will keep us in their city by plain force as their own slaves, while we are now free either to go or to stay.' Fearing the destruction of their one means of safety, the captains and crews sealed their ships and sat tight. All day bombardment of the land walls continued with unbridled ferocity. The urgency of the situation forced the council to meet again the following day and amend its plans. This time the captain of the two long galleys, Gabriel Trevisano, agreed to disarm his ships and take his 400 men to join the defence at the St Romanus Gate. It took four days to persuade the men to co-operate and to move the equipment. By the time they arrived on 13 May it was almost too late.

Although Mehmet had concentrated his fire on the area of the St Romanus Gate, some guns continued to blast away at a spot near the palace where the Theodosian wall formed its awkward junction with the single wall. By 12 May the guns had demolished a section of outer wall and Mehmet decided to make a concentrated night attack on this spot. Towards midnight a huge force advanced on the breach. The defenders were taken by surprise and forced back from the wall by a force commanded by Mustapha, the standard-bearer of the Anatolian army. Further reinforcements rushed from other sections of the wall but the Ottomans continued to push them back and began to mount scaling ladders against the wall. Terror broke out in the narrow streets around the palace. The townspeople ran fleeing from the wall and many 'believed that night that the city was lost'.

At this moment, according to Nestor-Iskander, a grim council of war was taking place three miles away in the porch of St Sophia. It had become unavoidable to confront the gravity of the situation. The defenders were being relentlessly thinned out day after day: 'if it continues on, all of us will perish and they will take the city'. Confronted with this reality, Constantine was laying a series of blunt options before his commanders: they could either sally out of the city at night and try to defeat the Ottomans in surprise attack or they could sit tight and await the inevitable, hoping for rescue by the Hungarians or the Italians. Lucas Notaras was suggesting that they should continue to hold out while others were again begging Constantine to leave the city, when word arrived that 'the Turks were already ascending the wall and overpowering the townspeople'.

Constantine galloped towards the palace. In the darkness he met citizens and soldiers fleeing from the breach. In vain he tried to turn them back but the situation was deteriorating by the minute. Ottoman cavalry had started to penetrate the city and the fighting was now taking place inside the walls. The arrival of Constantine and his bodyguard managed to rally the Greek soldiers: 'the Emperor arrived, cried out to his own men, and made them stronger'. With the help of Giustiniani he forced the intruders back, trapped them in the maze of narrow streets and divided their forces in two. Cornered, the Ottomans counter-attacked fiercely, trying to get at the emperor. Unscathed and excited by the chase Constantine drove some of them back as far as the breach – and would have galloped after them 'but the nobles of the imperial suite and his German guards stopped him and prevailed on him to ride back'. The Ottoman troops who could not escape were massacred in the dark lanes. Next morning the townspeople dragged the corpses up to the walls and hurled them into the ditch for their comrades to collect. The city had survived but each attack was lengthening the odds of survival.

This was to be Mehmet's last major assault on the palace section of wall. Despite its failure he must have felt that success was within his grasp. He seems now to have decided to concentrate all his firepower on the weakest stretch of all – the St Romanus Gate. On 14 May, when he learned that the Christians had disarmed some of their galleys and withdrawn the majority of their fleet into a small harbour back from the boom, he concluded that his ships in the Horn were relatively safe from attack. He then moved his guns from Galata Hill round to the land walls. At first he stationed them to bombard the wall near the palace; when this proved ineffectual he moved them again to St Romanus. Increasingly the guns were concentrated at one spot rather than being spread out along a broad front. The bombardments became ever more furious: 'Day and night these cannon did not stop firing at our poor walls, battering large portions of wall to the ground, and we in the city worked day and night to effect good repairs where the walls were smashed, with barrels and brushwood and earth and whatever else was necessary to do this.' It was here that the fresh men from the long galleys under Trevisano were stationed with 'good cannon and good guns and a large number of crossbows and other equipment'.

At the same time Mehmet ensured that the ships defending the boom were kept under constant pressure. On 16 May at the twenty-second hour some brigantines were seen to detach themselves from the main Ottoman fleet out in the straits and head at full speed for the boom. The watching sailors assumed them to be Christian conscripts escaping from the fleet 'and we Christians who were at the chain waited them with great pleasure'. As they drew near however, they loosed shots at the defenders. At once the Italians launched their own brigantines to see them off and the intruders turned to escape. The Christian ships nearly caught them before 'they hurriedly started rowing and escaped back to their fleet'. The following day the Ottomans tested the boom again with five fast *fustae*. They were seen off with a hail of 'more than seventy shots'.

A third and final assault on the boom was mounted before daybreak on 21 May, this time by the whole fleet. They came rowing hard towards the chain 'with a great sounding of their tambourines and castanets in an attempt to frighten us', then stopped, eyeing up the strength of their opponents. The ships at the boom were armed and ready and a major sea battle seemed about to unfold when suddenly the alarm was heard from within the city signalling a general attack. At this, all the ships in the Horn rushed to action stations and the Ottoman fleet appeared to have second thoughts. It turned about and sailed back to the Double Columns, so that 'two hours after sunrise there was complete calm on both sides, as if no attack by sea had taken place'. It was the last attempt on the boom. In all likelihood the morale in the Ottoman fleet, largely manned by Christian rowers, was now too low to mount a serious challenge to the Christian ships, but these manoeuvres ensured that the defenders could never relax.

Elsewhere the Muslims were ominously busy. On 19 May Ottoman engineers finished the construction of a pontoon bridge ready to swing across the Horn just beyond the walls. It was another extraordinary feat of improvisation. The pontoons comprised a thousand large barrels, doubtless obtained from the wine-drinking Christians at Galata, tied together in pairs lengthways and planked on top to provide a carriageway wide enough for five soldiers to walk abreast and solid enough to support a cart. The aim was to shorten communications round the top of the Horn between the two wings of his army. Barbaro suggests that Mehmet was preparing the pontoon bridge in readiness for a general attack when he might want to move his men quickly, but that it was only floated into its final position across the Horn at the end of the siege, for 'if the bridge had been stretched across the Horn before the all-out attack, a single shot from a cannon would have broken it'. All these preparations could be seen from the city walls. They provided the defenders with an ominous sense of the huge resources of manpower and materials that Mehmet could bring to the siege, but it was engineering work that they could not yet see that was soon to throw the Christians into deeper panic.

By the middle of May Mehmet had stretched the defences of the city to the limit but they had still not cracked. He had employed the resources of his army and navy to the full, in assault, bombardment and blockade, three of the key techniques of medieval siege warfare. There remained one classic strategy as yet largely untried – mining.

Within the Ottoman vassal states in Serbia lay Novo Brdo, the most important city in the interior of the Balkans, famed throughout Europe for the wealth of its silver mines. The Slav troops conscripted for the campaign included a band of skilled miners from the city, probably Saxon immigrants, 'masters in the art of digging and cutting away mountains, to whose tools marble was as wax and the black mountains as piles of dust'. They had made an early attempt at mining under the walls in the central section, but this had been abandoned because the ground was unsuitable. In mid-May, as other methods failed and the siege dragged on into its second month, another initiative was started, this time near the single wall of the palace. Mining, although laborious, was one of the most successful techniques for bringing down walls, and had been profitably employed by Muslim armies for hundreds of years. By the end of the twelfth century Saladin's successors had learned to capture the great crusader castles within six weeks through a combination of bombardment and mining.

Sometime in mid-May the Saxon silver miners, hidden by palisades and bunkers, started to dig the 250 yards to the wall from behind the Ottoman trenches. It was skilled, exhausting work and nightmarishly difficult. Lit by smoking torches, the miners excavated narrow subterranean tunnels, propping them with timber supports as they went. Attempts to undermine the walls in earlier Ottoman sieges had proved unsuccessful, and it was the received wisdom of old men in the city that mining would inevitably fail because the ground beneath the walls was mostly solid rock. In the dead of night on 16 May the defenders were aghast to discover the falsity of this notion. By chance soldiers on the ramparts heard the clink of pickaxes and the sound of muffled voices coming from the ground inside the wall. The mine had evidently passed under the ramparts and was intended to provide a secret point of entry into the city. Notaras and Constantine were quickly notified. A panicky conference was called and a search was made throughout the city for men with mining experience to confront this new threat. The man chosen to organize the defence against attack from underground was something of a curiosity: 'John Grant, a German, a skilful soldier, highly trained in military matters', had come to the siege in the company of Giustiniani. He was in fact a Scotsman who had apparently worked in Germany. It is impossible to guess at the sequence of events that had brought him to Constantinople. He was evidently a highly skilled professional soldier, siege specialist and engineer and for a brief moment he occupied a central role in one of the strangest sub-plots in the story of the struggle.

Grant evidently knew his business. The position of the enemy mine was located by the sound of the work. A countermine was dug with speed and stealth. The defenders had the advantage of surprise. Bursting into the enemy tunnel in the dark, they fired the pit props and collapsed the tunnel on the miners, leaving them to suffocate in the dark. The danger posed by this mine banished any complacency within the city. Henceforth, full precautions were taken to watch for mining activity. Grant must have instituted the standard practices of the time. Bowls or buckets of water would be placed at regular intervals on the ground by the wall and were observed for telltale ripples on the surface that would indicate subterranean vibrations. The greater skill was to locate the direction of the mine and to intercept it quickly and stealthily. Over the following days a grim underground struggle unfolded with its own skills and disciplines that echoed the contest for the wall and the boom in the daylight world. For a few days after 16 May, Christian sappers found no sign of movement. On the 21st another mine was detected. It had again passed under the foundations with the intention of letting troops into the city. Grant's men intercepted the tunnel but failed to surprise the Ottomans who withdrew, burning the props behind them so that it collapsed.

Thereafter it became a game of cat and mouse fought out in the dark under horrific conditions. The following day 'at the hour of Compline' the defenders discovered a tunnel into the city near the Calegaria Gate, which they intercepted. They burned the miners alive with Greek fire. A few hours later telltale vibrations indicated yet another mine near by, but this one proved harder to intercept. However, the pit props collapsed of their own accord and killed all the miners inside.

The Saxon miners were indefatigable. Not a day went by without underground warfare. Each time, Giacomo Tetaldi recalled, 'the Christians dug counter-mines, and listened, and located them . . . they suffocated the Turks in their mines with smoke, or sometimes with foul and evil-smelling odours. In some places they drowned them with a flood of water, and often found themselves fighting hand to hand.'

While the tunnelling continued, Mehmet's engineers contrived another remarkable and totally unexpected initiative in the world above. At daybreak on the morning of 19 May, the watchers on the wall near the Charisian Gate stirring themselves for another day looked out over the distant sea of enemy tents – and were staggered by what they saw. Ten paces in front of them and positioned on the lip of the ditch was an enormous tower, 'overtopping the walls of the barbicans', that had somehow appeared from nowhere overnight. The defenders were amazed and mystified by how the Ottomans had managed to erect this structure so rapidly, which had been wheeled forward from the enemy lines in the dark and now overtopped the ramparts. It was built on a framework of stout beams covered with camel skins and a double layer of hurdles to protect the men inside. Its lower half had been filled with earth and embanked with earth on the outside 'so that shots from cannon or handguns could not harm it'. Each storey inside was connected by ladders that could also be used to bridge the gap between the tower and the wall. Overnight a huge body of men had also constructed a covered causeway from it back to the Ottoman lines 'half a mile long . . . and over it two layers of hurdles and on top of them camel skins, by means of which they could go from the tower to the camp under cover, in such a way that they could not be harmed by bullets or crossbow bolts or by stones from small cannon'. Armed men rushed to the wall to view the incredible sight. The siege tower was almost a throwback to the era of classical warfare, though it seemed to Archbishop Leonard to be a device 'such as the Romans could scarcely have constructed'. It had been designed specifically to fill in the troublesome ditch in front of the wall. Inside the tower, teams of men were excavating earth and hurling it out through small openings in the protective screen into the ditch in front. They kept at it all day: while from the higher storeys archers shot a covering fire of arrows into the city, 'it seemed, from sheer high spirits'.

It was a signature project for Mehmet – conceived in secret on a grand scale and executed, like the transportation of the ships, with extraordinary speed. Its psychological impact was profound. The resourcefulness and the resources of the besieging army must have struck the defenders like a recurring nightmare. Constantine and his commanders hurried to the battlements to confront yet another emergency, 'and when they saw it they were all struck down with fear like dead men, and they were continuously concerned that this tower might cause them to lose the city because it overtopped the barbicans'. The threat from the tower was palpable. It was closing up the ditch in front of their eyes, and the covering fire from its archers made it difficult to mount any response. By nightfall the Ottomans had made remarkable progress. They had filled the ditch with logs, dried branches and earth. The siege tower, pushed from within, moved further forward and closer to the wall. The panicky defenders decided that immediate action was imperative – another day under the shadow of the overhanging tower could prove fatal. After dark, packed barrels of gunpowder were prepared behind the walls and rolled off the ramparts towards the tower, with fuses sputtering. There was a series of huge explosions: 'suddenly the earth roared like great thunder and lifted up the siege turrets and the men to the clouds, like a mighty storm'. The tower cracked and exploded: 'people and logs fell from high'. The defenders hurled barrels of burning pitch down on the wounded groaning below. Advancing out from the walls they massacred any further survivors and burned the bodies along with other siege equipment that had been drawn up nearby: 'long battering rams and wheeled ladders, and waggons with protective turrets on them'. Mehmet observed this failure from a distance. Furious, he withdrew his men. Similar towers which had been advanced at other points along the wall were also withdrawn or burned by the defenders. The siege towers were evidently too vulnerable to fire and the experiment was not repeated.

Underground the tunnel war intensified. On 23 May the defenders detected and entered yet another mine. As they advanced down the narrow shaft by the flickering light of flares, they found themselves suddenly face to face with the enemy. Hurling Greek fire, they brought down the roof, burying the miners, but managed to capture two officers and bring them back to the surface alive. The Greeks tortured these men until they revealed the location of all the other workings; 'and when they had confessed, their heads were cut off, and their bodies were thrown from the walls on the side of the city where the Turkish camp was; and the Turks, when they saw their men thrown from the walls, became enraged and felt great bitterness towards the Greeks and us Italians'.

The following day the silver miners changed their tactics. Instead of passing straight under the walls to create passageways into the city, they turned their tunnel sideways on reaching the wall to run directly under it for a distance of ten paces. The tunnel was propped on timbers and prepared for firing with the aim of collapsing a section of wall. The work was only just discovered in time; the intruders were repulsed and the wall was bricked up again underneath. It caused great disquiet in the city. On 25 May one last attempt was made to repeat this operation. The miners again managed to prop a long section of wall ready for firing before being intercepted and repulsed. In the eyes of the defenders it was the most dangerous of any of the tunnels to be found and its discovery signalled the end of the tunnel war. The Saxon miners had worked ceaselessly for ten days; they had constructed fourteen tunnels but Grant had destroyed them all. Mehmet acknowledged the failure of both towers and mines – and kept the guns firing.

*

Away to the west of Constantinople, far from the sound of firing and the night attacks, another small but significant drama was being played out. In one of the island harbours of the eastern Aegean a sailing ship was rocking at anchor. It was the Venetian brigantine that had slipped away from the city. During mid-May it swept the archipelago, looking for signs of a rescue fleet. The crew found nothing. They had received no positive reports from passing vessels. They now knew that there were no ships. In fact the Venetian fleet was off the coast of Greece cautiously seeking information about Ottoman naval intentions, whilst the galleys that the Pope had ordered from Venice were still under construction. The crew fully understood the implications of their situation. On deck a heated debate was in progress about what to do next. One sailor made a strong case for sailing away from the city and back to 'a Christian land, because I know very clearly that by this time the Turks will have taken Constantinople'. His companions turned to him and replied that the emperor had entrusted them with this task, and that it was their bounden duty to complete it: 'and so we want to return to Constantinople, if it is in the hands of the Turks or the Christians, if it is to death or to life, let us go on our way'. The democratic decision was taken to return, whatever the consequences.

The brigantine swept back up the Dardanelles on the south wind, reassumed its Turkish disguise and approached the city shortly before daybreak on 23 May. This time the Ottoman fleet was not deceived. They had been patrolling attentively, fearing the arrival of Venetian galleys, and took the small sailing boat for their outrider. They rowed forward to intercept but the brigantine outstripped them and the boom opened to let it back in. That day the crew went to make their report to the emperor that they had found no fleet. Constantine thanked them for returning to the city and 'began to weep bitterly for grief'. The final realization that Christendom would send no ships snuffed out any hopes of rescue; 'and seeing this the Emperor decided to put himself in the hands of our most merciful Lord Jesus Christ and of his Mother Madonna Saint Mary, and of Saint Constantine, Defender of his City, that they might guard it'. It was the forty-eighth day of the siege.

12 Omens and Portents
24–26 MAY 1453

We see auguries in the replies and salutations of men. We note the cries of domestic birds, the flight of crows and we draw omens from them. We take note of dreams and believe that they foretell the future . . . it is these sins and others like them that make us worthy of the punishments with which God visits us.

Joseph Bryennios, fourteenth-century Byzantine writer

Prophecy, apocalypse, sin: as the siege entered the final weeks of May deepening religious dread gripped the people of the city. A belief in portents had always been a feature of the life of Byzantium. Constantinople itself had been founded as the result of a mystical sign – the vision of a cross that had appeared to Constantine the Great before the crucial battle at the Milvian Bridge twelve hundred and forty years earlier – and omens were eagerly sought and interpreted. With the inexorable decline of the empire, these became increasingly linked to a profound pessimism. There was a widely held belief that the Byzantine Empire was to be the last empire on earth, whose final century had started around 1394. People remembered the ancient prophetic books from the time of the earlier Arab sieges; their gnomic, oracular verses were widely recited: 'misfortune to you, city of seven hills, when the twentieth letter is proclaimed on your ramparts. Then the fall will be near and the destruction of your sovereigns.' The Turks, in their turn, were seen as an apocalyptic people signifying the last judgement, a scourge sent by God as a punishment for Christian sin.

Monograms inscribed on the walls

In this climate people unceasingly scrutinized signs that might foretell the end of empire – or of the world itself: epidemics, natural phenomena, angelic apparitions. The city itself, old beyond the comprehension of its inhabitants, had become enshrouded in legend, ancient prophecy and supernatural meanings. Its 1,000-year-old monuments, whose original purpose had been lost, were said to be magical cryptograms in which the future might be read: the sculpted frieze on the base of the statue in the Forum of the Bull contained an encoded prophecy of the city's end, and the great equestrian statue of Justinian pointing east no longer expressed confident dominion over the Persians. It foretold the direction from which the final destroyers of the city would come.

Against this background, presentiments of the last judgement gained an incremental force as the siege wore on. The unseasonable weather and the terror of unceasing artillery bombardment convinced the Orthodox faithful that the end was drawing nigh in explosions and black smoke. The Antichrist, in the shape of Mehmet, was at the gate. Prophetic dreams and portents were widely circulated: how a child had seen the angel who guarded the city walls abandon his post; how oysters had been gathered that dripped blood; how a great serpent was drawing near, devastating the land; how the earth tremors and hailstorms that struck the city made it clear 'that universal ruin was approaching'. Everything pointed to a belief that time was nearly completed. In the monastery of St George there was an oracular document, divided into squares, showing the succession of emperors, one emperor to each square: 'in time the squares were all filled, and they say that only one last square was still empty' – the square to be occupied by Constantine XI. Byzantine notions that time was circular and symmetrical were further confirmed by a second imperial prophecy: that the city would be both founded and lost by an Emperor Constantine whose mother was called Helen. Both Constantine I and Constantine XI had mothers of that name.

In this fevered climate, the morale of the civilian population seemed to be disintegrating. Continuous services of intercession were held throughout the city. Day and night an endless cycle of prayer arose from the churches, with the exception of St Sophia, which remained empty and unvisited. Nestor-Iskander witnessed 'all of the people assembled in the holy churches of God, weeping, sobbing, raising their arms to heaven, and petitioning the grace of God'. To the Orthodox, prayer was a work as essential to the survival of the city as the nightly toil of carrying stones and branches to repair the stockade. It supported the forcefield of divine protection that ringed the city. The more hopeful remembered a set of counter-prophecies: that the city was personally shielded by Mary, Mother of God, and could never be taken because it contained the relics of the True Cross; and that even if the enemy succeeded in entering the city they could only proceed as far as the column of Constantine the Great before an angel would descend from heaven with a sword and put them to flight.

Despite this, apocalyptic anxiety had been fuelled by the disheartening news from the Venetian brig on 23 May and it reached a crescendo on the night of the full moon. This was probably the next day, 24 May, though dates are uncertain. The moon held a haunting place in the city's psyche. Rising over the copper dome of St Sophia, shimmering on the calm waters of the Horn and over the Bosphorus, it had been the symbol of Byzantium since ancient times. Like a gold coin dug from the Asian hills night after night, its ebb and flow expressed the antiquity of the city and the endlessly repeated cycles of time through which it had lived – fluctuating, timeless and ominous. Earth's final millennium was considered to be ruled by the moon, when 'life will be short, fortune unstable'. By late May particular fear focused on a certain belief that the city could never be taken on a waxing moon; after the 24th the moon would start to wane again and the future would be uncertain. The prospect of this date filled the populace with dread. The whole prophetic history of the city seemed to be drawing to a point.

It was with apprehension that the people waited for twilight on 24 May. After another day of heavy bombardment the evening suddenly gave way to silence. By all accounts it was a beautiful spring night, a time when Constantinople was at its most magical, the last light still glimmering in the west, the distant sound of water lapping the sea walls. 'The air was clear and unclouded,' remembered Barbaro, 'pure as crystal.' However as the moon rose at the first hour after sunset the watchers were met by an extraordinary sight. Where there should have been a complete circle of gold, they could see a moon 'only three days old, with little of it visible'. For four hours it remained sickly and minimal, then agonizingly, it 'grew little by little to its full circle, and at the sixth hour of the night, it formed the complete circle'. The partial eclipse struck the defenders with the force of prophecy. Was not the crescent moon the symbol of the Ottomans, visible on standards fluttering over Mehmet's camp? According to Barbaro 'the Emperor was greatly afraid of this sign, and all of his lords . . . but the Turks held a great celebration in their camp at the sign, because it seemed now that victory was theirs'. For Constantine, struggling to maintain the morale of the populace, it was a heavy blow.

Seal showing the Hodegetria

The next day a decision was taken, perhaps at the instigation of Constantine, to lift the spirits of the people by making another direct appeal to the Virgin. Huge belief was placed in the supernatural powers of the Mother of God. Her most holy icon, the Hodegetria, 'the one who shows the way', was a talisman credited with miraculous powers. It was believed to have been painted by St Luke the Evangelist, and had an ancient and honourable role in successful defences of the city. It had been processed along the ramparts during the Avar siege of 626. Again in 718 the Hodegetria was credited with saving Constantinople from the Arabs. Accordingly a huge crowd gathered on the morning of 25 May at the icon's shrine, the church of St Saviour in Chora near the city walls, to seek protection from the Virgin. The Hodegetria, mounted on a wooden pallet, was lifted onto the shoulders of a team of men drawn from the confraternity of the icon, and a penitent procession set off down the steep, narrow streets in traditional order: in front a cross-bearer; behind, the black robed priests swinging their censers, then the laity, men, women and children probably walking barefoot. Cantors led the people in holy song. The haunting quartertones of the hymns, the lamentations of the people, the clouds of incense and the traditional prayers to the protecting Virgin – all rose in the morning air. Over and over the citizens repeated their powerful cry for psychic protection: 'Do thou save thy city, as thou knowest and willest. We put thee forward as our arms, our rampart, our shield, our general: do thou fight for thy people.' The exact route for these processions was said to be dictated by a force emanating from the icon itself, like the tug of a divining rod.

In this charged atmosphere of fear and devotion, what followed was utterly devastating. The icon suddenly and inexplicably slipped from the hands of the bearers 'without any reason or visible force and fell on the ground'. Horror-stricken, people rushed forward with wild shouts to restore the Virgin to her stand, but the icon seemed to have become fastened to the earth as if weighted with lead. It was impossible to lift. For a considerable time, the priests and bearers struggled, with shouts and prayers, to wrestle the miraculous image from the mud. Eventually it was raised again but everyone was struck with fear at this ill-omened event. And worse was soon to follow. The shakily reformed procession had hardly gone further when it was hit by a violent storm. Thunder and lightning cracked and spat across the noon sky; torrential rain and stinging hail lashed the bedraggled procession so violently that people 'were unable either to stand up against it or move forward'. The icon came to an unsteady halt. Torrents of floodwater surged down the narrow street with ominous force, threatening to sweep children away in their path: 'many following were in danger of being carried away and drowned by the force and terrible power of the water if some of the men had not quickly grabbed them and with difficulty hauled them out of the rushing torrent'. The procession had to be abandoned. The crowd dispersed, taking with them a clear interpretation of their plight. The Virgin had refused their prayers; the storm 'certainly foretold the imminent destruction of everything and that, like the torrential, violent water, it would carry off and destroy everything'.

The next morning they awoke to discover the city blanketed in thick fog. There was evidently no wind; the air was still and the fog clung to the city all day. Everything was muffled, silent, invisible. The eerie atmosphere tightened the mood of hysteria. It was as if the weather itself were undermining the will of the defenders. There could only be one possible interpretation for such unseasonable fog. It indicated the 'departure of God and his leaving the city, forsaking and turning

The God-protected city

away from it completely. For God hides himself in cloud and so appears and again disappears.' Towards evening the atmosphere seemed to grow even thicker and a 'great darkness began to gather over the city'. And something even stranger was witnessed. Initially the sentries on the walls observed Constantinople to be illuminated by lights as if the enemy were burning the city. Alarmed, people ran to see what was happening and cried aloud when they looked up at the dome of St Sophia. A strange light was flickering on the roof. The excitable Nestor-Iskander described what he saw: 'at the top of the window, a large flame of fire issuing forth; it encircled the entire neck of the church for a long time. The flame gathered into one; its flame altered, and there was an indescribable light. At once it took to the sky. Those who had seen it were benumbed; they began to wail and cry out in Greek: 'Lord have mercy! The light itself has gone up to heaven.' It seemed clear to the faithful that God had abandoned Constantinople. In the Ottoman camp the unnaturally heavy atmosphere and the unearthly light had a similar effect on the troops. There was uncertainty and panic at these apparitions. Within his tent, Mehmet had been unable to sleep. When he saw the glow over the city he was initially troubled and sent for his mullahs to interpret the portents. They came and duly proclaimed the omens favourable to the Muslim cause: 'This is a great sign: The city is doomed.'

The following day, a deputation of priests and ministers went to Constantine to express their forebodings. The mysterious light was duly described and they tried to persuade the emperor to seek a safer place from which to mount effective resistance to Mehmet: 'Emperor: weigh all of what has been said about this city. God granted the light in the time of Emperor Justinian for the preservation of the great holy church and this city. But in this night, it departed for heaven. This signifies that God's grace and generosity have gone from us: God wishes to hand over our city to the enemy . . . we beseech you: Leave the city so that we will not all perish!' From a mixture of emotion and sheer exhaustion, Constantine collapsed to the ground in a dead faint and remained unconscious for a long time. When he came round, his response was unchanged: to leave the city would be to invite immortal ridicule on his name. He would remain and die with his subjects if need be. He furthermore ordered them not to spread words of discomfort among the people: 'do not allow them to fall into despair and weaken their effort in battle'.

Others responded differently. On the night of 26 May, a Venetian sea captain, one Nicholas Giustiniani – unrelated to Giovanni Giustiniani, the hero of the siege – slipped the chain and sailed off under the wing of night. A few smaller boats put out from the small harbours along the Marmara sea walls, dodged the naval blockade and made for the ports of the Greek-speaking Aegean. Some of the richer citizens sought refuge on the Italian ships within the Horn, judging them to offer the best chance of escape in the event of a final catastrophe. Others began to look for safe bolt-holes within the city. Few had any illusions what defeat might bring.

*

Within the mystical framework of the medieval world, the astrological portents and unseasonable weather that destroyed the city's morale were clear signs of the will of God. In fact the most likely explanation for these terrifying phenomena lay far away in the Pacific Ocean and rivalled even the most lurid vision of Armageddon. Some time around the start of 1453 the volcanic island of Kuwae, 1,200 miles east of Australia, literally blew itself up. Eight cubic miles of molten rock were blasted into the stratosphere with a force two million times that of the Hiroshima bomb. It was the Krakatoa of the Middle Ages, an event that dimmed the world's weather. Volcanic dust was propelled across the earth on global winds, lowering temperatures and blighting harvests from China to Sweden. South of the Yangtze River, an area with a climate as mild as Florida, it snowed continuously for forty days. Contemporary tree-ring records from England show years of stunted growth. The sulphur-rich particles from Kuwae could well have been responsible for the unseasonably cool and unstable mixture of rain, hail, fog and snow that blighted the city throughout the spring. Suspended in the atmosphere they would also have created lurid sunsets and strange optical effects. It could have been volcanic particles, alone or in conjunction with the effect of St Elmo's fire – the glow from the discharges of atmospheric electricity – that bathed the copper dome of the cathedral in ominous ribbons of fire on 26 May, and conjured for the defenders these visions of oblivion. (Lurid light effects after the Krakatoa eruption in 1883 similarly alarmed people in New York, but living in a more scientific age, they tended to assume huge fires were raging and sent for the fire brigade.)

The febrile atmosphere of foreboding was not confined to the city. By the last week of May the Ottoman camp was also suffering a severe crisis of morale. A muffled discontent fluttered among the Islamic banners. It was now the fifth month of the Arabian lunar year; for seven weeks they had assaulted the city by land and sea. They had endured wretched spring weather and had suffered terrible casualties at the walls. Unknown numbers of trampled dead had been carried away from the choked ditches; day after day the smoke of funeral pyres rose over the plain. And yet as they looked up from the sea of ordered tents, the walls still stood; and where they had been demolished by the great guns, the long earth rampart surmounted by barrels had risen in their place as the taunt of a stubborn enemy. The double-headed eagle of the emperor still fluttered over the ramparts while the lion of St Mark over the imperial palace served as the reminder of the presence of Western aid, and the fear that reinforcements might be on their way. No armoured host could sustain a lengthy siege as effectively as the Ottomans. They understood the essential rules of camp life better than any Western army – the rapid burning of corpses, the protection of water sources and the sanitary disposal of excrement were essential disciplines in Ottoman warfare – but gradually the mathematics of the siege were stacking against them. It has been estimated that in the Middle Ages a besieging army of 25,000 men, a third the size of that at Constantinople, must transport 9,000 gallons of water and thirty tons of fodder a day to provision itself. In a sixty-day siege such an army would need to remove 1 million gallons of human and animal urine and 4,000 tons of solid biological waste. Soon the summer heat would add to the Muslims' material discomforts and the threat of disease. The clock was ticking on Ottoman resolve.

In reality, after seven weeks of warfare, an immense weariness was affecting both sides. There was recognition that a final outcome could not long be postponed. Nerves were strained to breaking point. In this climate the struggle for Constantinople had become a personal contest between Mehmet and Constantine for the morale of their men. While Constantine watched confidence disintegrate inside the city, an identical affliction mysteriously struck the rank and file of the Ottoman army. The exact sequence and dating of events remains uncertain. The arrival of the Venetian brigantine on 23 May, bringing news that that there was no relieving fleet, was perhaps perceived by the Ottomans as the outrider of that fleet. The next day word spread quickly among the tents that a powerful fleet was approaching the Dardanelles while a Hungarian crusader army under John Hunyadi, 'the redoubtable white knight', had already crossed the Danube and was marching on Edirne. The most likely explanation is that Constantine had allowed this message to seep out in a last attempt to undermine Ottoman morale. It was immediately successful. Uncertainty and alarm rippled across the plain. The men remembered, in the words of the chronicler, that 'many kings and sultans had aspired . . . and had assembled and equipped large armies, but no one had reached the foot of the fortress. They had withdrawn in pain, wounded and disillusioned.' A mood of despondency gripped the camp, and if Leonard of Chios is to be believed, 'the Turks began to shout against their Sultan'. For the second time doubt and a sense of danger gripped the Ottoman high command and the old divisions over the conduct of the siege started to resurface.

For Mehmet it was the moment of crisis. Failure to take the city might prove fatal to his reputation but time and the patience of his army were running out. He needed to regain the confidence of his men and to act decisively. The night of the eclipse provided a lucky moment to bolster flagging morale. The religious zeal of the mullahs and dervishes who had come to the siege ensured that a favourable interpretation of the lunar eclipse was spread throughout the camp, but the decision to continue with the siege remained uncertain. With a characteristic mixture of shrewdness and cunning, he decided to make one more attempt to persuade Constantine to surrender peacefully.

Probably around 25 May he sent an emissary to the city, Ismail, a renegade Greek nobleman, to confront the Byzantines with their probable fate. He appealed to the hopelessness of their situation: 'Men of Greece, your fate is indeed balanced on a razor's edge. Why then do you not send an ambassador to discuss peace with the Sultan? If you will entrust this matter to me, I shall arrange for him to offer you terms. Otherwise, your city will be enslaved, your wives and your children will be sent into slavery, and you yourselves will utterly perish.' Cautiously they decided to investigate the proposition, but resolved to hedge their bets by sending a man 'not of high rank', rather than risk the life of one of the leaders of the city. This unfortunate individual was brought to the red and gold tent to prostrate himself before the sultan. Mehmet tersely offered two choices: the city could either offer a huge annual tribute of 100,000 bezants, or the whole population could abandon the city, 'taking their possessions with them, and go wherever each one of them wished'. The offer was relayed to the emperor and his council. Paying the tribute was clearly beyond the means of the poverty-stricken city, and the notion of sailing away and abandoning Constantinople remained inconceivable to Constantine. His reply was to the effect that he would surrender all that he had, with the exception of the city. Mehmet retorted that the only choices left were surrender of the city, death by the sword or conversion to Islam. Perhaps underlying this, there was a feeling in the city that Mehmet's offer had not been sincere, that he had sent Ismail 'as a means of testing the state of mind of the Greeks . . . to find out what the Greeks thought of their situation, and how secure their position was'. For Mehmet, however, voluntary surrender was still the preferred option. It would preserve the fabric of a city that he intended for his capital; under the laws of Islam, he would be compelled to allow his troops three days of pillage if it had to be taken by force.

No one knows how close the city came to a voluntary surrender. It has been suggested that the Genoese, whose colony at Galata was also indirectly threatened, exerted pressure on the emperor to refuse the surrender offer, but it seems unlikely that Constantine, whose approach remained remarkably consistent, was ever seriously minded to hand over Constantinople. For both sides it was probably too late for negotiated surrender. There was too much bitterness. For fifty days they had taunted and slaughtered each other across the walls and executed prisoners in full view of their compatriots. It was a case of either lifting the siege or conquering the city. Doukas probably caught the true tenor of Constantine's reply: 'Impose as large an annual tribute as you can, then agree a peace treaty and withdraw, for you don't know if you will gain victory or be deceived. It is not in my power, nor in that of any citizen, to hand over the city to you. It is our universal resolve to die rather than have our lives spared.'

If Constantine had released the rumour of approaching Western armies into the Ottoman camp it was a double-edged weapon. Outside the walls there was uncertainty what to do, but the threat of relief accelerated decisive action. The categoric reply from Constantine refocused debate in the Ottoman camp. Probably on the next day, 26 May, Mehmet called a council of war to resolve the matter one way or the other – either to lift the siege or proceed to an all-out assault. The argument that followed was a reprise of the earlier crisis meeting after the naval defeat on 21 April. Once again the old Turkish vizier, Halil Pasha, rose to speak. He was cautious, fearful of the consequences of the young sultan's rashness and the risk of provoking Christendom into a united response. He had witnessed the vicissitudes of fortune under Mehmet's father and knew the dangers of an uneasy army. He spoke with passion for peace: 'Your power, which is already very great, you can increase more by peace than by war. For the outcome of war is uncertain – more often you see adversity rather than prosperity accompany it.' He raised the spectre of an advancing Hungarian army and an Italian fleet and urged Mehmet to demand heavy penalties from the Greeks and lift the siege. Again Zaganos Pasha, the Greek convert, argued for war, pointing out the huge discrepancy in forces, the daily erosion of the defenders' strength and their near total exhaustion. He scorned the notion that help would come from the West, and showed a good knowledge of the realities of Italian politics: 'The Genoese are split into factions, the Venetians are under attack from the Duke of Milan – neither would give any help at all.' He appealed to Mehmet's desire for glory and demanded 'the chance of making one short sharp general assault, and if we fail, we shall afterwards do whatever you think best'. Zaganos was again supported by other generals, such as Turahan Bey, the commander of the European army, and by a strong religious faction, led by Sheikh Akshemsettin and Mullah Gurani.

The debate was heated. It was the decisive moment in a power struggle between two factions at the Ottoman court that had been raging for ten years. The outcome was to be hugely influential for the future of the Ottoman state, but both sides also knew that that they were arguing for their lives – a failed policy would lead inexorably to the hangman's noose or the strangler's bowstring. In the event Mehmet was persuaded by the appeal to military glory to blot out the possibility of failure or military revolt; it is possible that he dispatched Zaganos to tour the camp and report back on the mood of the army before finally deciding. If so, the answer was naturally unequivocal – Zaganos dutifully 'discovered' that the army was full of enthusiasm for the final attack. Mehmet decided that the moment for hesitation was past: 'Decide the day of battle, Zaganos. Prepare the army, surround Galata so that it can't help the enemy and make all these preparations quickly.'

The word was spread throughout the camp that an attack was to be prepared within the next few days. Mehmet knew that he needed to seize the moment to raise the faltering morale of his troops in readiness for the final assault – and to dumbfound the enemy. As night fell on 26 May heralds walked among the tents crying out the sultan's orders. In front of each tent torches and fires were to be lit. 'And all the tents in the camp lit two fires, and the fires were so big, that from their great light it seemed to be day time.' From the battlements the defenders gazed out in wonder and confusion as the ring of fire gradually spread in a widening circle to embrace the whole horizon – from the camp in front of them to the hills around Galata and across the water to the Asian shore. It was so bright that tents could be counted individually. 'This strange spectacle was indeed incredible,' recorded Doukas. 'The surface of the sea flashed like lightning.' 'It seemed that the sea and land were on fire,' Tetaldi remembered. Accompanying the brilliant illumination of the night sky, came the slowly rising crescendo of drums and cymbals and the repeated accelerating shouts of the faithful, '*Illala, Illala, Mahomet Russolalla*' – 'God is, and will always be, and Muhammad is his servant' – so loudly that it seemed 'the sky itself would burst open'. Within the Ottoman camp there were extraordinary scenes of enthusiasm and joy at the full-hearted commitment to a final attack. Initially some on the walls optimistically mistook the illuminations for a fire rampaging through the enemy tents. They scrambled up to watch the spectacle – then understood the true significance of the glittering horizon, the wild shouting. The ring of fire had its desired effect within the city, draining the defenders of courage to the extent that 'they appeared to be half-dead, unable to breathe either in or out'. Amazement at the display of religious fervour gave way to panic. Fervent pleas were addressed to the Virgin and repeated prayers for deliverance: 'Spare us, O Lord.' If they needed any confirmation of what the shouting and the flames meant, it soon came. Under cover of darkness, Christian conscripts in the sultan's army shot stealthy arrows over the battlements with letters attached that outlined the coming attack.

By the light of the fires ominous preparations were underway. The landscape was alive with figures advancing brushwood and other materials ready to fill up the ditch. The guns had been directing a withering bombardment at Giustiniani's stockade in the Lycus valley all that day. It was probably the day of the great fog, when the nerves of the defenders were already shredded by the terrible omens. There was a non-stop hail of stone shot. Gaping holes started to appear in the defences. 'I cannot describe all that the cannon did to the wall on this day,' reported Barbaro. 'We had great suffering and great fear.' Night fell and the exhausted defenders under the direction of Giustiniani prepared yet again to plug the gaps, but in the brilliant light of the flames, the walls were clearly illuminated and the firing continued far into the night. And then, with a startling suddenness, towards midnight the fires were extinguished, the cries of exaltation suddenly died, the bombardment stopped and an unnerving silence fell upon the May night that appalled the watchers on the ramparts as much as the wild celebrations. Giustiniani and the citizens laboured on through what was left of the short period of darkness to make good the rampart.

At about this time the gradual destruction of the wall forced the defenders to make one other small alteration to their defensive arrangements. They had been in the habit of undertaking surprise sallies from the gates in the outer fortifications to disrupt the activities of the enemy. As the wall was destroyed and was replaced with the stockade, it became harder to make inconspicuous raids from their own lines. Some old men knew of a blocked-up sally port concealed below the royal palace at the point where the sharp angle was created by the meeting of the Theodosian wall with the more irregular wall of Komnenos. This ancient doorway was known variously as the Circus Gate or the Wooden Gate, and was so named because it had once led to a wooden circus outside the city. The small doorway was screened by solid walls but would allow men to sally out and disrupt the enemy within the terrace outside. Constantine gave orders for the door to be unblocked so that disruptive raiding could continue. It seemed that no one remembered another ancient prophecy. At the time of the first Arab siege of 669, a strange prophetic book had appeared, the so-called Apocalypse of Pseudo-Methodius. Among its many predictions were these lines: 'Misfortune to you Byzantium, because Ismail [Arabia] will take you. And each horse of Ismail will cross over, and the first among them will set up his tent in front of you, Byzantium, and will begin the battle and break the gate of the Wooden Circus and enter as far as the Ox.'

13 'Remember the Date'
27–28 MAY 1453

These tribulations are for God's sake. The sword of Islam is in our hands. If we had not chosen to endure these tribulations, we would not be worthy to be called gazis. We would be ashamed to stand in God's presence on the day of Judgement.
Mehmet II

There is a fable about Mehmet's methods of conquest told by the Serbian chronicler, Michael the Janissary. In it, the sultan summoned his nobles and ordered 'a great rug to be brought and to be spread before them, and in the centre he had an apple placed, and he gave them the following riddle, saying: "Can any of you take up that apple without stepping on the rug?" And they reckoned among themselves, thinking about how that could be, and none of them could get the trick until (Mehmet) himself, having stepped up to the rug took the rug in both hands and rolled it before him, proceeding behind it; and so he got the apple and put the rug back down as it had been before.'

Mehmet now held the moment right for taking the apple. It was obvious to both sides that the final struggle was under way. The sultan hoped that, like a section of wall tottering under the weight of cannon fire, one last massive assault would collapse all resistance at a stroke. Constantine understood from spies, and possibly from Halil himself, that if they could survive this attack, the siege must be lifted and the church bells could ring for joy. Both commanders gathered for a supreme effort.

Inscription on the land walls: 'The Fortune of Constantine, our God-protected Sovereign, triumphs'

Mehmet propelled himself into a frenzy of activity. In these final days he seems to have been continuously in motion, on horseback among the men, holding audience in the red and gold tent, raising morale, giving orders, promising rewards, threatening punishments, personally supervising the final preparations – above all being seen. The physical presence of the Padishah was held to be an essential inspiration in steadying the morale of the men as they prepared to fight and die. Mehmet knew this was his moment of destiny. Dreams of glory were within his grasp; the alternative was unthinkable failure. He was determined personally to ensure that nothing should be left to chance.

On the Sunday morning, 27 May, he ordered the guns to open up again. It was probably the heaviest bombardment of the whole siege. All day the great cannon hammered away at the central section of the wall, with the express aim of opening up substantial breaches for a full-scale assault and preventing effective repairs. It seems that massive granite balls struck the wall three times before bringing down a large section. By daylight, under this withering volley of fire, it was impossible to carry out running repairs, but no attempt was made to attack. All day, according to Barbaro, 'they did nothing apart from bombard the poor walls and brought a lot of them crashing to the ground, and left half of them badly damaged'. The gaps were getting larger and Mehmet ensured that it was increasingly difficult to plug them. He wanted to make certain the defenders should have no rest in the days before the final rush.

During the day Mehmet called a meeting of the officer corps outside his tent. The complete command structure assembled to hear their sultan's words: 'the provincial governors and generals and cavalry officers and corps commanders and captains of the rank and file, as well as commanders of a thousand, a hundred or fifty men, and the cavalry he kept around him and the captains of the ships and triremes and the admiral of the whole fleet'. Mehmet suspended in the air before his listeners the image of fabulous wealth which was now theirs for the taking: the hoards of gold in the palaces and houses, the votive offerings and relics in the churches, 'fashioned out of gold and silver and precious stones and priceless pearls', the nobles and beautiful women and boys available for ransom, marriage and slavery, the graceful buildings and gardens which would be theirs to live in and enjoy. He went on to stress not only the immortal honour that would follow from capturing the most famous city on earth, but also the necessity of doing so. Constantinople remained a palpable threat to the security of the Ottoman Empire so long as it rested in Christian hands. Captured, it would be the stepping-stone to further conquests. He presented the task ahead as now being easy. The land wall was badly shattered, the moat filled in and the defenders few and demoralized. He was at particular pains to play down the determination of the Italians, whose involvement in the siege was obviously something of a psychological problem for his audience. Almost certainly, although Kritovoulos, a Greek, does not mention it, Mehmet stressed the appeal to holy war – the long-held Islamic desire for Constantinople, the words of the Prophet and the attractions of martyrdom.

He then laid out the tactics for the battle. He believed, quite rightly, that the defenders were exhausted by constant bombardment and skirmishing. The time had come to bring the full advantage of numbers into play. The troops would attack in relays. When one division was exhausted, a second would replace it. They would simply hurl wave after wave of fresh troops at the wall until the weary defenders cracked. It would take as long as it took and there would be no let-up: 'once we have started fighting, warfare will be unceasing, without sleeping or eating, drinking or resting, without any let-up, with us pressing on them until we have overpowered them in the struggle'. They would attack the city from all points simultaneously in a co-ordinated onslaught, so that it was impossible for the defenders to move troops to relieve particular pressure points. Despite the rhetoric, limitless attack was impossible: the practical timeframe for a full-scale assault would be finite, compressed into a few hours. A stout resistance would inflict murderous slaughter on the rushing troops; if they failed to overwhelm the defenders quickly, withdrawal would be inevitable.

Precise orders were given to each commander. The fleet at the Double Columns was to encircle the city and tie down the defenders at the sea walls. The ships inside the Horn were to assist in floating the pontoon across the Horn. Zaganos Pasha would then march his troops across from the Valley of the Springs and attack the end of the land wall. Next, the troops of Karaja Pasha would confront the wall by the Royal Palace, and in the centre Mehmet would station himself with Halil and the Janissaries for what many considered to be the crucial theatre of operations – the shattered wall and the stockade in the Lycus valley. On his right Ishak Pasha and Mahmut Pasha would attempt to storm the walls down towards the Sea of Marmara. Throughout he laid particular emphasis on ensuring the discipline of the troops. They must obey commands to the letter: 'to be silent when they must advance without noise, and when they must shout to utter the most bloodcurdling yells'. He reiterated how much hung on the success of the attack for the future of the Ottoman people, and promised personally to oversee it. With these words he dismissed the officers back to their troops.

Later he rode in person through the camp, accompanied by his Janissary bodyguard in their distinctive white headdresses, and his heralds who made the public announcement of the coming attack. The message cried amongst the sea of tents was designed to ignite the enthusiasm of the men. There would be the traditional rewards for storming a city: 'You know how many governorships are at my disposal in Asia and in Europe. Of these I will give the finest to the first to pass the stockade. And I shall pay him the honours which he deserves, and I shall requite him with a position of wealth, and make him happy among the men of our generation.' All major Ottoman battles were preceded by the promise of a graduated series of stated honours designed to spur the men on. There was a matching set of punishments: 'But if I see any man lurking in the tents and not fighting at the wall, he will not be able to escape a lingering death.' It was one of the psychological ploys of Ottoman conquest that it bound men into an effective reward system that linked honour and profit to the recognition of exceptional effort. It was implemented by the presence on the battlefield of the sultan's messengers, the *chavushes*, a body of men who reported directly to the sultan. Their single account of an act of bravery could lead to instant promotion. The men knew that great acts could be rewarded.

Mehmet went further. In accordance with the dictates of Islamic law, it was decreed that since the city had not surrendered it would be given to the soldiers for three days of plunder. He swore by God, 'by the four thousand prophets, by Muhammad, by the soul of his father and his children and by the sword he strapped on, that he would give them everything to sack, all the people, men and women, and everything in the city, both treasure and property, and that he would not break his promise'.

The prospect of the Red Apple, rich in plunder and marvels, was a direct appeal to the very soul of the nomadic raider, an archetype of the horseman's longing for the wealth of cities. After seven weeks of suffering in the spring rain it must have struck the men with the force of hunger. To a large extent the city they imagined did not exist. The Constantinople conjured by Mehmet had been ransacked by Christian crusaders two and a half centuries earlier. Its fabulous treasures, its gold ornaments, its jewel-encrusted relics had largely gone in the catastrophe of 1204 – melted down by Norman knights or shipped off to Venice with the bronze horses. What was left in May 1453 was an impoverished, shrunken shadow of its former self, whose main wealth was now its people. 'Once the city of wisdom, now a city of ruins,' Gennadios had said of the dying Constantinople. A few rich men may have had hoards of gold hidden in their houses and the churches still had precious objects, but the city no longer possessed the treasure troves of Aladdin that the Ottoman troops longingly imagined as they stared up at the walls.

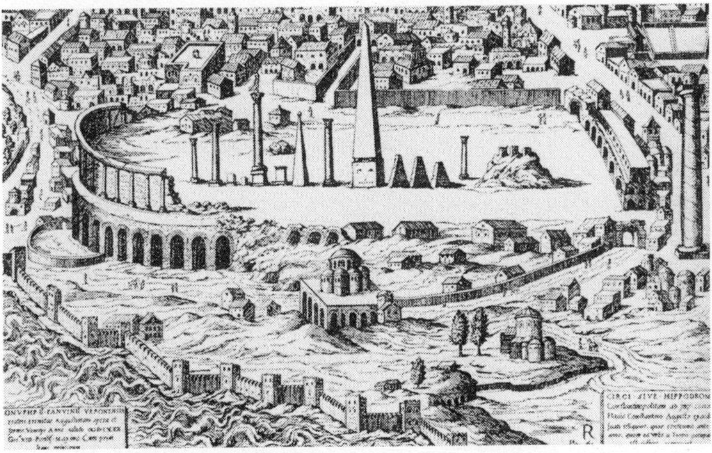

City of ruins: the crumbling hippodrome and empty spaces of the city

Nevertheless the proclamation whipped the listening army into a fever of excitement. Their great shouts were carried to the exhausted defenders watching from the walls. 'O, if you had heard their voices raised to heaven,' recorded Leonard, 'you would indeed have been paralysed.' The looting of the city was probably a promise that Mehmet had not wanted to make, but it had become the necessary lever for fully winning over the grumbling troops. A negotiated surrender would have prevented a level of destruction that he was hoping to avoid. The Red Apple was not for Mehmet just a chest of war booty to be plundered; it was to be the centre of his empire and he was keen to preserve it intact. With this in mind a stern caveat was attached to the promise: the buildings and walls of the city were to remain the property of the sultan alone; under no circumstances were they to be damaged or destroyed once the city had been entered. The capture of Istanbul was not to be a second sacking of Baghdad, the most fabulous city of the Middle Ages, committed to the flames by the Mongols in 1258.

The attack was fixed for the day after next – Tuesday 29 May. In order to work the soldiers to a pitch of religious zeal and to quash any negative thoughts, it was announced that the following day, Monday 28, was to be given over to atonement. The men were to fast during daylight hours, to carry out their ritual ablutions, to say their prayers five times and to ask God's aid in capturing the city. The customary candle illuminations were to continue for the next two nights. The mystery and awe that the illuminations, combined with prayers and music, worked on both the men and their enemies were powerful psychological tools, employed to full effect outside the walls of Constantinople.

In the meantime the work in the Ottoman camp went on with renewed enthusiasm. Vast quantities of earth and brushwood were collected ready to fill up the ditch, scaling ladders were made, stockpiles of arrows were collected, wheeled protective screens drawn up. As night fell the city was again ringed by a brilliant circle of fire; the rhythmic chanting of the names of God rose steadily from the camp to the steady beating of drums, the clash of cymbals and the skirl of the *zorna*. According to Barbaro the shouting could be heard across the Bosphorus on the coast of Anatolia, 'and all us Christians were in the greatest terror'. Within the city it had been the feast day of All Saints, but there was no comfort in the churches, only penitence and continual prayers of intercession.

At the day's end Giustiniani and his men again set about repairing the damage to the outer wall, but in the brilliantly illuminated darkness the cannon fire continued unabated. The defenders were horribly conspicuous and it was now, according to Nestor-Iskander, that Giustiniani's personal luck started to run out. As he directed operations, a fragment of stone shot, probably a ricochet, struck the

Genoese commander, piercing his steel breastplate and lodging in his chest. He fell to the ground and was carried home to bed.

It is difficult to overestimate the importance of Giustiniani to the Byzantine cause. From the moment that he had stepped dramatically onto the quayside in January 1453 with 700 skilled fighters in shining armour, Giustiniani had been an iconic figure in the defence of the city. He had come voluntarily and at his own expense, 'for the advantage of the Christian faith and for the honour of the world'. Technically skilful, personally brave and utterly tireless in his defence of the land walls, he alone had been able to command the loyalty of both the Greeks and Venetians – to the extent that they were forced to make an exception to their general hatred of the Genoese. The construction of the stockade was a brilliant piece of improvisation whose effectiveness chipped away at the morale of the Ottoman troops. The unreliable testimony of his fellow countryman, Leonard of Chios, suggests that Mehmet was moved to exasperated admiration of his principal opponent and tried to bribe him with a large sum of money. Giustiniani was not to be bought. Despair seems to have gripped the defenders at the felling of their inspirational leader. Wall repairs were abandoned in disarray. When Constantine was told, 'right away his resolution vanished and he melted away into thought'.

At midnight the shouting again suddenly died down and the fires were extinguished. Silence and darkness fell abruptly over the tents and banners, the guns, horses and ships, the calm waters of the Horn and the shattered walls. The doctors who watched over the wounded Giustiniani 'treated him all night long and laboured in sustaining him'. The people of the city enjoyed little rest.

Mehmet spent Monday 28 May making final arrangements for the attack. He was up at dawn giving orders to his gunners to prepare and aim their guns on the wrecked parts of the wall, so that they might target the vulnerable defenders when the order was given later in the day. The leaders of the cavalry and infantry divisions of his guard were summoned to receive their orders and were organized into divisions. Throughout the camp the order was given, to the sound of trumpets, that all the officer corps should stand to their posts under pain of death, in readiness for tomorrow's attack.

When the guns did open up, 'it was a thing not of this world', according to Barbaro, 'and this they did because it was the day for ending the bombardment'. Despite the intensity of the cannon fire there were no attacks. The only other visible activity was the steady collection of thousands of long ladders, which were carried up close to the walls, and a huge number of wooden hurdles, which would provide protection for the advancing men as they struggled to climb the stockade. Cavalry horses were brought in from pasture. It was a late spring day and the sun was shining. Within the Ottoman camp the men went about their preparations: fasting and prayer, sharpening blades, checking fastenings on shields and armour, resting. A mood of introspection stilled the troops as they steadied themselves for the final assault. The religious quietness and discipline of the army unnerved the watchers on the walls. Some hoped that the lack of activity was a preparation for withdrawal; others were more realistic.

Mehmet had worked hard on the morale of his men, tuning their responses over several days through cycles of fervour and reflection that were designed to build morale and distract from internal doubt. The mullahs and dervishes played a key role in creating the right mentality. Thousands of wandering holy men had come to the siege from the towns and villages of upland Anatolia, bringing with them a fervent religious expectation. In their dusty robes they moved about the camp, their eyes alight with excitement. They recited relevant verses from the Koran and the Hadith and told tales of martyrdom and prophecy. The men were reminded that they were following in the footsteps of the companions of the Prophet killed at the first Arab siege of Constantinople. Their names were passed from mouth to mouth: Hazret Hafiz, Ebu Seybet ul-Ensari, Hamd ul-Ensari and above all Ayyub, whom the Turks called Eyüp. The holy men reminded their listeners, in hushed tones, that to them fell the honour of fulfilling the word of the Prophet himself:

> The Prophet said to his disciples: 'Have you heard of a city with land on one side and sea on the other two sides?' They replied: 'Yes, O Messenger of God.' He spoke: 'The last hour [of Judgement] will not dawn before it is taken by 70,000 sons of Isaac. When they reach it, they will not do battle with arms and catapults but with the words "There is no God but Allah, and Allah is great." Then the first sea wall will collapse, and the second time the second sea wall, and the third time the wall on the land side will collapse, And, rejoicing, they will enter in.'

The words attributed to the Prophet may have been spurious, but the sentiment was real. To the army fell the prospect of completing a messianic cycle of history, a persistent dream of the Islamic peoples since the birth of Islam itself, and of winning immortal fame. And for those killed in battle blessed martyrdom and the prospect of paradise lay ahead: 'Gardens watered by running streams, where they shall dwell for ever; spouses of perfect chastity: and grace from God.'

It was a heady mixture but there were those in the camp, including Sheikh Akshemsettin himself, who were extremely realistic about the authentic motivation of some of the troops. 'You well know', he had written to Mehmet earlier in the siege, 'that most of the soldiers have in any case been converted by force. The number of those who are ready to sacrifice their lives for the love of God is extremely small. On the other hand, if they glimpse the possibility of winning booty they will run towards certain death.' For them too, there was encouragement in the Koran: 'God has promised you rich booty, and has given you this with all promptness. He has stayed your enemies' hands, so that He may make your victory a sign to true believers and guide you along a straight path.'

Mehmet embarked on a final restless tour of inspection. With a large troop of cavalry he rode to the Double Columns to give Hamza instructions for the naval assault. The fleet was to sail round the city, bringing the ships within firing range to engage the defenders in continuous battle. If possible, some of the vessels should be run aground and an attempt made to scale the sea walls, although the chances of success in the fast currents of the Marmara were not considered great. The fleet in the Horn was given similar orders. On the way back he also stopped outside the chief gate of Galata and ordered the chief magistrates of the town to present themselves to him. They were sternly warned to ensure that no help was given to the city on the following day.

In the afternoon he was again on horseback, making a tour of inspection of the whole army, riding the four miles from sea to sea, encouraging the men, addressing the individual officers by name, stirring them up for battle. The message of 'carrot and stick' was reiterated: both great rewards were at hand and terrible punishments for those who failed to obey. They were ordered under pain of death to follow the orders of their officers to the letter. Mehmet probably addressed his sternest words to the impressed and reluctant Christian troops under Zaganos Pasha. Satisfied with these preparations he returned to his tent to rest.

*

Within the city a set of matching preparations was underway. Somehow, against the worst fears of Constantine and the doctors, Giustiniani had survived the night. Disturbed and obsessed by the state of the outer wall, he demanded to be carried up to the ramparts to oversee the work again. The defenders set about the business of plugging the gaps once again and made good progress until they were spotted by the Ottoman gunners. At once a torrent of fire forced them to stop. Later it seems that Giustiniani was well enough to take active command of the defences of the crucial central area once more.

Elsewhere preparations for the final defence were hampered by friction between the various national and religious factions. The deep-rooted rivalries and conflicting priorities of the different interest groups, the difficulty of providing sufficient food, the exhaustion of continuous work and the shock of bombardment – after fifty-three days of siege, nerves were stretched to breaking point and disagreements flared into open conflict. As they prepared for the coming attack, Giustiniani and Lucas Notaras nearly came to blows over the deployment of their few precious cannon. Giustiniani demanded that Notaras should hand over the cannon under his control for the defence at the land walls. Notaras refused, believing that they might be required to defend the sea walls. A furious row took place. Giustiniani threatened to run Notaras through with his sword.

A further quarrel broke out about provisioning the land walls. The shattered battlements needed to be topped by effective defensive structures to provide protection against enemy missiles. The Venetians set about making mantlets – wooden hurdles – in the carpenters' workshops of their quarter, the Plateia, down by the Horn. Seven cartloads of mantlets were collected in the square. The Venetian bailey ordered the Greeks to take them the two miles up to the walls. The Greeks refused unless they were paid. The Venetians accused them of greed; the Greeks, who had hungry families to feed and were resentful of the arrogance of the Italians, needed time or money to get food before the end of the day. The dispute rumbled on so long that the mantlets were not delivered until after nightfall, by which time it was too late to use them.

These flaring antagonisms had a deep history. Religious schism, the sacking of Constantinople in the Fourth Crusade, the commercial rivalry of the Genoese and the Venetians – all contributed to the accusations of greed, treachery, idleness and arrogance that were hurled back and forward in the tense final days. But beneath this surface of discord and despair, there is evidence that all sides generally did their best for the common defence on 28 May. Constantine himself spent the day organizing, imploring, rallying the citizens and the assorted defenders – Greek, Venetian, Genoese, Turkish and Spanish – to work together for the cause. Women and children toiled throughout the day, lugging stones up to the walls to hurl down on the enemy. The Venetian bailey put out a heartfelt plea 'that all who called themselves Venetians should go to the land walls, firstly out of love for God, then for the good of the city and for the honour of all Christendom and that they should all stand to their posts and be willing to die there with a good heart'. In the harbour the boom was checked and all the ships stood to in battle order. Across the water, the people of Galata watched the preparations for a final struggle with growing concern. It seems likely that the podesta also put out a last, clandestine appeal to the men of the town to cross the Horn in secret and join the defence. He realized that the fate of the Genoese enclave was now dependent on Constantinople's survival.

In contrast to the silence of the Ottoman camp, Constantinople was animated by noise. All day church bells were rung and drums and wooden gongs beaten to rally the people to make final preparations. The endless cycle of prayers, services and cries of intercession had intensified after the terrible omens of the previous days. They reached a mighty crescendo on the morning of 28 May. The religious fervour within the city matched that on the plain outside. Early in the morning a great procession of priests, men, women and children formed outside St Sophia. All the most holy icons of the city were brought out from their shrines and chapels. As well as the Hodegetria whose previous procession had proved so ill-omened, they carried forth the bones of the saints, the gilded and jewelled crosses containing fragments of the True Cross itself and an array of other icons. The bishops and priests in their brocade vestments led the way. The laity walked behind, penitent and barefoot, weeping and beating their chests, asking absolution for sins and joining in the singing of the psalms. The procession went throughout the city and along the full length of the land walls. At each important position, the priests read the ancient prayers that God would protect the walls and give victory to His faithful people. The bishops raised their crosiers and blessed the defenders, sprinkling them with holy water from bunches of dried basil. For many it was a day of fasting also, broken only at sunset. It was the ultimate method of raising the defenders' morale.

The emperor probably joined the procession himself and when it was over he called together the leading nobles and commanders from all the factions within the city to make a last appeal for unity and courage. His speech was the mirror image of Mehmet's. It was witnessed by Archbishop Leonard and recorded in his own way. Constantine addressed each group in turn, appealing to their own interests and beliefs. First he spoke to his own people, the Greek residents of the city. He praised them for their stout defence of their home for the past fifty-three days and entreated them not to be afraid of the wild shouts of the untrained mob of 'evil Turks': their strength lay 'in God's protection' but also in their superior armour. He reminded them of how Mehmet had started the war by breaking a treaty, building a fortress on the Bosphorus, 'pretending peace'. In an appeal to home, religion and the future of Greece, he reminded them that Mehmet intended to capture 'the city of Constantine the Great, your homeland, the support of Christian fugitives and the protection of all the Greeks, and to profane the sacred temples of God by turning them into stables for his horses'.

Turning first to the Genoese then the Venetians, he praised them for their courage and commitment to the city: 'You have decorated this city with great and noble men as if it were your own. Now raise your lofty souls for this struggle.' Finally he addressed all the fighting men as a body, begged them to be utterly obedient to orders, and concluded with an appeal for earthly or heavenly glory almost identical to that of Mehmet: 'Know that today is your day of glory, on which, if you shed even one drop of blood, you will prepare for yourself a martyr's crown and immortal glory.' These sentiments had their desired effect on the audience. All present were encouraged by Constantine's words and swore to stand firm in the face of the coming onslaught, that 'with God's help we may hope to gain the victory'. It seems that they all resolved to put aside their personal grievances and problems and to join together for the common cause. Then they departed to take up their posts.

In reality Constantine and Giustiniani knew how thinly their forces were now stretched. After seven weeks of attritional fighting it is likely that the original 8,000 men had dwindled to about 4,000, to guard a total perimeter of twelve miles. Mehmet was probably right when he had told his men that in places there were 'only two or three men defending each tower, and the same number again on the ramparts between the towers'. The length of the Golden Horn, some three miles, which might be subject to attack by the Ottoman ships at the Springs and by troops advancing over the pontoon bridge, was guarded by a detachment of 500 skilled crossbowmen and archers. Beyond the chain, right round the sea walls, another five miles, only a single skilled archer, crossbowman or gunner was assigned to each tower, backed up by an untrained band of citizens and monks. Particular parts of the sea walls were allotted to different groups – Cretan sailors held some towers, a small band of Catalans another. The Ottoman pretender Orhan, the sultan's uncle, held a stretch of wall overlooking the Marmara. His band was certain to fight to the death if it came to a final struggle. For them, surrender would not be an option. In general however, it was reckoned that the sea wall was well protected by the Marmara currents and that all the men who could possibly be spared must be sent to the central section of the land wall. It was obvious to everyone that the most concerted assault must come in the Lycus valley, between the Romanus and the Charisian gates, where the guns had destroyed sections of the outer wall. The last day was given to making all possible repairs to the stockade and to assigning troops to its defence. Giustiniani was in charge of the central section with 400 Italians and the bulk of the Byzantine troops – some 2,000 men in all. Constantine also set up his headquarters in this section to ensure full support.

By mid-afternoon the defenders could see the troops gathering beyond their walls. It was a fine afternoon. The sun was sinking in the west. Out on the plain the Ottoman army started to deploy into regimental formations, turning and wheeling, drawing up its battle standards, filling the horizon from coast to coast. In the vanguard, men continued to work to fill in the ditches, the cannon were advanced as close as possible, and the inexorable accumulation of scaling equipment continued unchecked. Within the Horn the eighty ships of the Ottoman fleet that had been transported overland prepared to float the pontoon bridge up close to the land walls; and beyond the chain, the larger fleet under Hamza Pasha encircled the city, sailing past the point of the Acropolis and round the Marmara shore. Each ship was loaded with soldiers, stone-throwing equipment and long ladders as high as the walls themselves. The men on the ramparts settled down to wait, for there was still time to spare.

Late in the afternoon the people of the city, seeking religious solace, converged for the first time in five months on the mother church of St

Sophia. The dark church, which had been so conspicuously boycotted by the Orthodox faithful, was filled with people, anxious, penitent and fervent, and for the first time since the summer of 1064, in the ultimate moment of need, it seems that Catholic and Orthodox worshipped together in the city, and the 400-year-old schism and the bitterness of the crusades were put aside in a final service of intercession. The huge space of Justinian's 1,000-year-old church glittered with the mysterious light of candles, and reverberated with the rising and falling notes of the liturgy. Constantine took part in the service. He occupied the imperial chair at the right side of the altar and partook of the sacraments with great fervour, and 'fell to the ground, and begged God's loving kindness and forgiveness for their transgressions'. Then he took leave of the clergy and the people, bowed in all directions – and left the church. 'Immediately', according to the fervent Nestor-Iskander, 'all clerics and people present cried out; the women and children wailed and moaned; their voices, I believe, reached to heaven.' All the commanders returned to their posts. Some of the civilian population remained in the church to take part in an all night vigil. Others went to hide. People let themselves down into the echoing darkness of the great underground cisterns, to float in small boats among the columns. Above ground, Justinian still rode on his bronze horse, pointing defiantly to the east.

As evening fell, the Ottomans went to break their fast in a shared meal and to prepare themselves for the night. The pre-battle meal was a further opportunity to build group solidarity and a sense of sacrifice among the soldiers gathered around the communal cooking pots. Fires and candles were lit, if anything larger than on the previous two nights. Again the criers swept through accompanied by pipes and horns, reinforcing the twin messages of prosperous life and joyful death: 'Children of Muhammad, be of good heart, for tomorrow we shall have so many Christians in our hands that we will sell them, two slaves for a ducat, and will have such riches that we will all be of gold, and from the beards of the Greeks we will make leads for our dogs, and their families will be our slaves. So be of good heart and be ready to die cheerfully for the love of our Muhammad.' A mood of fervent joy passed through the camp as the excited prayers of the soldiers slowly rose to a crescendo like the breaking of a mighty wave. The lights and the rhythmical cries froze the blood of the waiting Christians. A massive bombardment opened up in the dark, so heavy 'that to us it seemed to be a very inferno'. And at midnight silence and darkness fell on the Ottoman camp. The men went in good order to their posts 'with all their weapons and a great mountain of arrows'. Pumped up by the adrenalin of the coming battle, dreaming of martyrdom and gold, they waited in total silence for the final signal to attack.

There was nothing left to be done. Both sides understood the climactic significance of the coming day. Both had made their spiritual preparations. According to Barbaro, who of course gave the final say in the outcome to the Christian god, 'and when each side had prayed to his god for victory, they to theirs and we to ours, our Father in Heaven decided with his Mother who should be successful in this battle that would be so fierce, which would be concluded next day'. According to Sa'd-ud-din, the Ottoman troops, 'from dusk till dawn, intent on battle . . . united the greatest of meritorious works . . . passing the night in prayer'.

There is an afterword to this day. One of the chronicles of George Sphrantzes sees Constantine riding through the dark streets of the city on his Arab mare and returning late at night to the Blachernae Palace. He called his servants and household to him and begged them for forgiveness, and thus absolved, according to Sphrantzes 'the Emperor mounted his horse and we left the palace and began to make the circuit of the walls in order to rouse the sentries to keep watch alertly and not lapse into sleep'. Having checked that all was well, and that the gates were securely locked, at first cockcrow they climbed the tower at the Caligaria Gate, which commanded a wide view over the plain and the Golden Horn, to witness the enemy preparations in the dark. They could hear the wheeled siege towers creaking invisibly towards the ramparts, long ladders being dragged over the pounded ground and the activity of many soldiers filling in the ditches beneath the shattered walls. To the south, on the glimmering Bosphorus and the Marmara the outlines of the larger galleys could be discerned as distant, ghostly shapes moving into position beyond the bulking dome of St Sophia, while within the Horn the smaller *fustae* worked to float the pontoon bridge over the straits and to manoeuvre close to the walls. It is a haunting, introspective moment and an enduring image of the long-suffering Constantine – the noble emperor and his faithful friend standing on the outer tower listening to the ominous preparations for the final attack, the world dark and still before the moment of final destiny. For fifty-three days their tiny force had confounded the might of the Ottoman army; they had faced down the heaviest bombardment in the Middle Ages from the largest cannon ever built – an estimated 5,000 shots and 55,000 pounds of gunpowder; they had resisted three full-scale assaults and dozens of skirmishes, killed unknown thousands of Ottoman soldiers, destroyed underground mines and siege towers, fought sea battles, conducted sorties and peace negotiations, and worked ceaselessly to erode the enemy's morale – and they had come closer to success than they probably knew.

This scene is accurate in geographical and factual detail; the guards on the highest ramparts of the city could hear the Ottoman troops manoeuvring in the darkness below the walls and would have commanded a wide view over both land and sea, but we have no idea if Constantine and Sphrantzes were actually there. The account is possibly an invention, concocted a hundred years later by a priest with a reputation for forgery. What we do know is that at some point on 28 May Constantine and his minister parted, and that Sphrantzes had a presentiment of this day and its meaning. The two men were lifelong friends. Sphrantzes had served his master with a faithfulness conspicuously absent among those who surrounded the emperor in the quarrelsome final years of the Byzantine Empire. Twenty-three years earlier, he had saved Constantine's life at the siege of Patras. He had been wounded and captured for his pains, and had languished in leg irons in a verminous dungeon for a month before being released. He had undertaken endless diplomatic missions for his master over a thirty-year period, including a fruitless three-year embassy round the Black Sea in search of a wife for the emperor. In return Constantine made Sphrantzes governor of Patras, had been the best man at his wedding and the godfather of his children. Sphrantzes had more at stake than many during the siege: he had his family with him in the city. Whenever the two men parted on 28 May it must have been with foreboding on Sphrantzes' part. Two years earlier to the day he had had a premonition while away from Constantinople: 'On the same night of May 28 [1451] I had a dream: it seemed to me that I was back in the City; as I made a motion to prostrate myself and kiss the Emperor's feet, he stopped me, raised me, and kissed my eyes. Then I woke up and told those sleeping by me: "I just had this dream. Remember the date."'

14 The Locked Gates

1.30 A.M. 29 MAY 1453

There is no certainty of victory in war, even when the equipment and numerical strength that cause victory exist. Victory and superiority in war come from luck and chance.

Ibn Khaldun, fourteenth-century Arab historian

By nightfall on Monday 28 May, the great guns had been firing at the land walls for forty-seven days. Over time Mehmet had come to concentrate his batteries in three places: to the north between the Blachernae Palace and the Charisian Gate, in the central section around the Lycus River, and to the south towards the Marmara at the Third Military Gate. Severe damage had been inflicted at all these points, so that when he addressed his commanders before the battle he could claim, with convenient exaggeration, that 'the moat has all been filled up and the land wall at three points has been so broken down that not only heavy and light infantry like yourselves, but even the horses and heavily armed cavalry can easily penetrate it'. In fact it had been clear to both sides for some time that a concerted attack would be focused on only one spot, the middle section, the Mesoteichion, the shallow valley between the gates of St Romanus and Charisius. This was the Achilles heel of the defensive system and it was here that Mehmet had expended his greatest firepower.

By the eve of the total assault, there were nine substantial holes in the outer wall, some about thirty yards long and mostly in the valley,

Ottoman military band: designed to terrify and inspire

which had been replaced piecemeal by Giustiniani's stockade. It was a ramshackle structure that patched up the defences whenever a stretch of wall gave way. Baulks of timber lashed together provided its basic framework, along with hardcore from the fallen wall augmented by any other materials readily to hand: brushwood, branches, bundles of reeds and loose stones, all in-filled with earth, which had the advantage of absorbing the shock of the cannon balls more effectively than any stone structure. In time it was evidently nearly as high as the original wall, and wide enough to provide a good fighting platform. The defenders were protected from enemy fire by barrels and wicker containers full of earth that served as battlements, and whose removal was always the initial objective of Ottoman attacks. Since 21 April the maintenance of the stockade had been the city's highest priority. Both soldiers and civilians worked unceasingly to mend and extend it. Men, women and children, monks and nuns had all contributed, lugging stones, timber, cartloads of earth, branches and vine cuttings up to the front line in an exhausting and apparently unceasing cycle of destruction and repair. They had worked under cannon fire and attack, by day and by night, rain and sun to plug gaps wherever they appeared. The stockade represented the collective energy of the population and under Giustiniani's direction it had repaid their efforts, repulsing every attempt on the city and demoralizing the enemy.

It was behind this stockade that the pick of the available fighting troops took up their positions late on the sunny afternoon of 28 May. According to Doukas, here were 'three thousand Latins and Romans' – the remainder of the 700 crack Italian troops who had come with Giustiniani, sailors from the Venetian galleys plus the bulk of the Byzantine troops. In all probability the figure was nearer 2,000. They were well armoured and helmeted in chainmail and plate, and equipped with a variety of weapons: crossbows, rifles, small cannon, long bows, swords and maces – all the equipment for mowing down their attackers at a distance and fighting them hand to hand at the barricades. In addition a large number of rocks had been brought up to the front line by civilians, as well as inflammatory materials – barrels of Greek fire and pitchers of tar. The troops entered the enclosure through the gates in the inner wall and spread out down the length of the stockade to fill the Mesoteichion for 1,000 yards. The enclosure was only twenty yards deep, backed by the higher inner wall and a scooped out ditch at its foot where earth had been removed to fortify the stockade. There was just room for horsemen to gallop up and down the line behind the men pressed to the stockade. In the whole stretch there were only four entry points through the inner walls: two posterns by the gates of St Romanus and Charisius to left and right on the brow of the hills, the forbidding Fifth Military Gate that led only into the enclosure halfway up the northern slope, and another postern at an unidentified point that had been created by Giustiniani to make entry into the city more convenient. It was obvious to everyone that the battle would be won or lost at the stockade; there could be no retreat from this station. A decision was therefore taken that the posterns back into the city should be locked behind the defenders once they had entered the enclosure and the keys entrusted to their commanders. They would do or die with their backs to the inner wall and their leaders with them. As night fell they settled down to wait. A heavy shower of rain fell in the dark but the Ottoman troops continued to advance siege equipment outside. Later Giustiniani entered the enclosure, then Constantine and his inner retinue of nobles: the Spaniard Don Francisco of Toledo, his cousin Theophilus Palaiologos and his faithful military companion John Dalmata. They waited on the stockade and the wall for the first signs of an attack. Though perhaps few would have shared the optimism of the Podesta of Galata who declared that 'victory was assured', they were not without confidence in their ability to weather one final storm.

The Ottoman troops were readied for battle in the small hours of the morning. In the darkness of his tent, Mehmet performed the ritual ablutions and prayers, and entreated God for the city's fall. In all likelihood his personal preparations would have included the donning of a talismanic shirt, richly embroidered with verses from the Koran and the names of God, as a magical protection against bad luck. Turbanned and caftanned, with a sword strapped to his waist, and accompanied by his key commanders, he set out on horseback to direct the attack.

The preparations for a simultaneous assault by land and sea had been carefully made and closely followed. The ships in the Horn and Marmara were in position; troops were massed to make assaults at key locations along the land walls, with the focus being on the Lycus valley. Mehmet decided to commit large numbers of men to the stockade and to deploy his regiments in ascending order of usefulness and skill. He ordered that the first attack should be made by irregulars – the *azaps* and foreign auxiliaries – unskilled troops recruited for booty or impressed for the campaign under the laws of vassalage. A large number of these seem to have been 'Christians, kept in his camp by force', according to Barbaro, 'Greeks, Latins, Germans, Hungarians – people from all the Christian realms' according to Leonard – an ill-assorted mix of races and creeds armed in a variety of ways; some with bows, slings or muskets, but the majority simply with scimitars and shields. It was in no sense a disciplined fighting force, but Mehmet's aim was to use expendable infidels to wear down the enemy before committing more valuable troops to the killing zone. These men were brought up from the north end of the wall, equipped with scaling ladders and readied to attack along the whole front of the Mesoteichion and the stockade in particular. Thousands of them waited in the darkness for the moment to go.

At one-thirty in the morning horns, drums and cymbals signalled the attack. The cannon opened up and from all directions, from both land and sea, Ottoman forces moved forward. The irregulars were under strict orders to advance at a steady pace and in silence. Within range, they unleashed a volley of fire 'with arrows from the archers, slingshot from the slingers and iron and lead balls from the cannon and arquebuses'. At a second command, they ran forward across the filled ditch, yelling and hurling themselves at the walls 'with javelins and pikes and spears'. The defenders were well prepared. As the irregulars attempted to scale the walls, the Christians pushed their ladders away and hurled fire and hot oil down on those scrambling at the foot of the stockade. The darkness and confusion were lit only by pale hand-held flares and the sound of 'violent yelling and blasphemies and curses'. Giustiniani marshalled his men and the presence of the emperor lent encouragement to the defence. Advantage lay with the defenders who 'threw big stones down on them from the battlements' and shot arrows and bullets into their close-packed ranks, 'so that few escaped alive'. Those coming up behind started to waver and turn back. However, Mehmet had determined to press his irregular troops to the limit. In the rear he stationed a line of *chavushes* – Mehmet's military police – as enforcers, armed with clubs and whips to turn them back; and behind them a line of Janissaries with scimitars to cut down any who broke through this cordon and ran for it. Horrible cries rose from the wretched men caught between the hail of missiles in front and the systematic pressure from behind, 'so that they had a choice of dying on one side or the other'. They turned again to assault the stockade, struggling with furious desperation to raise their ladders against the steady bombardment from above – and were decimated. Despite heavy losses these expendable men served their purpose. For two hours they wore away at the energy of the enemy on the stockade, until Mehmet permitted the remnant to withdraw from the slaughter and limp back behind the lines.

There was a moment of pause. It was three-thirty in the morning, still dark, the plain lit by flares. On the stockade the men drew breath; there was time to reorganize and make running repairs. Elsewhere up and down the line, the irregulars' attack had been pressed less vigorously; the strength of the intact walls made progress difficult. It was more a diversionary tactic to ensure that men were tied down along the whole sector and could not be moved to refresh those under pressure in the Mesoteichion. The forces were stretched so thinly that the troops kept in reserve on the central ridge near the Church of the Holy Apostles, a mile away, had been whittled down to a force of 300. Staring out over the plain, the men at the wall vainly hoped that the enemy might withdraw for the night, but it was not to be.

The moment had come to escalate the conflict. Mehmet rode over to the Anatolian troops on his right flank stationed just beyond the St Romanus Gate. These men were heavy infantry, well equipped with chain armour, experienced, disciplined – and fired by a strong Muslim zeal for the cause. He addressed them in the colloquial, paternal tones a twenty-one-year-old sultan could rightly adopt with his tribe: 'Advance, my friends and children! Now is the moment to prove yourselves worthy men!' They advanced down the edge of the valley, wheeled to face the stockade and pressed forward in a tightly packed mass, calling out the name of Allah 'with shouts and fearful yells'. They came on, said Nicolo Barbaro, 'like lions unchained against the walls'. The purposeful advance threw the defenders into alarm. Throughout the city church bells clanged, summoning every man back to his post. Many of the population came running up to the walls to help. Others redoubled their cycle of prayer in the churches. Three miles away, outside St Sophia, the clergy offered their own support; 'When they heard the bells, they took the divine icons, went out before the church, stood, prayed, and blessed with crosses the entire city; in tears did they recite: "Bring us to life again, Lord God, and help us lest we perish in the end."'

The Anatolians crossed the ditch at a run, moving forward in a tightly packed mass of compressed steel. They were riddled by fire from crossbows and cannon that 'killed an incredible number of Turks'. Still they came on, shielding themselves from the hail of rocks and missiles, trying to force themselves up onto the stockade. 'We hurled deadly missiles down on them', said Archbishop Leonard, 'and fired crossbows into their massed ranks.' By sheer force of numbers the Anatolians managed to prop ladders against the stockade. These were hurled down again and the attackers were crushed by rocks and burned by hot pitch. For a short while the Ottomans drew back, but quickly pressed forward again. Behind the stockade the defenders were amazed and appalled by the spirit of their foe, who seemed motivated by a force beyond the limits of the human. There was evidently no need for extra motivation; this group were 'all brave men', recorded Barbaro. 'They continued to raise their shouts to the skies and they unfurled their standards all the more eagerly. O you would have marvelled at these beasts! Their army was being destroyed, but with limitless bravery they kept trying to get to the fosse.' The Anatolians were hindered by their numbers and their own dead as successive waves surged forward. Men trampled and scrabbled over each other in a human pyramid as they tried to reach the top of the stockade. Some managed to get there, slashing and hacking wildly at their opponents. Hand to hand fighting developed on the earth platform, man pressed against man. With limited space to move, it was as much physical pressure as armed combat that determined whether the Anatolians forced their enemy backwards or were hurled down onto the scrabbling, shouting, cursing pile of dead and dying men, discarded weapons, helmets, turbans and shields.

The situation shifted from moment to moment. 'Sometimes the heavy infantry clambered over the walls and stockades, pressing their way forcefully forward without wavering. At other times they were violently repulsed and driven back.' Mehmet himself galloped forward, urging them on with shouts and cries, sometimes throwing fresh waves of men into the narrow gap as those in front wavered and died. He ordered the match to be put to the big cannon. Volleys of stone shot sprayed the walls, peppering the defenders and felling the Anatolians from behind. Everything was dark and confused in the predawn of the summer morning, the extraordinary noise of the battle so deafening 'that the very air seemed to split apart' with the visceral thump of the kettledrums, the braying of pipes, the crash of cymbals, the clang of church bells, the thock of arrows whipping through the night air, the amplified subterranean roar of the Ottoman cannon vibrating the ground, the flat crack of handguns. Swords clattered harshly against shields, more softly as blades severed windpipes, arrowheads puckered into chests, lead bullets shattered ribs, rocks crushed skulls – and behind these sounds the more terrible hubbub of human voices: prayers and battle cries, shouts of encouragement, curses, howls, sobs and the softer moan of those approaching death. Smoke and dust drifted across the front line. Islamic banners were held hopefully aloft in the dark. Bearded faces, helmets and armour were lit by smoking handheld flares; for brief seconds the gun crews became a frozen tableau backlit by the vivid flash of the cannon; smaller tongues of flame from the handguns sparked sharply in the darkness; buckets of Greek fire arced downwards over the walls like golden rain.

An hour before dawn one of the big cannon landed a direct hit on the stockade and smashed a hole. Clouds of dust and cannon smoke obscured the front line, but the Anatolians, quickest to react, pressed forward into the breach. Before the defence could react, 300 had swept inside. For the first time the Ottomans had penetrated the enclosure. Chaos reigned inside. The defenders desperately regrouped and faced the Anatolians in the narrow space between the two walls. The gap was evidently not large enough to permit a larger flood of men to surge in and the attackers soon found themselves surrounded and cornered. Systematically the Greeks and Italians hacked them to pieces. None survived. Cheered by this local victory the defenders drove the Anatolians back from the stockade. Discouraged, the Ottoman troops faltered for the first time and were pulled back. It was half past five. The defenders had been fighting, unrested, for four hours.

By this stage of the morning little substantive progress had been made elsewhere by Ottoman troops. Within the Horn, Zaganos Pasha had succeeded in getting the pontoon bridge in position overnight and moving a good number of troops onto the shore near the end of the land walls. At the same time he brought the light galleys up close so that archers and musketeers could rake the walls with fire. He advanced ladders and wooden towers to these walls and tried to get his infantry to storm the ramparts. The attempt failed. Halil's seaborne landing on the Marmara had been equally unsuccessful. The currents made steadying the ships difficult and the dominant position of the sea walls, which looked straight over the water, provided no foreshore on which to establish a bridgehead. Although the ramparts were very lightly manned and in part were entrusted solely to monks, the intruders were easily repulsed or captured and beheaded. South of the Mesoteichion, Ishak Pasha maintained some pressure on the defenders but his best Anatolian troops had been diverted to tackle the stockade. A more serious attempt was made by Karaja Pasha's men in the area of the Blachernae Palace – one of the places Mehmet had targeted for easy access into the city. It was 'where the city's defences were tottering' because of the state of the wall, but the defence was managed by the three Genoese Bocchiardi brothers who were skilful professional soldiers. According to Archbishop Leonard 'they were frightened by nothing – neither the walls collapsing under fire nor the explosions of the cannon . . . day and night they showed the greatest vigilance with their crossbows and terrible guns'. At times they made sallies from the Circus Gate postern to disrupt enemy activity. Karaja's men could make no progress. The lion of St Mark still fluttered over the dark palace.

The failure of the irregulars and the Anatolian divisions after four hours of fierce fighting seems to have enraged Mehmet. More than that: it made him anxious. He had only one body of fresh troops left – his own palace regiments, the 5,000 crack professional troops of his own bodyguard: 'men who were very well-armed, bold and courageous, who were far more experienced and brave than the others. These were the army's crack troops: heavy infantry, archers and lancers, and with them the brigade called the Janissaries.' He decided to commit them to the battle at once before the defenders had time to regroup. Everything depended on this manoeuvre; if they failed to break the line within another few hours the momentum would be lost, the exhausted troops would have to be withdrawn and the siege effectively lifted.

Within the enclosure there was no time to pause. Casualties had been heavier during the second wave of attacks, and the tiredness of the men increased accordingly. However, the spirit of resistance remained firm; according to Kritovoulos they were deterred by nothing: 'neither hunger pressing on them, nor the lack of sleep, nor unremitting and continuous fighting, nor wounds and slaughter, nor the death of their relatives in front of their eyes, nor any other frightful spectacle could make them give in or weaken their eagerness and sense of purpose'. In fact they had no option but to stand and fight; they could not be replaced – there were no other troops – but the Italians were fighting under the command of Giustiniani and the Greeks in the presence of their emperor, figures as motivating as the sultan was to the Ottoman army.

Mehmet knew he must strike again before the attack faltered. Now, if ever, his paid soldiers needed to earn their keep. Riding forward on his horse, he urged his troops to prove themselves as heroes. Clear orders were issued and Mehmet himself personally led the men at a steady pace to the edge of the ditch. It was still an hour to sunrise but the stars were fading and 'the blackness of night was drawing towards dawn'. They stopped at the ditch. There he ordered 'the bowmen, slingers and rifle men to stand at a distance and shoot to the right at those defending the stockade and battered outer wall'. A firestorm swept towards the walls: 'there were so many culverins and arrows being fired, that it was impossible to see the sky'. The defenders were forced to duck beneath the stockade under 'the rain of arrows and other projectiles falling like snowflakes'. At another signal the infantry advanced 'with a loud and terrifying war cry' 'not like Turks but like lions'. They pressed towards the stockade propelled on a huge wall of sound, the ultimate psychological battle weapon of Ottoman armies, so loud that it could be heard on the Asian shore, five miles from their camp. The sound of drums and pipes, the shouts and exhortations of their officers, the thunderous roll of the cannon, and the piercing cries of the men themselves calculated both to liberate their own adrenalin and to shatter the nerve of the enemy – all had their desired effect. 'With their great shouting they took away our courage and spread fear throughout the city,' recorded Barbaro. The attack was simultaneous along the whole four-mile front of the land wall, like the crash of a breaking wave. Again the church bells rang in warning and the non-combatants hastened to their prayers.

The heavy infantry and Janissaries were 'eager and fresh for battle'. They were fighting in the presence of their sultan both for honour and for the prize of being first onto the ramparts. They advanced on the stockade without any wavering or hesitancy, 'like men intent on entering the city' who knew their business. They ripped down the barrels and wooden turrets with hooked sticks, tore at the framework of the stockade, propped ladders against the rampart, and raising their shields over their heads attempted to force their way up beneath a withering bombardment of rocks and missiles. Their officers stood behind yelling instructions, and the sultan himself wheeled back and forth on his horse shouting and encouraging.

From the opposite side the weary Greeks and Italians joined battle. Giustiniani and his men, and Constantine, accompanied by 'all his nobles and his principal knights and his bravest men', pressed forward to the barricades with 'javelins, pikes, long spears and other fighting weapons'. The first wave of palace troops 'fell, struck by stones, so that many died', but others stepped up to replace them. There was no wavering. It was soon a hand-to-hand, face-to-face struggle for control of the rampart with each side fighting with total belief – for honour, God and great rewards on one side, for God and survival on the other. In the pressed close-up combat it was the terrible sound of shouting voices that filled the air – 'taunts, those stabbing with their spears, others being stabbed at, killers and being killed, those doing all kinds of terrible things in anger and fury'. Behind, the cannon fired their huge shot and smoke drifted across the battlefield, alternately concealing and revealing the combatants to each other. 'It seemed', said Barbaro, 'like something from another world.'

For an hour the fighting continued, with the palace regiments making little headway. The defenders never stepped back. 'We repelled them vigorously,' reported Leonard, 'but many of our men were now wounded and pulled back from fighting. However, Giustiniani our commander still stood firm and the other captains remained in their fighting positions.' There came a moment, imperceptibly at first, when those inside the stockade felt the pressure from the Ottomans ease a fraction. It was the pivotal moment, the instant when a battle turns. Constantine noticed it and urged the defenders on. According to Leonard he called out to his men: 'Brave soldiers, the enemy's army is weakening, the crown of victory is ours. God is on our side – keep fighting!' The Ottomans faltered. The weary defenders found new strength.

And then two strange moments of fortune swung the battle away from them. Half a mile up the line towards the Blachernae Palace, the

Bocchiardi brothers had been successful in repulsing the troops of Karaja Pasha, occasionally making sorties from the Circus Gate, the postern hidden in an angle of the walls. This gate was now to live up to ancient prophecy. Returning from a raid, one of the Italian soldiers failed to close the postern behind him. In the growing light, some of Karaja's men spotted the open door and burst in. Fifty managed to get access via a flight of stairs up to the wall and to surprise the soldiers on top. Some were cut down, others preferred to jump to their death. Exactly what happened next is unclear; it appears that the intruders were successfully isolated and surrounded before too much further damage could be done, but they managed to tear down the flag of St Mark and the emperor's standard from some towers and replace them with Ottoman standards.

Down the line at the stockade Constantine and Giustiniani were unaware of these developments. They were confidently holding the line, when bad luck dealt a more serious blow. Giustiniani was wounded. To some it was the God of the Christians or the Muslims answering or refusing prayers who created this moment. To bookish Greeks it was a moment straight from Homer: a sudden reversal in battle, caused, according to Kritovoulos, by 'wicked and merciless fortune', the instant when a serene and merciless goddess, surveying the battle with Olympian detachment, decides to tilt the outcome – and swipes the hero to the dust and turns his heart to jelly.

There is no clear agreement on what happened, but everyone knew its significance: it caused immediate consternation amongst his Genoese troops. In the light of subsequent events, the accounts become fragmentary and quarrelsome: Giustiniani, 'dressed in the armour of Achilles', falls to the ground in a dozen ways. He is hit on the right leg by an arrow; he is struck in the chest by a crossbow bolt; he is stabbed from below in the belly while struggling on the ramparts; a lead shot passes through the back of his arm and penetrates his breastplate; he is struck in the shoulder by a culverin; he is hit from behind by one of his own side by accident – or on purpose. The most probable versions suggest that his upper body armour was punctured by lead shot, a small hole concealing grave internal damage.

Giustiniani had been fighting continuously since the start of the siege and was undoubtedly exhausted beyond endurance. He had been wounded the day before, and this second wound seems to have broken his spirit. Unable to stand and more seriously injured than any bystander could see, he ordered his men to carry him back to his ship to seek medical attention. They went to the emperor to ask for the key to one of the gates. Constantine was appalled by the danger presented by the withdrawal of his principal commander and begged Giustiniani and his officers to stay until the danger was over, but they would not. Giustiniani entrusted command of the troops to two officers and promised to return after attending to his wound. Reluctantly Constantine handed over the key. The gate was opened and his bodyguard carried him away down to his galley at the Horn. It was a catastrophic decision. The temptation of the open gate was too much for the other Genoese; seeing their commander departing, they streamed through the gate after him.

Desperately Constantine and his entourage attempted to stem the tide. They forbade any of the Greeks to follow the Italians out of the enclosure, and ordered them to close ranks and step up to fill the empty spaces in the front line. Mehmet seems to have perceived that the defence was slackening, and rallied his troops for another assault. 'Friends, we have the city!' he called out. 'With just a little more effort the city is taken!'

A group of Janissaries under the command of one of Mehmet's favourite officers, Cafer Bey, ran forward shouting '*Allahu Akbar* – God is great'. With the cry of the sultan ringing in their ears – 'Go on my falcons, march on my lions!' – and remembering the promised reward for raising the flag on the walls, they surged towards the stockade. At the front, carrying the Ottoman flag, was a giant of a man, Hasan of Ulubat, accompanied by thirty companions. Covering his head with his shield, he managed to storm the rampart, throwing back the wavering defenders and establishing himself on top. For a short while he was able to maintain his position, flag in hand, inspiring the onrush of the Janissary corps. It was a defining and thrilling image of Ottoman courage – the Janissary giant finally planting the flag of Islam on the walls of the Christian city – and destined to pass into the nation-making mythology. Before long however, the defenders regrouped and retaliated with a barrage of rocks, arrows and spears. They threw back some of the thirty and then cornered Hasan, finally battering him to his knees and hacking him to pieces – but all around more and more Janissaries were able to establish themselves on the ramparts and to penetrate gaps in the stockade. Like a flood breaching coastal defences thousands of men started to pour into the enclosure, remorselessly pushing back the defenders by weight of numbers. In a short time they were hemmed in towards the inner wall, in front of which a ditch had been excavated to provide earth for the stockade. Some were pushed into it and were trapped. Unable to clamber out, they were massacred.

Ottoman troops were pouring into the enclosure along a broadening front; many were killed by the defenders bombarding them from the stockade, but the flood was now unstoppable; according to Barbaro there were 30,000 inside within fifteen minutes, uttering 'such cries that it seemed to be hell itself'. At the same time the flags planted by the few enemy intruders on towers near the Circus Gate were spotted and the cry went up, 'The city is taken!' Blind panic seized the defenders. They turned and ran, seeking a way to escape the locked enclosure back into the city. At the same time, Mehmet's men were starting to climb the inner wall as well and were firing down on them from above.

There was only possible exit route – the small postern through which Giustiniani had been carried away. All the other gates were locked. A struggling mass of men converged on the gateway, trampling each other in their attempts to get out, 'so that they made a great mound of living men by the gate which prevented anyone from having passage'. Some fell underfoot and were crushed to death; others were slaughtered by the Ottoman heavy infantry now sweeping down the stockade in orderly formation. The mound of bodies grew and choked off any further chance of escape. All the surviving defenders in the stockade perished in the slaughter. By each of the other gateways – the Charisian, the Fifth Military Gate – lay a similar pile of corpses, the men who had fled there unable to get out of the locked enclosure. And somewhere in this choking, panicking, struggling mêlée, Constantine is glimpsed for the last time, surrounded by his most faithful retinue – Theophilus Palaiologos, John Dalmata, Don Francisco of Toledo – his last moments reported by unreliable witnesses who were almost certainly not present, struggling, resisting defiantly, falling, crushed underfoot, until he vanishes from history into the afterlife of legend.

A posse of Janissaries clambered over the dead bodies and forced open the Fifth Military Gate. Making their way up the inside of the city walls, some turned left towards the Charisian gate and opened it from the inside; others going right opened the gate of St Romanus. From tower after tower Ottoman flags fluttered in the wind. 'Then all the rest of the army burst violently into the city . . . and the Sultan stood before the mighty walls, where the great standard was and the horsetail banners, and watched the events.' It was dawn. The sun was rising. Ottoman soldiers moved among the fallen, beheading the dead and dying. Large birds of prey circled overhead. The defence had collapsed in less than five hours.

لتفتحن القسطنطينية
فلنعم الأمير أميرها ولنعم الجيش ذلك الجيش

15 A Handful of Dust
6 A.M. 29 MAY 1453

Tell me please how and when the end of this world will be? And how will men know that the end is close, at the doors? By what signs will the end be indicated? And whither will pass this city, the New Jerusalem? What will happen to the holy temples standing here, to the venerated icons, the relics of the Saints, and the books? Please inform me.

Epiphanios, tenth-century Orthodox monk to St Andrew the Fool for Christ

As the Ottoman troops poured into the city and their flags were seen flying from the towers, panic spread through the civilian population. The cry, 'The city is lost!' rang through the streets. People started to run. The Bocchiardi brothers at the walls near the Circus Gate saw soldiers fleeing past their position. They mounted their horses and drove at the enemy, temporarily forcing them back. However, they too soon realized the hopelessness of the situation. Ottoman troops on the ramparts hurled missiles down on them and Paolo was wounded on the head. They realized that they were in imminent danger of being surrounded. Paolo was captured and killed, but his brothers fought their way out and back down to the Horn with their men. At the harbour, the wounded Giustiniani learned that the defence had crumbled, and 'ordered his trumpeters to sound the signal to recall his men'. For others it was too late. The Venetian bailey, Minotto, and many of the leading Venetians and the sailors who had come from the galleys to fight were surrounded and captured at the Palace of Blachernae, while

'Verily they will conquer Constantinople. Truly their commander will be an excellent one. Truly that army will be an excellent one!': a saying attributed to the Prophet

further up the land wall towards the sea of Marmara, where the defence had remained firm, the soldiers now found themselves attacked from the rear. Many were killed; others, including the commanders, Philippo Contarini and Demetrios Cantacuzenos surrendered and were captured.

Within the city, confusion spread with extraordinary speed. The collapse at the front line was so dramatic and unexpected that many were taken by surprise. While some of those who had escaped from the land walls were fleeing towards the Horn in the hope of getting on board the ships, others were running towards the front line. Alerted by the sound of battle, some of the civilians were making their way up to the walls to offer help to the troops when they met the first marauding bands of Ottoman soldiers pressing into the city, who 'attacked them with great anger and fury' and cut them down. It was a mixture of fear and hatred that sparked the initial slaughter in the city. Suddenly finding themselves in the maze of narrow streets, the Ottoman soldiers were confused and apprehensive. They expected to meet a large and determined army; it was impossible to believe that the 2,000 routed in the stockade comprised the total military resources of the city. At the same time weeks of suffering and the taunts hurled over the battlements by the Greeks had marked the conflict with a bitterness that made them savage. Now the city would pay for failing to accept negotiated surrender. They killed initially 'to create universal terror'; for a short while 'everyone they found they dispatched at the point of a scimitar, women and men, old and young, of any condition'. This ruthlessness was probably intensified by pockets of spirited resistance from the populace who 'threw bricks and paving stones at them from above . . . and threw fire upon them'. The streets became slippery with blood.

The flags of the sultan fluttering from the high towers on the land walls spread the word quickly down the Ottoman line. Along the Golden Horn the Ottoman fleet redoubled its attacks and as defenders slipped away, the sailors forced open the sea gates one after another. Soon the Plateia Gate, close to the Venetian quarter, was opened and detachments of men started to penetrate the heart of the city. Further round the coast, the word reached Hamza Bey and the Marmara fleet. Eager to join in the opportunity for plunder, the sailors brought their ships back inshore and threw ladders up against the walls.

For a short while indiscriminate slaughter continued to rage: 'The whole city was filled with men killing or being killed, fleeing or pursuing,' according to Chalcocondylas. In the panic everyone now consulted his own best interests. While the Italians made for the Horn and the safety of the ships, the Greeks fled home to protect their wives and children. Some were captured on the way; others got home to find 'their wives and children abducted and their possessions plundered'. Yet others, on reaching home, 'were themselves bound and fettered with their closest friends and wives'. Many who reached home before the intruders, realizing the likely outcome of surrender, decided to die in defence of their families. People hid themselves away in cellars and cisterns or wandered about the city in dazed confusion waiting to be captured or killed. A pathetic scene took place at the church of Theodosia down near the Golden Horn. It was the saint's feast day, kept with adoration and zeal down hundreds of years of worship to a faithfully preserved ritual. The facade was adorned with early summer roses. Within, the customary all-night vigil had taken place at the saint's sepulchre, the lighted candles glimmering in the short summer night. In the early morning, a procession of men and women were wending their way towards the church, blindly trusting in the miraculous power of prayer. They were carrying the customary gifts, 'beautifully embellished and adorned candles and incense', when they were intercepted by soldiers and carried off; the whole congregation was taken prisoner; the church, which was rich with the offerings of worshippers, was stripped. Theodosia's bones were thrown to the dogs. Elsewhere women awoke in their beds to the sight of intruders bursting through the door.

As the morning wore on and the Ottomans realized the truth – that there no longer was any organized resistance – the principles of slaughter became more discriminating. The Ottoman soldiers acted, according to Sa'd-ud-din, in accordance with the precept, 'Slaughter their aged and capture their youth.' The emphasis shifted to taking live prisoners as booty. The hunt began for valuable slaves – young women, beautiful children – with the irregular troops of many 'nations, customs and languages', including Christians, being in the forefront, 'plundering, destroying, robbing, murdering, insulting, seizing and enslaving men, women, children, old and young, priests and monks – people of every age and rank'. The accounts of the atrocities were largely written by Christians, more coyly by Ottoman chroniclers, but there is no doubt that the morning unfolded in scenes of terror. They have left a series of vivid snapshots, sights 'terrible and pitiful and beyond all tragedies', according to Kritovoulos, the generally pro-Ottoman Greek writer. Women were 'dragged violently from their bed chambers'. Children were snatched from their parents; old men and women who were unable to flee their houses were 'slaughtered mercilessly', along with 'the weak-minded, the old, the lepers and the infirm'. 'The newborn babies were hurled into the squares.' Women and boys were raped, then ill-assorted groups of captives were tied together by their captors, 'dragging them out savagely, driving them, tearing at them, manhandling them, herding them off disgracefully and shamefully into the crossroads, insulting them and doing terrible things'. Those who survived, particularly the 'young and modest women, nobly born and wealthy, who were used to staying in their homes' were traumatized beyond life itself. Rather than undergo this fate, some of the girls and married women preferred to throw themselves into wells. Among the pillagers fights broke out over the most beautiful girls, which were sometimes fought to the death.

Churches and monasteries were particularly sought out. Those near the land walls – the military church of St George by the Charisian Gate, the Church of St John the Baptist at Petra and the Chora Monastery – were quickly plundered. The miracle-working icon of the Hodegetria was hacked into four pieces and divided among the soldiers for its valuable frame. Crosses were smashed from the roofs of the churches; the tombs of saints were cracked open and searched for treasures; their contents torn to pieces and thrown into the streets. The church treasures – chalices, goblets and 'holy artefacts and precious and sumptuous robes embroidered with much gold and glittering with precious stones and pearls' – were carted away and melted down. The altars were torn down and the 'walls of churches and sanctuaries were ransacked . . . looking for gold'. 'The consecrated images of God's saints' witnessed scenes of rape, according to Leonard. Entering the convents, nuns were 'led to the fleet and ravished'; the monks were killed in their cells or 'hauled out of the churches where they had sought sanctuary, and driven away with insults and dishonour'. The tombs of the emperors were smashed open with iron bars in search of hidden gold. These 'and ten thousand other terrible things were done', Kritovoulos mournfully recorded. In a few hours a thousand years of Christian Constantinople largely disappeared.

In front of this tidal wave, those who could, panicked and ran. Many headed for St Sophia guided by instinct and superstition. They remembered the old prophecy that the enemy would penetrate the city as far as the Column of Constantine, near the great church, when an avenging angel would descend, sword in hand, and inspire the defenders to drive them out of the city 'and from the West and from Anatolia itself to the place called the Red Apple tree on the borders of Persia'. Inside the church, a large congregation of clergy and laity, men, women and children gathered for the service of matins and to put their faith in God. The massive bronze doors of the church were swung shut and barred. It was eight in the morning.

The doors of St Sophia

Elsewhere, some of the outlying areas of the city were able to negotiate wholesale surrender. By the middle of the fifteenth century the population of Constantinople was so shrunk within its outer walls that some parts of the city were separate villages, protected by their own walls and palisades. Some of these – Studion on the Marmara and the fishing village of Petrion near the Horn – voluntarily opened their gates on condition that their houses would be spared the general ransack. The headman in each case was conducted to the sultan to make formal surrender of his village and Mehmet probably detailed a detachment of military police to protect the houses. Such acts of surrender could be held to secure immunity under Islamic laws of war, and a number of churches and monasteries survived intact as a result. Elsewhere, heroic or desperate pockets of resistance continued. Down on the Horn, a group of Cretan sailors barricaded themselves into three towers and refused to surrender. All morning they resisted Ottoman attempts to dislodge them. Many on the sea walls furthest from the land wall also battled on, often ignorant of the true situation until they suddenly found the enemy in their rear. Some threw themselves from the battlements, others surrendered to the enemy unconditionally. Prince Orhan, the pretender to the Ottoman throne, and his small band of Turks had no such options. They fought on, as did the Catalans stationed further along the sea wall near the Bucoleon Palace.

In the midst of this unfolding destruction, the Ottoman sailors took a fateful decision. When they saw the army within the walls, and fearing that they would miss the chance to plunder, they drove their ships up onto the shore and abandoned them 'to search for gold, jewels and other riches'. So keen were the sailors to get ashore down on the Horn that they ignored the Italians fleeing over the walls the other way. It was to be a rare stroke of luck.

The search for booty became obsessive. The Jewish quarter down by the Horn was an early target for plundering, due to its traditional trade in gems, and Italian merchants similarly were eagerly sought out. As the day wore on booty collection became more organized. The first troop to enter a house raised a flag outside to indicate that it had already been stripped; other parties automatically moved on to look elsewhere: 'and so they put their flags everywhere, even on monasteries and churches'. The men worked in teams, carting off the prisoners and plunder back to the camp or the ships, then returning for more. No corner was left untouched: 'churches, old vaults and tombs, cloisters, underground chambers and hidden places and crannies and caves and holes. And they searched in all the hidden corners, and if there was anyone or anything hidden there, they dragged it into the light.' Some even engaged in secondary activity, stealing the unguarded booty deposited back in the camp.

Meanwhile the struggle for survival went on. During the course of the morning hundreds of individual fates were decided by luck. Cardinal Isidore, the Archbishop of Kiev, with the help of his servants, managed to swap his sumptuous episcopal robes for those of a soldier lying dead in the street. Ottoman troops soon came across the corpse dressed in the bishop's robes, cut off the head and carried it in triumph through the streets. The elderly Isidore was himself quickly captured but, unrecognized, seemed too wretched to be worth the bother of dragging off into slavery. For a small sum of money he bought his freedom from his captors on the spot and managed to get aboard one of the Italian ships in the harbour. Prince Orhan was less fortunate. Dressed as a soldier and with a fluent command of Greek he sought to make good his escape from the sea walls but was recognized and pursued. Seeing that his situation was hopeless he hurled himself off the battlements. The severed head was taken to Mehmet, who had been anxious to know his fate. Other leading notables were captured alive – Lucas Notaras and his family were taken, probably in their palace, George Sphrantzes and his family likewise. The monk Gennadios, who had led the anti-unionist cause, was captured in his cell. The Catalans fought on until they were all killed or captured, but the Cretans in their towers beside the Golden Horn proved impossible to dislodge. Eventually someone reported their resistance to Mehmet. In a characteristically quixotic gesture, he offered them a truce and the chance to sail away in their ships. After some hesitation they accepted the offer and departed, free men.

For many, the Horn seemed to offer the best chance of escape. During the early morning hundreds of soldiers and civilians streamed down the narrow lanes hoping to clamber aboard the Italian ships in the harbour. The scene at the sea gates was one of confusion and panic. In headlong flight many hurled themselves into crowded rowing boats that capsized and sank, drowning their occupants. The sense of tragedy was magnified by a decision taken by some of the gatekeepers. Seeing their Greek compatriots fleeing to the shore and remembering the prophecy that the enemy could be turned back at the statue of Constantine, they decided that the defenders could be persuaded to turn and drive the enemy out if their exit was barred. Accordingly they threw the keys away from the top of the wall and prevented further escape. As any means of reaching the Italian galleys offshore disappeared, the scene on the foreshore became increasingly pitiful – 'men, women, monks and nuns crying pitifully, beating their breasts, imploring the ships to come in and rescue them' – but the situation aboard the galleys was also panic-stricken and the captains were torn on how best to proceed. By the time the Florentine merchant Giacomo Tetaldi reached the shore, two hours after the collapse of the front line, there was nothing for it but to swim or await 'the fury of the Turks'. Preferring to risk death by drowning, he stripped off his clothes and struck out for the ships and was hauled aboard. He was just in time. Looking back, he saw about forty more soldiers, seized by the Ottomans in the very act of removing their armour to follow him.

'May God help them,' he wrote. Some of the distraught figures lining the shore were rescued from across the water by the Podesta of Galata and persuaded to accept the comparative safety of the Genoese colony: 'not without great danger, I brought back into the town those at the palisade; you never saw such a terrible thing'.

On board the Italian ships there was paralysing indecision. They had heard the defiant clanging of the church bells die away in the early morning, the sound of screaming floating across the water as the Ottoman sailors brought their ships ashore and stormed the walls of the Horn. The Venetians had seen too the pitiful spectacle of the population imploring the captains to bring their craft inshore or drowning in their attempts to reach them, but it was too dangerous to risk approaching the shore; apart from the obvious danger of being captured by the enemy, a sudden stampede by desperate people at the water's edge could easily risk the safety of a vessel. In addition a large part of the Italian galley crews had been sent to man the walls and ships were alarmingly short-crewed. Yet the behaviour of the Ottoman fleet which had abandoned its vessels to take part in the plunder was a massive stroke of good luck and presented, doubtless only for a short time, the possibility of escape. It was imperative that the galley fleet acted decisively before Ottoman naval discipline was restored.

The mood of uncertainty was mirrored in Galata. When it was obvious that the city had been taken the people panicked. 'I always knew that if Constantinople was lost, this place was also lost,' recorded Angelo Lomellino, the podesta, afterwards. The question was how to react. Mehmet's attitude to the Genoese, whom he considered to be guilty of collaboration in the defence of the city, was uncertain. The majority of its able-bodied men were indeed fighting across the water, including the podesta's own nephew. There were only 600 men left in the town. Many were tempted to quit Galata at once. A large number of people boarded a Genoese ship to make their escape, abandoning their homes and possessions; another boat, largely carrying women, was captured by Ottoman ships, but Lomellino decided to set an example and sit tight. He reckoned that if he himself abandoned the city, sack would be inevitable.

In the midst of these deliberations the captain of the Venetian fleet, Aluvixe Diedo, accompanied by his armourer and the surgeon Nicolo Barbaro, put ashore to consult with the podesta on what to do: should the Genoese and Venetian ships jointly confront the Ottomans, openly declaring a state of war between the Italian Republics and the sultan, or should they make good their escape? Lomellino begged them to wait while he sent an ambassador to Mehmet, but for the Venetian captains time was pressing. They had delayed as long as possible to collect those survivors who could swim away from the stricken city and they dared wait no longer, given the difficulty of preparing their ships for sea. Diedo and his companions in Galata could see the galleys getting ready to depart in the bay below them and were hurrying back through the streets to rejoin their ships, when they discovered, to their horror, that Lomellino had barred the gates to prevent a mass exodus. 'We were in a terrible situation,' Barbaro recalled. 'We were shut in their town, the galleys suddenly began to raise their sails, spreading them and drawing in their oars, ready to leave without their captain.' They could see their ships preparing to sail away and it was certain that Mehmet would not deal kindly with the captain of the enemy fleet. Desperately they implored the podesta to let them go. Finally he permitted the gates to be opened. Just in time they made it to the foreshore and were taken back on board. The galleys slowly kedged their way up to the chain, which still barred the mouth of the bay. Two men leaped down into the water with axes and hacked away at one of the wooden floating sections of the boom until it gave way. One by one the ships hauled themselves out into the Bosphorus, while Ottoman commanders watched from the shore in impotent fury. The flotilla of ships rounded the point of Galata and formed up in the now empty Ottoman harbour at the Double Columns. There they waited in the hope of taking their shipmates and other survivors on board but by midday it was clear that all had been killed or captured and they could wait no longer. For a second time fate smiled on Christian ships. The south wind which had propelled the Genoese ships up the straits so helpfully in late April was now blowing a powerful twelve knots from the north. Without this stroke of luck, Barbaro acknowledged, 'all of us would have been captured'.

And so, 'at midday with the help of the Lord God, Master Aluvixe Diedo, the captain of the Tana fleet, set sail on his galley', and with him a small flotilla of ships and galleys from Venice and Crete. One of the great galleys from Trebizond, which had lost 164 of its crew, had great difficulty hoisting its sails, but there was no one to oppose them and they surged down the Marmara, past the corpses of Christians and Muslims floating out to sea, 'like melons along a canal', and away towards the Dardanelles with a mixture of relief at their good fortune and regret for the memory of their lost shipmates, 'some of whom had been drowned, some dead in the bombardment or killed in the battle in other ways', including Trevisano himself. They carried 400 survivors rescued in the final chaotic hours, as well as a surprising number of Byzantine nobles who had already boarded before the city fell. Seven ships from Genoa also got away, among them the galley carrying the wounded Giustiniani. Even as they did so Hamza Bey managed to regroup the Ottoman fleet, which swept round into the mouth of the Horn and captured fifteen ships, belonging to the emperor, Ancona and the Genoese, which were still lying there, some too overcrowded with refugees to sail. Other pitiful groups of figures stood on the foreshore, wailing and beseeching the departing galleys. Ottoman marines simply rounded them up and herded them onto their own vessels.

It is three miles from the land walls to the heart of the city. By dawn determined bands of Janissaries were already forcing their way down the central thoroughfare from the St Romanus Gate, intent on St Sophia. Alongside the legend of the Red Apple there was a belief, widely circulated in the Ottoman camp, that the crypt of St Sophia, so visible on the distant skyline during the weeks of fruitless siege, contained an enormous treasure of gold, silver and precious stones. The Janissaries clattered through the destitute squares and deserted highways – past the Forum of the Ox and the Forum of Theodosius and down the Mese, the Middle Way that led into the heart of the city. Others came through the Charisian Gate further north past the Church of the Holy Apostles, which remained unsacked: it seems that Mehmet had placed a guard on the church to limit the wholesale devastation of the city's monuments. There was little resistance. When they reached the Forum of Constantine where the founder of the city gazed down from his imperial column, no angel turned them back with a fiery sword. At the same time sailors from the Horn and Marmara fleets were storming through the bazaars and churches at the tip of the peninsula. By seven in the morning both groups had reached the centre of the city and poured into the forum of the Augusteum. Here stood the greatest remaining trophies of Byzantium's imperial splendour – Justinian still riding towards the rising sun, the Milion, the milepost from which all distances in the empire were measured; beyond it on one side lay the Hippodrome and some of Constantine the Great's original plunder – ornaments that linked the city to an even more ancient past: the strange triple-headed brass serpent column from the temple of Apollo at Delphi, a commemorative token for a Greek victory against the Persians at the battle of Plataea in 479 BC, and even older, the Egyptian column of the Pharaoh Tutmose III. The perfectly preserved hieroglyphs on its polished granite surface were already three thousand years old when Ottoman troops looked up at them for the first time. On the other side stood St Sophia itself, the Great Church, rising 'to the very heavens'.

Inside, the service of matins had begun and the nine massive brass-fronted wooden doors, surmounted by their protective crosses, were barred shut. The huge congregation prayed for a miracle to save them from the enemy at the gate. The women had taken their usual places in the gallery, the men downstairs. The priests were at the altar conducting the service. Some people hid themselves in the furthest recesses of the great structure, climbing up into the service passages and onto the roof. When the Janissaries surged into the inner courtyard and found the doors barred, they started to batter down the central one, the imperial gate, reserved for the entrance of the emperor and his entourage. Under repeated axe blows, the four-inch thick door shuddered and crashed open and the Ottoman troops poured into the great building. Above them the mosaic figure of Christ in blue and gold watched impassively, his right hand raised in blessing, and in his left a book inscribed with the words 'Peace be with you, I am the light of the world.'

If there is any precise moment when Byzantium could be said to have died, it is now with the final blow of an axe. St Sophia had witnessed many of the great dramas of the imperial city. A church had stood on the site for 1,100 years; the great church of Justinian for 900. The mighty building reflected and had lived the turbulent spiritual and secular life of the city. Every emperor, with the ominous exception of the last, had been crowned here, many of the defining dramas of the empire had been played out under the great dome 'suspended from heaven by a golden chain'. Blood had been spilled on its marble floors before; riots had taken place; patriarchs and emperors had taken sanctuary from mobs and plotters, or been dragged from it by force. Three times the dome had collapsed in earthquakes. Its imposing doorways had seen the papal legates march in with their bull of excommunication. Vikings had carved graffiti on its walls; barbarian Frankish crusaders had pillaged it mercilessly. It was here that the whole population of Russia had been converted to Christianity as a result of the unearthly beauty of the Orthodox liturgy, here too that the great religious controversies had been played out and ordinary people had worn the floors smooth with their feet and their prayers. The history of the Church of the Holy Wisdom was the reflection of Byzantium – sacred and profane, mystical and sensuous, beautiful and cruel, irrational, divine and human, and after 1,123 years and 27 days it was nearly over.

A wail of fear arose from the cowering population as the soldiers burst in. Cries were raised to God but it made no difference; they were 'trapped as in a net'. There was little bloodshed. A few who resisted and perhaps some of the old and infirm were slaughtered but the majority surrendered 'like sheep'. The Ottoman troops had come for plunder and profit. They ignored the screaming of men, women and children, as each soldier struggled to secure his own prize. Young women were almost torn apart in the race to secure the most valuable slaves. Nuns and noble women, young and old, masters and servants were bound together and dragged out of the church. The women were secured with their own veils, whilst the men were tied up with rope. Working in teams each man would lead his captives to 'a certain spot, and placing them in safekeeping, returned to take a second and even a third prize'. Within an hour the whole congregation had been bound up. 'The infinite chains of captives', recorded Doukas, 'who like herds of cattle and flocks of sheep poured out of the temple and the temple sanctuary made an extraordinary spectacle!' A terrible noise of lamentation filled the morning air.

The soldiers then turned their attention to the fabric of the church. They hacked the icons to pieces, stripping away the valuable metal frames and seized 'in an instant the precious and holy relics which were kept safe in the sanctuary, the vessels of gold and silver and other valuable materials'. Then rapidly all the other fixtures and fittings followed, things that the Muslims considered both idolatrous affronts to God and rightful booty for soldiers – the chains, candelabra and lamps, the iconostasis, the altar and its coverings, the church furniture, the emperor's chair – in a short time everything was either seized and carried off or destroyed in situ, leaving the great church 'ransacked and desolate', according to Doukas. The great church reverted to a shell. This defining moment of loss for the Greeks gave rise to a legend so typical of their enduring belief in the power of miracles and their yearning for the holy city. At the moment that the soldiers approached the altar, the priests took the holy vessels and approached the sanctuary and – the story goes – the wall opened to admit them, and closed again behind them; and there they will remain safe until an Orthodox emperor restores St Sophia to a church. The basis for this story may lie in the possibility that some of the priests were able to get away through one of the old passages that connected the church to the patriarch's residence behind, and so escape. And there was one other small, grim consolation. The Ottomans smashed open the tomb of the hated Venetian doge, Enrico Dandolo, who had wrought a similar devastation on the city two hundred and fifty years earlier. They found no treasure but they hurled his bones into the street for the dogs to gnaw.

All morning Mehmet remained in his camp outside the walls, awaiting reports of the city's capitulation and its sack. He received a steady stream of news and frightened deputations of citizens. Ambassadors came from the Podesta of Galata with gifts, seeking assurance that the pact of neutrality should remain in place, but he made no categoric reply. Soldiers brought the head of Orhan, but it was the face of Constantine that Mehmet was most anxious to look on. The fate of the emperor and the verification of his death remain confused and apocryphal. For a long time there was no definitive report of his end and it seems that Mehmet may have ordered a search of the battlefield for his body. Later in the day some Janissaries, possibly Serbs, brought a head to the sultan; according to Doukas, the Grand Duke Lucas Notaras was present at this scene and confirmed the identity of his master. The head – or a head – was then fixed on the column of Justinian opposite St Sophia as a proof to the Greeks that their emperor was dead. Later the skin was peeled off, the head stuffed with straw and was progressed with elaborate ceremony around the principal courts of the Muslim world as an emblem of power and conquest.

How – or even, according to some, if – he died is uncertain. No reliable eyewitness was present at the scene and the truth splinters and fragments into partisan and apocryphal accounts. The Ottoman chroniclers unite in presenting a disparaging but quite specific account, many versions of which were written long after the event and seem to draw on one another: 'the blind-hearted emperor' tried to flee when it was obvious that the battle was lost. He was making his way down to the steep streets to the Horn or the Marmara with his retinue to look for a ship when he ran into a band of *azaps* and Janissaries bent on plunder. 'A desperate battle ensued. The Emperor's horse slipped as he was attacking a wounded azap, whereupon the *azap* pulled himself together, and cut off the Emperor's head. When they saw this, the rest of the enemy troops lost hope and *azaps* managed to kill or capture most of them. A great quantity of money and precious stones in the possession of the Emperor's retinue were also seized.'

The Greek accounts see him generally charging into the fray at the wall with his faithful band of nobles as the front line collapses. In the version of Chalcocondylas 'the Emperor turned to Cantacuzenos and the few that were with them, and said, "Let us then go forward, men, against these barbarians." Cantacuzenos, a brave man, was killed, and the Emperor Constantine himself was forced back and was relentlessly pursued, struck on the shoulder and then killed.' There are many variants of this story that end in a mound of bodies at the St Romanus Gate or near one of the locked posterns; all of them provided the Greek people with enduring legends about the emperor. 'The Emperor of Constantinople was killed,' recorded Giacomo Tetaldi with unvarnished simplicity. 'Some say his head was cut off, others that he died in the crowd pressed against the gate. Both stories could very well be true.' 'He was killed and his head was presented to the Lord of the Turks on a lance,' wrote Benvenuto, the consul of Ancona in the city. The fact that there was no clear identification of the body suggests that Constantine may well have stripped off his imperial regalia at the final onslaught and died like a common soldier. Many of the corpses were decapitated and it would subsequently have been difficult to distinguish the fallen. Apocryphal stories abounded, some that he had escaped by ship, but these may be discounted, others that Mehmet gave his body to the Greeks for burial in one of several locations in the city, but no sure site can be identified. The uncertainty of his ending would become the focus for a growing body of Greek legend, a sense of yearning for lost glory, reflected in songs and lamentations:

Weep Christians of the East and the West, weep and cry over this great destruction. On Tuesday the 29th day of May in the year 1453, the sons of Hagar took the town of Constantinople . . . And when Constantine Dragases . . . heard the news . . . he seized his lance, strapped on his sword, he mounted his mare, his mare with white feet and struck the Turks, the impious dogs. He killed ten pashas and sixty Janissaries, but his sword broke and his lance broke and he remained alone, alone without any help . . . and a Turk struck him on the head and poor Constantine fell from his mare; and he lay stretched out on the earth in the dust and the blood. They cut off his head and fixed it on the end of a lance, and they buried his body under a laurel tree.

The 'unfortunate emperor' was forty-nine years old when he died. Whatever the circumstances of his death, it seems clear that he tried to the very end to keep the flame of Byzantium alight. 'The ruler of Istanbul was brave and asked for no quarter', declared the chronicler Oruch, in a rare note of begrudging respect from the Ottomans. He had been a redoubtable opponent.

Later in the day, when the chaos had died down and some semblance of order had been restored, Mehmet made his own triumphant entry into Constantinople. He passed through the Gate of Charisius – that was to become in Turkish, the Edirne gate – on horseback, accompanied on foot by his viziers, beylerbeys, the ulema and commanders and by his crack troops, his bodyguards and foot soldiers, in a show of pageantry that has been amplified by legend. The green banners of Islam and the red banners of the sultan were unfurled as the cavalcade jingled through the archway. After portraits of Kemal Ataturk, it is probably the single most famous image in Turkish history, endlessly memorialized in poems and pictures. In nineteenth-century prints the bearded Mehmet sits upright on his proudly stepping horse, his face turned to one side. He is flanked by sturdy moustachioed Janissaries carrying matchlocks, spears and battle axes, imams whose white beards symbolize the wisdom of Islam, and behind the waving banners and a thicket of clustered spears stretch deep to the horizon. To the left a black warrior, muscled like a body builder, stands proudly erect as a representative of all the other nations of the Faith welcoming the *gazi* warriors into the inheritance promised by the Prophet. His scimitar points to a heap of fallen Christians at the sultan's feet, whose shields are surmounted with crosses – a memory of the crusades and a symbol of the triumph of Islam over Christianity. According to legend, Mehmet stopped and gave thanks to God. Then he turned to congratulate his 'seventy or eighty thousand Muslim heroes, crying out: "Halt not Conquerors! God be praised! You are the Conquerors of Constantinople!"' It is the iconic moment at which he assumes the name by which he has always been known in Turkish – *Fatih*, the

Conqueror – and the instant at which the Ottoman Empire comes fully into its own. He was twenty-one years old.

Mehmet then processed into the heart of the city to inspect the buildings that he had visualized so clearly from afar – past the church of the Holy Apostles and the mighty aqueduct of Valens towards St Sophia. He was probably sobered rather than impressed by what he saw. It resembled a human Pompeii more than the City of Gold. Uncontrolled, the army had forgotten the edict to leave the fabric of the buildings untouched. They had fallen on Constantinople, according to Kritovoulos with a measure of exaggeration, 'like a fire or a whirlwind . . . the whole city was deserted and emptied and appeared ravaged and charred as if by fire . . . the only houses left had been devastated, so ruined that they struck fear in the hearts of all that saw them because of the enormous devastation'. Although he had promised his army three days of looting it had effectively been picked clean in one. In order to prevent even greater destruction he broke his promise and ordered an end to the looting by nightfall on the first day – and it says something for the underlying discipline of his army that the *chavushes* were able to enforce obedience.

Mehmet rode on, stopping to inspect particular landmarks along the way. According to legend, as he passed the serpent column of Delphi, he struck it with his mace and broke off the under jaw of one of the heads. Passing the statue of Justinian, he rode up to the front doors of St Sophia and dismounted. Bowing down to the ground, he poured a handful of dust over his turban as an act of humility to God. Then he stepped inside the wrecked church. He seems to have been both amazed and appalled by what he saw. As he walked across the great space and stared up at the dome, he caught sight of a soldier smashing away at the marble pavement. He asked the man why he was demolishing the floor. 'For the Faith,' the man replied. Infuriated by this visible defiance of his orders to preserve the buildings, Mehmet struck the man with his sword. He was dragged off half-dead by Mehmet's attendants. A few Greeks, who were still hiding in the furthest recesses of the building, came out and threw themselves at his feet and some priests re-appeared – possibly those who had miraculously been 'swallowed up' by the walls. In one of those unpredictable acts of mercy that characterized the sultan, Mehmet ordered that these men should be allowed to go home under protection. Then he called for an imam to go up into the pulpit and recite the call to prayer, and he himself climbed onto the altar and bowed down and prayed to the victorious God.

Later, according to the Ottoman historian Tursun Bey, Mehmet, 'mounting as [Jesus] the spirit of God ascending to the fourth sphere of heaven', climbed up through the galleries of the church out onto the dome. From here he could look out over the church and the ancient heart of the Christian city. Below, the decay of a once-proud empire was all too apparent. Many of the buildings surrounding the church had collapsed, including most of the raised seating of the Hippodrome and the old Royal Palace. This building, once the centre of imperial power, had long been a ruin, totally wrecked by the crusaders in 1204. As he surveyed the desolate scene, 'he thought of the impermanence and instability of this world, and its ultimate destruction', and remembered a couplet of poetry that recalled the obliteration of the Persian Empire by the Arabs in the seventh century:

> The spider is curtain-bearer in the Palace of Chosroes
> The owl sounds the relief in the castle of Afrasiyab.

It is a melancholy image. Mehmet had achieved everything he had dreamed of; at the end of an enormous day when he had confirmed the Ottoman Empire as the great superpower of the age, he had already stared over the edge of its own decline. He rode back through the wrecked city. Long lines of captives were being herded into makeshift tents outside the fosse. Almost the whole population of 50,000 had been led away to the ships and the camp; maybe 4,000 had been killed in the day's fighting. Separated from their families, children could be heard calling out for their mothers, men for their wives, all 'dumbfounded by such a catastrophe'. In the Ottoman camp there were fires and festivities, singing and dancing to pipes and drums. Horses were dressed in the robes of priests and the crucifix was mockingly paraded through the Ottoman camp, topped with a Turkish cap. Booty was traded, precious stones bought and sold. Men were said to become rich overnight 'by buying jewels for a few pence', 'gold and silver were traded for the price of tin'.

If the day had unfolded in pitiful scenes and terrible instances of massacre, there was nothing particular to Islam in this behaviour. It was the expected reaction of any medieval army that had taken a city by storm. The history of Byzantium could produce many similar incidents that were only incidentally conducted on religious grounds. It was no worse that the Byzantine sack of the Saracen city of Candia on Crete in 961, when Nicephorus Phocas – a man nicknamed 'the white death of the Saracens' – lost control of his army for three days of appalling carnage; no worse than the crusader sack of Constantinople in 1204 itself, and more disciplined than an irrational outburst of xenophobia that had preceded it in 1183, when the Byzantines butchered nearly every Latin in the city, 'women and children, the old and infirm, even the sick from the hospitals'. But when night fell on the Bosphorus and on the city on 29 May 1453, and slanted in through the windows of the dome of St Sophia and obliterated the mosaic portraits of emperors and angels, the porphyry columns, the onyx and marble floors, the smashed furniture and the pools of dried blood, it carried Byzantium away with it too, once and for all.

The ruined palace of Hormisdas on the Marmara shore

16 The Present Terror of the World 1453–1683

Whichever way I look, I see trouble.
Angelo Lomellino, Podesta of Galata, to his brother, 23 June 1453

The reckoning followed hard on the heels of the fall. The next day, there was a distribution of the booty: according to custom, Mehmet as commander was entitled to a fifth of everything that had been taken. His share of the enslaved Greeks he settled in the city in an area by the Horn, the Phanar district, which would continue as a traditional Greek quarter down to modern times. The vast majority of the ordinary citizens – about 30,000 – were marched off to the slave markets of Edirne, Bursa and Ankara. We know the fates of a few of these deportees because they were important people who were subsequently ransomed back into freedom. Among these was Matthew Camariotes, whose father and brother were killed, and whose family was dispersed; painstakingly he set about finding them. 'I ransomed my sister from one place, my mother from somewhere else; then my brother's son: most pleasing to God, I obtained their release.' Overall, though, it was a bitter experience. Beyond the death and disappearance of loved ones, most shattering to Camariotes was the discovery that 'of my brother's four sons, in the disaster three – alas! – through the fragility of youth, renounced their Christian faith . . . maybe this wouldn't have happened, had my father and brother survived . . . so I live, if you can call it living, in pain and grief'. Conversion was a not

A medal showing the ageing Mehmet, dated 1481, the year of his death uncommon occurrence, so traumatic had been the failure of prayers and relics to prevent the capture of the God-protected city by Islam. Many more captives simply disappeared into the gene pool of the Ottoman Empire – 'scattered across the whole world like dust', in the lament of the Armenian poet, Abraham of Ankara.

The surviving notables in the city suffered more immediate fates. Mehmet retained all the significant personages whom he could find, including the Grand Duke Lucas Notaras and his family. The Venetians, whom Mehmet identified as his key opponents in the Mediterranean basin, came in for especially harsh treatment. Minotto, the bailey of their colony, who had played a spirited part in the defence of the city, was executed, together with his son and other Venetian notables; a further twenty-nine were ransomed back to Italy. The Catalan consul and some of his leading men were also executed, whilst a vain hunt was conducted for the unionist churchmen, Leonard of Chios and Isidore of Kiev, who managed to escape unrecognized. A search in Galata for the two surviving Bocchiardi brothers was similarly unsuccessful; they hid and survived.

The Podesta of Galata, Angelo Lomellino, acted promptly to try to save the Genoese colony. Its complicity in the defence of Constantinople made it immediately vulnerable to retribution. Lomellino wrote to his brother that the sultan 'said that we did all we could for the safety of Constantinople . . . and certainly he spoke the truth. We were in the greatest danger, we had to do what he wanted to avoid his fury.' Mehmet ordered the immediate destruction of the town's walls and ditch, with the exception of the sea wall, destruction of its defensive towers and the handing over of the cannon and all other weapons. The podesta's nephew was taken off into the service of the palace as a hostage, in common with a number of sons of the Byzantine nobility – a policy that would both ensure good behaviour and provide educated young recruits for the imperial administration.

It was in this context that the fate of the Grand Duke Lucas Notaras was decided. The highest-ranking Byzantine noble, Notaras was a controversial figure during the siege, given a consistently bad press by the Italians. He was apparently against union; his oft repeated remark, 'rather the sultan's turban than the cardinal's hat', was held up by Italian writers as proof of the intransigence of Orthodox Greeks. It appears that Mehmet was initially minded to make Notaras prefect of the city – an indication of the deeper direction of the sultan's plans for

Constantinople – but was probably persuaded by his ministers to reverse the decision. According to the ever-vivid Doukas, Mehmet, 'full of wine and in a drunken stupor', demanded that Notaras should hand over his son to satisfy the sultan's lust. When Notaras refused, Mehmet sent the executioner to the family. After killing all the males, 'the executioner picked up the heads and returned to the banquet, presenting them to the bloodthirsty beast'. It is perhaps more likely that Notaras was unwilling to see his children taken as hostages and Mehmet decided that it was too risky to let the leading Byzantine nobility survive.

The work of converting St Sophia into a mosque began almost at once. A wooden minaret was rapidly constructed for the call to prayer and the figurative mosaics whitewashed over, with the exception of the four guardian angels under the dome, which Mehmet, with a regard for the spirits of the place, preserved. (Other powerful 'pagan' talismans of the ancient city also survived for a while intact – the equestrian statue of Justinian, the serpent column from Delphi and the Egyptian column; Mehmet was nothing if not superstitious.) On 2 June, Friday prayers were heard for the first time in what was now the Aya Sofya mosque 'and the Islamic invocation was read in the name of Sultan Mehmet Khan Gazi'. According to the Ottoman chroniclers, 'the sweet five-times-repeated chant of the Muslim faith was heard in the city' and in a moment of piety Mehmet coined a new name for the city: *Islambol* – a pun on its Turkish name, meaning 'full of Islam' – that somehow failed to strike an echo in Turkish ears. Miraculously Sheikh Akshemsettin also rapidly 'rediscovered' the tomb of Ayyub, the Prophet's standard-bearer who had died at the first Arab siege in 669 and whose death had been such a powerful motivator in the holy war for the city.

Despite these tokens of Muslim piety, the sultan's rebuilding of the city was to prove highly controversial to conventional Islam. Mehmet had been deeply disturbed by the devastation inflicted on Constantinople: 'What a city we have committed to plunder and destruction,' he is reported to have said when he first toured the city, and when he rode back to Edirne on 21 June he undoubtedly left behind a melancholy ruin, devoid of people. Reconstructing an imperial capital was to be a major preoccupation of his reign – but his model would not be an Islamic one.

*

The Christian ships that had escaped on the morning of 29 May carried word of the city's fall back to the West. At the start of June three ships reached Crete with the sailors whose heroic defence of the towers had prompted their release by Mehmet. The news appalled the island. 'Nothing worse than this has happened, nor will happen,' wrote a monk. Meanwhile the Venetian galleys reached the island of Negroponte off the coast of Greece and reduced the population to panic – it was only with difficulty that the bailey there managed to prevent a whole-scale evacuation of the island. He wrote post-haste to the Venetian Senate. As ships criss-crossed the Aegean exchanging news, the word spread with gathering speed to the islands and the sea ports of the eastern sea, to Cyprus, Rhodes, Corfu, Chios, Monemvasia, Modon, Lepanto. Like a giant boulder dropped into the basin of the Mediterranean a tidal wave of panic rippled outwards all the way to the Gates of Gibraltar – and far beyond. It reached the mainland of Europe at Venice on the morning of Friday 29 June 1453. The Senate was in session. When a fast cutter from Lepanto tied up at the wooden landing stage on the Bacino, people were leaning from windows and balconies avid for news of the city, their families and their commercial interests. When they learned that Constantinople had fallen, 'a great and excessive crying broke out, weeping, groaning . . . everyone beating their chests with their fists, tearing at their heads and faces, for the death of a father or a son or a brother, or for the loss of their property'. The Senate heard the news in stunned silence; voting was suspended. A flurry of letters was dispatched by flying courier across Italy to tell the news of 'the horrible and deplorable fall of the cities of Constantinople and Pera [Galata]'. It reached Bologna on 4 July, Genoa on 6 July, Rome on 8 July and Naples shortly after. Many at first refused to believe reports that the invincible city could have fallen; when they did, there was open mourning in the streets. Terror amplified the wildest rumours. It was reported that the whole population over the age of six had been slaughtered, that 40,000 people had been blinded by the Turks, that all the churches had been destroyed and the sultan was now gathering a huge force for an immediate invasion of Italy. Word of mouth emphasized the bestiality of the Turks, the ferocity of their attack on Christendom – themes that would ring loudly in Europe for hundreds of years.

If there is any moment at which it is possible to recognize a modern sensibility in a medieval event it is here in the account of reactions to the news of the fall of Constantinople. Like the assassination of Kennedy or 9/11 it is clear that people throughout Europe could remember exactly where they were when they first heard the news. 'On the day when the Turks took Constantinople the sun was darkened,' declared a Georgian chronicler. 'What is this execrable news which is borne to us concerning Constantinople?' wrote Aeneas Sylvius Piccolomini to the Pope. 'My hand trembles, even as I write; my soul is horrified.' Frederick III wept when word reached him in Germany. The news radiated outward across Europe as fast as a ship could sail, a horse could ride, a song could be sung. It spread outwards from Italy to France, Spain, Portugal, the Low Countries, Serbia, Hungary, Poland and beyond. In London a chronicler noted that 'in this year was the City of Constantine the noble lost by Christian men and won by the Prince of the Turks, Muhammad'; Christian I, King of Denmark and Norway, described Mehmet as the beast of the Apocalypse rising out of the sea. The diplomatic channels between the courts of Europe hummed with news and warnings and ideas for projected crusades. Across the Christian world there was a huge outpouring of letters, chronicles, histories, prophecies, songs, laments and sermons translated into all the languages of the Faith, from Serbian to French, from Armenian to English. The tale of Constantinople was heard not just in palaces and castles but also at crossroads, market squares and inns. It reached the furthest corners of Europe and the humblest people: in due course even the Lutheran prayer book in Iceland would beg God's salvation from 'the cunning of the Pope and the terror of the Turk'. It was just the start of a huge renewal of anti-Islamic sentiment.

Within Islam itself, the word was greeted with joy by pious Muslims. On 27 October an ambassador from Mehmet arrived in Cairo, bearing news of the city's capture and bringing two highborn Greek captives as visible proof. According to the Muslim chronicler, 'The Sultan and all the men rejoiced at this mighty conquest; the good news was sounded by the bands each morning and Cairo was decorated for two days . . . people celebrated by decorating shops and houses most extravagantly . . . I say to God be thanks and acknowledgement for this mighty victory.' It was a victory of immense significance for the Muslim world; it fulfilled the old pseudo-prophecies attributed to Muhammad and seemed to restore the prospect of the world spread of the Faith. It brought the Sultan immense prestige. Mehmet also sent the customary victory letter to the leading potentates of the Muslim world that staked his claim to be the true leader of the holy war, taking the title of 'Father of the Conquest', directly linked 'by the breath of the wind of the Caliphate' to the early, glorious days of Islam. According to Doukas the head of Constantine, 'stuffed with straw', was also sent round 'to the leaders of the Persians, Arabs and other Turks', and Mehmet sent 400 Greek children each to the rulers of Egypt, Tunis and Granada. These were not mere gifts. Mehmet was laying claim to be the defender of the Faith and to its ultimate prize: protectorate of the holy places of Mecca, Medina and Jerusalem. 'It is your responsibility', he peremptorily scolded the Mamluk sultan in Cairo, 'to keep the pilgrimage routes open for the Muslims; we have the duty of providing gazis.' At the same time, he declared himself to be 'Sovereign of two seas and two lands', heir to the empire of the Caesars with ambitions to a world domination that would be both imperial and religious: 'There must . . . be only one empire, one faith and one sovereignty in the world.'

In the West the fall of Constantinople changed nothing and everything. To those close to events, it was clear that the city was undefendable. As an isolated enclave its capture was ultimately inevitable; if Constantine had managed to stave off the Ottoman siege it would only have been a matter of time before another assault succeeded. For those who cared to look, the fall of Constantinople or the capture of Istanbul – depending on religious perspective – was largely the symbolic recognition of an established fact: that the Ottomans were a world power, firmly established in Europe. Few were that close. Even the Venetians, with their spies and their endless flow of diplomatic information back to the Senate, were largely unaware of the military capabilities available to Mehmet. 'Our Senators would not believe that the Turks could bring a fleet against Constantinople,' remarked Marco Barbaro on the tardiness of the Venetian rescue effort. Nor had they understood the power of the guns or the determination and resourcefulness of Mehmet himself. What the capture of the city underlined was the extent to which the balance of power had already shifted in the Mediterranean – and clarified the threat to a host of Christian interests and nations that Constantinople, as a buffer zone, had encouraged them to ignore.

Throughout the Christian world the consequences were religious, military, economic and psychological. At once the terrible image of Mehmet and his ambitions were drawn into sharp focus for the Greeks, the Venetians, the Genoese, the Pope in Rome, the Hungarians, the Wallachians and all the peoples of the Balkans. The implacable figure of the Great Turk and his insatiable desire to be the Alexander of the age were projected wildly onto the screen of the European imagination. One source has the Conqueror entering the city with the words 'I thank Muhammad who has given us this splendid victory; but I pray that he will permit me to live long enough to capture and subjugate Old Rome as I have New Rome.' This belief was not without foundation. In Mehmet's imagination, the seat of the Red Apple had now moved westward – from Constantinople to Rome. Long before Ottoman armies invaded Italy they went into battle with the cry 'Roma! Roma!' Step by step the very incarnation of the Antichrist seemed to be moving inexorably against the Christian world. In the years following 1453, he would snuff out the Black Sea colonies of the Genoese and the Greeks one after another: Sinop, Trebizond and Kaffa all fell. In 1462 he invaded Wallachia, the following year Bosnia. The Morea fell under Ottoman rule in 1464. In 1474 he was in Albania, 1476 in Moldavia – the rolling tide of the Ottoman advance seemed irreversible. Its troops failed to take Rhodes in a famous siege in 1480 but it was only a temporary setback. The Venetians had more to fear than most: war with Mehmet opened in 1463 and ran for fifteen years – it was to be just the overture to a titanic contest. During this time they lost their prize trading-post at Negroponte, and worse: in 1477 Ottoman raiders plundered the hinterlands of the city; they came so near that the smoke of their fires could be seen from the campanile of St Mark's. Venice could feel the hot breath of Islam on its collar. 'The enemy is at our gates!' wrote Celso Maffei to the Doge. 'The axe is at the root. Unless divine help comes, the doom of the Christian name is sealed.' In July 1481 the Ottomans finally landed an army on the heel of Italy to march on Rome. When they took Otranto, the archbishop was felled at the altar of his cathedral, 12,000 citizens were put to death. In Rome the Pope considered flight and the people panicked, but at this moment news of Mehmet's death reached the army and the Italian campaign collapsed.

Under the impetus of the fall of Constantinople, popes and cardinals tried to breathe life back into the project of religious crusades that continued well into the sixteenth century. Pope Pius II, for whom the whole Christian culture was at stake, set the tone when he convened a congress at Mantua in 1459 to unify the fractious nations of Christendom. In a ringing speech that lasted two hours he outlined the situation in the bleakest terms:

> We ourselves allowed Constantinople, the capital of the east, to be conquered by the Turks. And while we sit at home in ease and idleness, the arms of these barbarians are advancing to the Danube and the Sava. In the Eastern imperial city they have massacred the successor of Constantine along with his people, desecrated the temples of the Lord, sullied the noble edifice of Justinian with the hideous cult of Muhammad; they have destroyed the images of the mother of God and other saints, overturned the altars, cast the relics of the martyrs to the swine, killed the priests, dishonored women and young girls, even the virgins dedicated to the Lord, slaughtered the nobles of the city at the sultan's banquet, carried off the image of our crucified Saviour to their camp with scorn and mockery amid cries of 'That is the God of the Christians!' and befouled it with mud and spittle. All this happened beneath our very eyes, but we lie in a deep sleep . . . Mehmet will never lay down arms except in victory or total defeat. Every victory will be for him a stepping-stone to another, until, after subjecting all the princes of the West, he has destroyed the Gospel of Christ and imposed the law of his false prophet upon the whole world.

Despite numerous attempts, such impassioned words failed to provoke practical action, just as the project to save Constantinople itself had failed. The powers of Europe were too jealous, too disunited – and in some senses too secular – ever to combine in the name of Christendom again: it was even rumoured that the Venetians had been complicit in the landing at Otranto. However it did reinvigorate deep European fears about Islam. It would be another two hundred years before the advance of the Ottomans into Europe was definitely halted, in 1683, at the gates of Vienna; in the interval Christianity and Islam would wage a long-running war, both hot and cold, that would linger long in the racial memory and that formed a long link in the chain of events between the two faiths. The fall of Constantinople had awakened in Islam and Europe deep memories of the crusades. The Ottoman peril was seen as the continuation of the perceived assault of Islam on the Christian world; the word 'Turk' replaced the word 'Saracen' as the generic term for a Muslim – and with it came all the connotations of a cruel and implacable opponent. Both sides saw themselves engaged in a struggle for survival against a foe intent on destroying the world. It was the prototype of global ideological conflict. The Ottomans kept the spirit of jihad alive, now linked to their sense of imperial mission. Within the Muslim heartlands the belief in the superiority of Islam was rejuvenated. The legend of the Red Apple had enormous currency; after Rome it attached successively to Budapest, then Vienna. Beyond these literal destinations, it was the symbol of messianic belief in the final victory of the Faith. Within Europe, the image of the Turk became synonymous with all that was faithless and cruel. By 1536 the word was in use in English to mean, in the words of the Oxford English Dictionary, 'anyone behaving as a barbarian or savage'. And what added fuel to these attitudes was a discovery that typified the very spirit of Renaissance enlightenment – the invention of printing.

The fall of Constantinople happened on the cusp of a revolution – the moment that the runaway train of scientific discovery started to gather speed in the West at the expense of religion. Some of these forces were at play in the siege itself: the impact of gunpowder, the superiority of sailing ships, the end of medieval siege warfare; the next seventy years would bring Europe, amongst other things, gold fillings in teeth, the pocket watch and the astrolabe, navigation manuals, syphilis, the New Testament in translation, Copernicus and Leonardo da Vinci, Columbus and Luther – and movable type.

Gutenberg's invention revolutionized mass communications and spread new ideas about the holy war with Islam. A huge corpus of crusader and anti-Islamic literature poured off the presses of Europe in the next 150 years. One of the earliest surviving examples of modern printing is the indulgence granted by Nicholas V in 1451 to raise money for the relief of Cyprus from the Turks. Thousands of copies of such documents appeared across Europe along with crusader appeals and broadsheets – forerunners of modern newspapers – that spread news about the war against 'the damnable menace of the Grand Turk of the infidels'. An explosion of books followed – in France alone, eighty books were published on the Ottomans between 1480 and 1609, compared to forty on the Americas. When Richard Knolles wrote his bestseller *The General History of the Turks* in 1603, there was already a healthy literature in English on the people he called 'the present terror of the world'. These works had suggestive titles: *The Turks' Wars*, *A Notable History of the Saracens*, *A Discourse on the Bloody and Cruel Battle lost by Sultan Selim*, *True News of a Notable Victory obtained against the Turk*, *The Estate of Christians living under the Subjection of the Turk* – the flood of information was endless.

Seeing your enemy: sixteenth-century German print of Ottoman cavalry

Othello was engaged in fighting the world war of the day – against the 'general enemy Ottoman', the 'malignant and turbaned Turk' – and for the first time, Christians far from the Muslim world could see woodcut images of their enemy in highly influential illustrated books such as Bartholomew Georgevich's *Miseries and Tribulations of the Christians held in Tribute and Slavery by the Turk*. These showed ferocious battles between armoured knights and turbaned Muslims, and all the barbarism of the infidel: Turks beheading prisoners, leading off long lines of captive women and children, riding with babies spitted on their lances. The conflict with the Turk was widely understood to be the continuation of a much longer-running contest with Islam – a thousand year struggle for the truth. Its features and causes were exhaustively studied in the West. Thomas Brightman, writing in 1644, declared that the Saracens were 'the first troop of locusts . . . about the year 630' who were succeeded by 'the Turks, a brood of vipers, worse than their parent, [who] did utterly destroy the Saracens their mother'. Somehow the conflict with Islam was always different: deeper, more threatening, closer to nightmare.

It is certainly true that Europe had much to fear from the wealthier, more powerful and better organized Ottoman Empire in the two hundred years after Constantinople, yet the image of its opponent, conceived largely in religious terms at a time when the idea of Christendom itself was dying, was highly partial. The inside and the outside of the Ottoman world presented two different faces, and nowhere was this clearer than in Constantinople.

Sa'd-ud-din might declare that after the capture of Istanbul 'the churches which were within the city were emptied of their vile idols, and cleansed from their filthy and idolatrous impurities' – but the reality was rather different. The city that Mehmet rebuilt after the fall hardly conformed to the dread image of Islam that Christendom supposed. The sultan regarded himself not only as a Muslim ruler but as the heir to the Roman Empire and set about reconstructing a multicultural capital in which all citizens would have certain rights. He forcibly resettled both Greek Christians and Turkish Muslims back into the city, guaranteed the safety of the Genoese enclave at Galata and forbade any Turks to live there. The monk Gennadios, who had so fiercely resisted attempts at union, was rescued from slavery in Edirne and restored to the capital as patriarch of the Orthodox community with the formula: 'Be Patriarch, with good fortune, and be assured of our friendship, keeping all the privileges that the Patriarchs before you enjoyed.' The Christians were to live in their own neighbourhoods and to retain some of their churches, though under certain restrictions: they had to wear distinctive dress and were forbidden from bearing arms – within the context of the times it was a policy of remarkable tolerance. At the other end of the Mediterranean, the final reconquest of Spain by the Catholic kings in 1492 resulted in the forced conversion or expulsion of all the Muslims and Jews. The Spanish Jews themselves were encouraged to migrate to the Ottoman Empire – 'the refuge of the world' – where, within the overall experience of Jewish exile, their reception was generally positive. 'Here in the land of the Turks we have nothing to complain of,' wrote one rabbi to his brethren in Europe. 'We possess great fortunes, much gold and silver are in our hands. We are not oppressed with heavy taxes and our commerce is free and unhindered.' Mehmet was to bear the brunt of considerable Islamic criticism for these policies. His son, the more pious Bayezit II, declared that his father 'by the counsel of mischief makers and hypocrites' had 'infringed the Law of the Prophet'.

Although Constantinople would become a more Islamic city over the centuries, Mehmet set the tone for a place that was astonishingly multicultural, the model of the Levantine city. For those Westerners who looked beneath the crude stereotypes, there were plenty of surprises. When the German Arnold von Harff came in 1499 he was amazed to discover two Franciscan monasteries in Galata where the Catholic mass was still being celebrated. Those who knew the infidel up close were quite clear. 'The Turks do not compel anyone to renounce his faith, do not try hard to persuade anyone and do not have a great opinion of renegades,' wrote George of Hungary in the fifteenth century. It was a stark contrast to the religious wars that fragmented Europe during the Reformation. The flow of refugees after the fall would be largely one way: from the Christian lands to the Ottoman Empire. Mehmet himself was more interested in building a world empire than in converting that world to Islam.

The fall of Constantinople was a trauma for the West; not only had it dented the confidence of Christendom, it was also considered the tragic end of the classical world, 'a second death for Homer and Plato'. And yet the fall also liberated the place from impoverishment, isolation and ruin. The city surrounded by 'the garland of waters',

Ottoman calligraphy

which Procopius had celebrated in the sixth century, now regained its old dash and energy as the capital of a rich and multicultural empire, straddling two worlds and a dozen trade routes; and the people whom the West believed to be tailed monsters spawned by the Apocalypse – 'made up of a horse and a man' – reincarnated a city of astonishment and beauty, different to the Christian City of Gold, but cast in equally glowing colours.

Constantinople once again traded the goods of the world through the labyrinthine alleys of the covered bazaar and the Egyptian bazaar; camel trains and ships once more connected it to all the principal points of the Levant, but for sailors approaching from the Marmara, its horizon acquired a new shape. Alongside Aya Sofya, the hills of the city started to bubble with the grey leaded domes of mosques. White minarets as thin as needles and as fat as pencils, grooved and fluted and hung with tiers of delicately traceried balconies, punctuated the city skyline. A succession of brilliant mosque architects created, under sprung domes, abstract and timeless spaces: interiors of calm light, tiled with intricate geometric patterns and calligraphy and stylized flowers whose sensuous colours – crisp tomato and turquoise and celadon and the clearest blue from the depths of the sea – created 'a reflection of the infinite garden of delight' promised in the Koran.

Ottoman Istanbul was a city that lived vividly in the eye and the ear – a place of wooden houses and cypress trees, street fountains and gardens, graceful tombs and subterranean bazaars, of noise and bustle and manufacture, where each occupation and ethnic group had its quarter, and all the races of the Levant in their distinctive garb and headdresses worked and traded, where the sea could be suddenly glimpsed, shimmering at the turn of a street or from the terrace of a mosque, and the

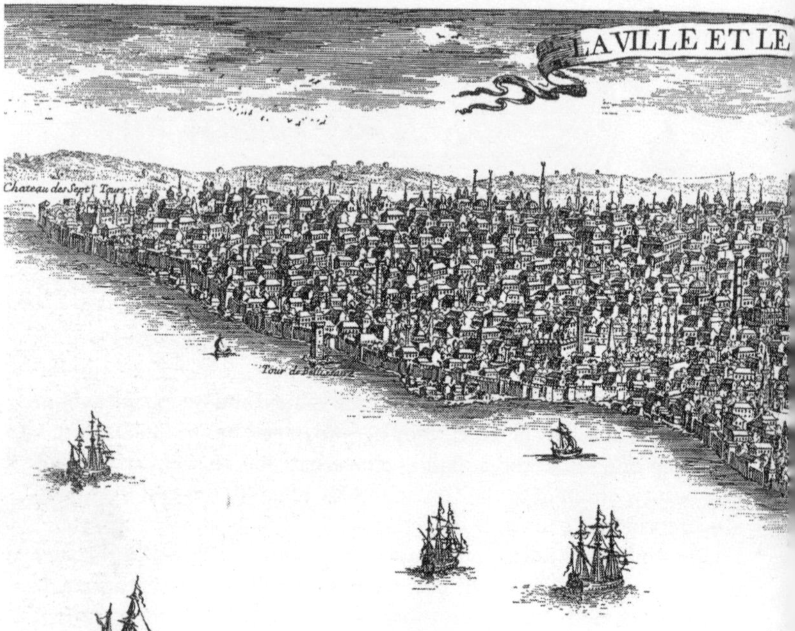

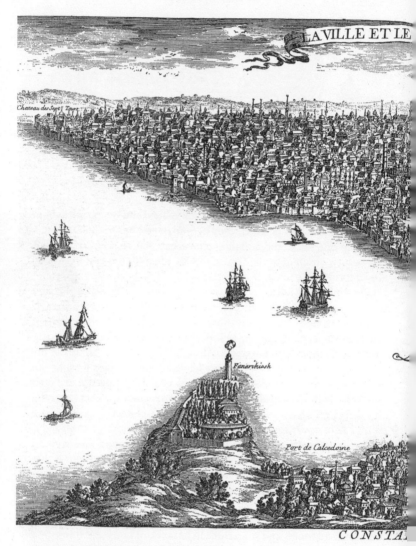

The new skyline: the Islamic city from the sea

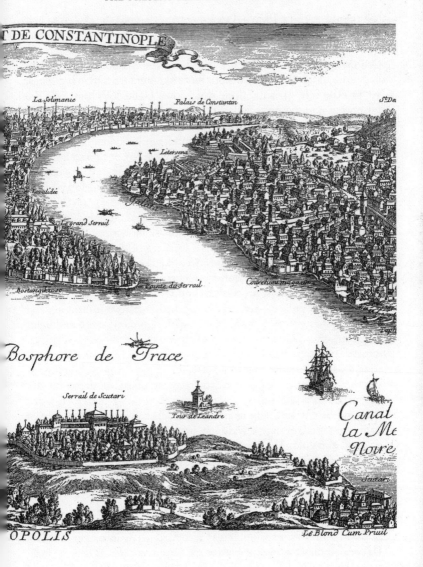

T DE CONSTANTINOPLE
La Solimanie
Palais de Constantin
Letersena
Le grand Serrail
Pointe du Serrail
Bosphore de Trace
Serrail de Scutari
Tour de Leandre
Canal
la Me
Noire
Scutari
OPOLIS
Le Blond Cum Priuil

call to prayer, rising from a dozen minarets, mapped the city from end to end and from dawn to dusk as intimately as the street cries of the local traders. Behind the forbidding walls of the Topkapi palace, the Ottoman sultans created their own echo of the Alhambra and Isfahan in a series of fragile, tiled pavilions more like solid tents than buildings, set in elaborate gardens, from which they could look out over the Bosphorus and the Asian hills. Ottoman art, architecture and ceremonial created a rich visual world that held as much astonishment for Western visitors as Christian Constantinople had done before it. 'I beheld the prospect of that little world, the great city of Constantinople,' wrote Edward Lithgow in 1640, 'which indeed yields such an outward splendor to the amazed beholder . . . whereof now the world makes so great account that the whole earth cannot equal it.'

Nowhere is the sensuous texture of Ottoman Istanbul recorded more vividly than in the endless succession of miniatures in which sultans celebrated their triumphs. It is a joyous world of primary colour patterned flat and without perspective, like the decorative devices on tiles and carpets. Here are court presentations and banquets, battles and sieges, beheadings, processions and festivities, tents and banners, fountains and palaces, elaborately worked kaftans and armour and beautiful horses. It is a world in love with ceremony, noise and light. There are ram fights, tumblers, kebab cooks and firework displays, massed Janissary bands that thump and toot and crash their way soundlessly across the page in a blare of red, tight-rope walkers crossing the Horn on ropes suspended from the masts of ships, cavalry squadrons in white turbans riding past elaborately patterned tents, maps of the city as bright as jewels, and all the visible exuberance of paint: vivid red, orange, royal blue, lilac, lemon, chestnut, grey, pink, emerald and gold. The world of the miniatures seems to express both joy and pride in the Ottoman achievement, the breathtaking ascent from tribe to empire in two hundred years, an echo of the words once written by the Seljuk Turks over a doorway in the holy city of Konya: 'What I have created is unrivalled throughout the world.'

In 1599 Queen Elizabeth I of England sent Sultan Mehmet III an organ as a gift of friendship. It was accompanied by its maker, Thomas Dallam, to play the instrument for the Ottoman ruler. When the master musician was led through the successive courts of the palace and into the presence of the sultan, he was so dazzled by the ceremonial that 'the sight whereof did make me almost to think that I was in another world'. Visitors had been emitting exactly the same gasps of astonishment since Constantine the Great founded the second Rome and the second Jerusalem in the fourth century. 'It seems to me', wrote the Frenchman Pierre Gilles in the sixteenth century, 'that while other cities are mortal, this one will remain as long as there are men on earth.'

Epilogue: Resting Places

It was fortunate for Christendom and for Italy that death checked the fierce and indomitable barbarian.

Giovanni Sagredo, seventeenth-century Venetian nobleman

In the spring of 1481, the sultan's horsetail banners were set up on the Anatolian shore across the water from the city, signifying that the year's campaign would be in Asia. It is typical of Mehmet's secrecy that no one, not even his leading ministers, knew its true objective. It was, in all likelihood, war against the rival Muslim dynasty of the Mamluks of Egypt.

For thirty years the sultan had worked to build the world empire, personally managing the affairs of state himself: appointing and executing ministers, accepting tribute, rebuilding Istanbul, forcibly resettling populations, reorganizing the economy, concluding treaties, visiting terrible death on recalcitrant peoples, granting freedom of worship, dispatching or leading armies year after year to east and west. He was forty-nine years old and in poor health. Time and self-indulgence had taken their toll. According to an unflattering contemporary report, he was fat and fleshy, with 'a short, thick neck, a sallow complexion, rather high shoulders, and a loud voice'. Mehmet, who collected titles like campaign medals – 'The Thunderbolt of War', 'The Lord of Power and Victory on Land and Sea', 'Emperor of the Romans and of the Terrestrial Globe', 'The World Conqueror' – could at times hardly walk. He was affected by gout and a deforming morbid corpulence, and shut himself away from human gaze in the Topkapi Palace.

View of the Ottoman city

The man whom the West called 'the Blood Drinker', 'the Second Nero', had taken on the appearance of a grotesque. The French diplomat Philippe de Commynes declared that 'men who have seen him have told me that a monstrous swelling formed on his legs; at the approach of summer it grew as large as the body of a man and could not be opened; and then it subsided'. Behind the palace walls Mehmet indulged in the untypical pursuits of a tyrant: gardening, handicrafts and the commissioning of obscene frescoes from the painter, Gentile Bellini, recently imported from Venice. Bellini's famous last portrait, framed in a golden arch and surmounted with imperial crowns, hints at some unappeased essence in the man: the World Conqueror remained, to the last, moody, superstitious and haunted.

Mehmet crossed the straits to Asia on 25 April for the year's campaign but was almost immediately struck down with acute stomach pains. After a few days of excruciating torment he died on 3 May 1481, near Gebze, where another would-be world conqueror, Hannibal, had committed suicide by poison. It is an end surrounded in mystery. The likeliest possibility is that Mehmet was also poisoned, by his Persian doctor. Despite numerous Venetian assassination attempts over the years, the finger of suspicion points mostly strongly at his son, Bayezit. Mehmet's law of fratricide had perhaps tempted the prince to make a pre-emptive – and successful – strike for the throne. Father and son were not close: the pious Bayezit detested Mehmet's unorthodox religious views – an Italian court gossip quotes Bayezit as saying 'his father was domineering and did not believe in the Prophet Muhammad'. Thirty years later Bayezit would in turn be poisoned by his son, Selim 'the Grim'; 'there are no ties of kinship between princes' goes the Arab saying. In Italy the news of Mehmet's death was greeted with particular joy. Cannon fired and bells rang; in Rome there were fireworks and services of thanksgiving. The messenger who brought the news to Venice declared, 'The great eagle is dead.' Even the Mamluk sultan in Cairo breathed a sigh of relief.

Today *Fatih* – the Conqueror – lies in a mausoleum in the mosque complex and the district of Istanbul that both bear his name. The choice of site was not accidental. It replaced one of the most famous and historical of all Byzantine churches: that of the Holy Apostles, where the city's founder, Constantine the Great, had been entombed with great ceremony in 337. In death, as in life, Mehmet assumed the imperial inheritance. The original mausoleum was shattered by earthquake and completely rebuilt so that the interior is now as ormolu as a nineteenth-century French drawing room, complete with grandfather clock, baroque ceiling decoration and pendent crystal chandelier, like the resting-place of a Muslim Napoleon. The richly decorated tomb, covered with a green cloth and surmounted by a stylized turban at one end, is as long as a small cannon. People come here to pray, to read the Koran and to take photographs. With the passing of time sainthood has come to Fatih – he has taken on some of the characteristics of a holy man for the Muslim faithful – so that he has a dual identity, sacred and secular. Like Churchill he is both a national brand – the name of a make of lorry, a bridge over the Bosphorus, the instantly recognizable image of a heroic galloping horseman on a commemorative stamp or a school building – and a symbol of piety. The Fatih district is the heartland of traditional and newly self-confident Muslim Istanbul. It is a peaceful spot: in the mosque courtyard, women in headscarves gather to talk under the plane trees after prayers; attendant children run round in circles; wandering salesmen sell sesame rolls, toy cars and helium balloons in the shape of animals. At the doorway of Mehmet's tomb there is a stone cannon ball placed like a votive offering.

The fates of the other principal Ottoman actors at the siege reflected the insecurities of serving the sultan. For Halil Pasha, who had consistently opposed the war policy, the end was quick. He was hanged at Edirne in August or September 1453 and replaced by Zaganos Pasha, the Greek renegade who had so actively supported the war. The fate of the old vizier marked a decisive shift in state politics: almost all successive viziers would be of converted slave origin rather than born Turks from the old aristocracy. Of Orban the cannon founder, a key architect of the victory, there is circumstantial evidence that he survived the siege to claim a reward from the sultan: after the capture of Istanbul there was an area called Gunner Verban District, suggesting that the Hungarian mercenary had taken up residence in the city whose walls he had done so much to destroy. And Ayyub, the Prophet's companion, whose death at the first Arab siege had been so inspirational to the *gazis*, now rests in his own mosque complex among plane trees in the pleasant backwater of Eyüp at the top of the Golden Horn, a venerated place for pilgrimage and for hundreds of years the coronation mosque of the sultans.

Amongst the defenders who escaped, fates were many and various. The Greek refugees generally experienced the typical fortunes of exile:

destitution in a foreign land and nostalgia for the lost city. Many eked out their lives in Italy – there were 4,000 Greeks in Venice alone by 1478 – or on Crete, which was a bastion of the Orthodox Church, but they were dispersed across the world as far away as London. The descendants of the family of Palaiologos gradually disappeared into the general pool of the lesser aristocracy of Europe. One or two, through homesickness or poverty, returned to Constantinople and threw themselves on the sultan's mercy. At least one, Andrew, converted to Islam and became a court official under the name Mehmet Pasha. The melancholy Greek reality of the fall is perhaps encapsulated in the experiences of George Sphrantzes and his wife. They ended their days in monasteries on Corfu where Sphrantzes wrote a short, painful chronicle of the events of his life. It starts: 'I am George Sphrantzes the pitiful First Lord of the Imperial Wardrobe, presently known by my monastic name Gregory. I wrote the following account of the events that occurred during my wretched life. It would have been fine for me not to have been born or to have perished in childhood. Since this did not happen, let it be known that I was born on Tuesday, August 30, 1401.' In laconic, strangulated tones Sphrantzes recorded the twin tragedies – personal and national – of the Ottoman advance. Both his children were taken into the seraglio; his son was executed there in 1453. Of September 1455 he wrote: 'My beautiful daughter Thamar died of an infectious disease in the Sultan's seraglio. Alas for me, her wretched father! She was fourteen years and five months.' He lived on until 1477, long enough to see the almost complete extinction of Greek freedom under the Turkish occupation. His testament ends with a reaffirmation of the Orthodox position on the *filioque* – the issue that had caused so much trouble during the siege: 'I confess with certainty that the Holy Ghost does not issue from the Father and the Son, as the Italians claim, but without separation from the very manifestation of the Father.'

Among the Italian survivors, fates were similarly diverse. The wounded Giustiniani made it back to Chios where – according to his fellow Genoese, Archbishop Leonard – he died not long afterwards, 'either from his wound or the shame of his disgrace', almost universally blamed for the final defeat. He was buried with the epitaph, now lost, that read: 'Here lies Giovanni Giustiniani, a great man and a noble of Genoa and Chios, who died on 8 August 1453 from a fatal wound, received during the storming of Constantinople and the death of the most gracious Constantine, last emperor and brave leader of the Eastern Christians, at the hands of the Turkish sovereign Mehmet.' Leonard himself died in Genoa in 1459; Cardinal Isidore of Kiev, who had come to bring union to the Greeks, was made Patriarch of Constantinople *in absentia* by the Pope on no legitimate authority; he succumbed to senile dementia and died in Rome in 1463.

For Constantine himself there is no certainty, no burial place. The emperor's death heralded the emphatic eclipse of the Byzantine world and the onset of the *Turkocratia* – the Turkish occupation of Greece – that would outlast Byron. Constantine's unknown fate became the focus of a deep yearning in the Greek soul for the lost glories of Byzantium and in time a rich vein of prophecy attached to his name. He became an Arthurian figure in Greek popular culture, the Once and Future King, sleeping in his tomb beside the Golden Gate, who would one day return through that gate and chase the Turks back east as far as the Red Apple Tree and reclaim the city. The Ottomans feared the talismanic figure of the emperor – Mehmet carefully watched Constantine's brothers and walled up the Golden Gate for good measure. These legends would ensure the unlucky Constantine a tragic afterlife. Towards the end of the nineteenth century, his legacy would get bound up with a Greek national vision, the Great Idea – the dream of re-incorporating the Greek populations of Byzantium into the Greek state. It provoked a disastrous intervention in Turkish Anatolia that was crushed by Kemal Ataturk in 1922 and the massacre of the Greek population of Smyrna and the subsequent exchange of populations. It was only then that hopes of rebuilding Byzantium finally died.

If the spirit of Constantine resides anywhere it is not in Istanbul, but a thousand miles away in the Peloponnese. Here for a time he had ruled the Morea as despot from the small medieval city of Mistra that for two hundred years witnessed an astonishing late flowering of the Byzantine tradition. It remains a shrine to the Byzantine soul: every lamppost in the modern village beneath the citadel bears the insignia of the double-headed eagle; in the square, the Platia Palaiologou, there is a statue of Constantine defending the faith with drawn sword – image of a man whose image is unknown. He stands in front of a marble plinth that carries a quotation from Doukas; above his head the Byzantine flag, a vivid yellow stamped with black eagles, hangs lifelessly against the blue Greek sky. Medieval Mistra rises up behind, a stacked green hillside of crumbling mansions, churches and halls interspersed with cypress trees. It is a poignant place. Here for a fragile moment, Constantinople rebuilt itself in miniature as a Greek Florence. It painted a brilliant humanist version of the gospels in radiant frescoes, rediscovered the teachings of Aristotle and Plato and dreamed of a golden future before the Ottomans came to snuff it out. In the little cathedral of St Demetrios, no bigger than an English country church, Constantine was possibly crowned; in the church of St Sophia, his wife Theodora lies buried. At the top of the site is the Palace of Despots with the bare Taygetus mountains behind and the Spartan mesa rolling away far below. The building is similar in style to the imperial palace on the walls of Constantinople, and it is easy to imagine the emperor looking out from the socketless windows of his airy hall down over the green plain where Spartan hoplites once trained for Thermopylae and the Byzantines grew oil, wheat, honey and silk. And on 29 May each year, while the Turks celebrate the capture of Istanbul with a military re-enactment at the Edirne Gate, Constantine, who died in heresy because of his support for union, is remembered in the small barrel-vaulted village churches of Crete and the great cathedrals of Greek cities.

In Istanbul itself, little of the Christian city now remains, though one can still walk through the great brass doors of St Sophia, battered open for the last time on 29 May 1453, and pass beneath the mosaic figure of Christ with his hand raised in blessing, into a space as astonishing now as it was in the sixth century. The city itself, contained within the two sides of the triangle made by the Horn and the Marmara, visibly retains the particular shape that determined so many of the key events. Ferries chug up into the mouth of the Bosphorus from the west in the wake of the four Christian ships, past the Acropolis point where the naval battle was fought, before making the identical turn across the wind into the mouth of the Horn, blocked now by a different boom – the bridge over to Galata. At the next stop up the Horn, boats put in at Kasimpasha – the Valley of the Springs – where Mehmet's ships splashed one by one into the calm water, while on the Bosphorus shore, Rumeli Hisari, the Throat Cutter, still straddles its extraordinary sloping site, and a red Turkish flag flutters brightly from the large tower at the water's edge that was Halil's contribution to the project.

Some of the sea walls of the city, particularly those along the Horn, are mere fragments now, but the great land wall of Theodosius, the third side of the triangle, that confronts the modern visitor arriving from the airport, seems to ride the landscape as confidently as ever. Up close, it shows its fifteen hundred years: sections are battered and crumbling, downright seedy in some places or incongruously restored in others; towers lean at strange angles, split by earthquakes or cannon balls or time; the fosse that caused the Ottoman troops so much trouble is now peacefully occupied by vegetables; the defences have been breached in places by arterial roads and undermined by a new metro system more effectively than the Serbian miners ever did, but despite the pressures of the modern world, the Theodosian wall is almost continuous for its whole length. One can walk it from sea to sea, following the lie of the land down the sloping central section of the Lycus valley where the walls have been ruined by medieval cannon fire, or stand on the ramparts and imagine Ottoman tents and pennants fluttering on the plain below, 'like a border of tulips', and galleys sliding noiselessly on the glittering Marmara or the Horn. Almost all the gateways of the siege have survived; the ominous shadow of their weighty arches retains the power to awe, though the Golden Gate itself, approached down an avenue of cannon balls from Orban's great guns, was long ago bricked up by Mehmet against the prophetic return of Constantine. For the Turks, the most significant is the Edirne Gate, the Byzantine Gate of Charisius, where Mehmet's formal entry into Istanbul is recorded by a plaque, but the most poignant of all the gateways that figured in the story of the siege stands completely forgotten a little further up towards the Horn.

Here the wall takes its sudden right-angle turn, and hidden nearby behind a patch of wasteland and directly abutting the shell of the Constantine's Palace, there is an unremarkable bricked-in arch, typical of the patchwork of alterations and repairs over the centuries. This is said by some to be the prophetic Circus Gate, the small postern left open in the final attack that first allowed Ottoman soldiers onto the walls. Or it might be somewhere else. Facts about the great siege shade easily into myths.

There is one other powerful protagonist of the spring of 1453 still to be discovered within the modern city – the cannon themselves. They lie scattered across Istanbul, snoozing beside walls and in museum courtyards – primitive hooped tubes largely unaffected by five hundred years of weather – sometimes accompanied by the perfectly spherical granite or marble balls that they fired. Of Orban's supergun

The blocked-up arch of the Circus Gate

there is now no trace – it was probably melted down in the Ottoman gun foundry at Tophane, followed sometime later by the giant equestrian statue of Justinian. Mehmet took the statue down on the advice of his astrologers, but it appears to have lain in the square for a long time before being finally hauled off to the smelting house. The French scholar Pierre Gilles saw some portions of it there in the sixteenth century. 'Among the fragments were the leg of Justinian, which exceeded my height, and his nose, which was over nine inches long. I dared not publicly measure the horse's legs as they lay on the ground but privately measured one of the hoofs and found it to be nine inches in height.' It was a last glimpse of the great emperor – and of the outsized grandeur of Byzantium – before the furnace consumed them.

About the Sources

There were so many events in this war that the pen can't describe them all, the tongue can't list them all.
Neshri, fifteenth-century Ottoman chronicler

The Fall of Constantinople – or the Capture of Istanbul – was a fulcrum moment in the Middle Ages. The news spread across the Muslim and Christian worlds with astonishing speed, and a hungry interest in the story has ensured the survival of a huge number of accounts, so that the event seems to be blessed with a unique assemblage of reports. On closer examination however, the sum of the parts is slightly less than the whole. The band of eyewitnesses is actually quite small, and largely Christian; many of their names will have become familiar to the readers of this book: Archbishop Leonard of Chios, the intemperate Catholic churchman, Nicolo Barbaro, the ship's doctor who wrote the most reliably dated diary, Giacomo Tetaldi, a Florentine merchant, the Russian Orthodox Nestor-Iskander, Tursun Bey, an Ottoman civil servant, and one or two others, such as George Sphrantzes, whose chronicles have proved something of a headache for modern historians. Behind these participants come a tight group of immediate successors who lived close to the moment and who probably heard the story soon afterwards at second hand – Doukas, the irrepressible Greek chronicler, vivid, unreliable and full of apocryphal stories, who imparts a lively energy to the story – and another Greek, Kritovoulos, a judge on the island of Imbros, unique in writing a Christian but pro-Ottoman version. (One of his many ambitions for his work was for it to be read 'by all the western nations', including those who inhabit the British Isles.) Successive centuries see a wealth of further versions from both sides; some of these are straight retellings, others add hearsay, lost oral accounts, myth and Christian or Ottoman imperial propaganda to create a heady mix of unverifiable information. It is out of such a bag of narratives that this book has been fashioned.

Many of the difficulties that arise from handling the sources are of course endemic to history, particularly history before the age of science. Eyewitnesses at the siege are notoriously prone to large round numbers when estimating army sizes and casualty figures, hazy on dates and times, given to the use of infuriatingly local systems of weights and measures and keen to exaggerate for a receptive audience. The chronological sequencing of events is usually a convention waiting to be invented and the distinction between fact, story and myth is a fine one. Religious superstitions are so deeply intertwined with events that the city's fall is a narrative about what people believed as well as what actually happened. And of course the notion of an objective account is entirely alien throughout.

Every writer has an angle and a motive for his version and it is necessary to pick carefully through the claims and special interests of each one. Judgements are routinely made on the basis of religion, nationality and creed. Venetians will automatically talk up the valour of their sailors and denigrate the treachery of the Genoese – and vice versa. Italians will accuse the Greeks of cowardice, laziness and stupidity. Catholics and Orthodox will hurl insults at each other over the parapets of schism. Within the Christian camp the search for an explanation, either theological or human, for the loss of the city is a prime motivation and the blame culture rings loudly through the pages. And of course all the Christian writers hurl routine abuse at the blood-drinker Mehmet – with the exception of Kritovoulos, who leans over backwards to ingratiate himself with the sultan. The Ottomans naturally return these insults in kind.

The tale that these witnesses tell is always vivid – they were conscious that they had witnessed, and survived the most extraordinary event – but the versions are full of strange silences. Given the huge significance of 1453 to the history of the Turkish people, it is surprising that there are so few contemporary Ottoman accounts of the capture of the city, no eyewitness narratives, almost no personal reports of the feelings and motivations of the Muslim soldiers, apart from Sheikh Akshemsettin's letter to Mehmet. The society was predominately preliterate; transmission of events was largely oral, with no tradition of recording individual stories. What does exist is in the form of terse chronicles, later reworked to serve in the creation of an Ottoman dynastic legend, so that the Ottoman perspective often has to be constructed by reading between the lines of Christian accounts: 1453 is unusual in being history largely written by the losers.

Almost as surprising is the shortage of testimony from Orthodox Greeks. Perhaps because many of the leading Byzantines were killed in the final sack, or were possibly too traumatized, like George Sphrantzes, to dwell on the details, the Christian story is largely relayed by Italians or pro-unionist Greeks who give the Orthodox defenders of the city, with the exception of Constantine, an unstintingly bad press.

As a consequence the story contains a large number of mysteries that will probably never be resolved. How the Ottomans transported their ships remains a lively subject for debate amongst Turkish historians, whilst the death of Constantine is maddeningly elusive – the competing versions divide neatly along party lines; indeed Constantine himself remains a shadowy figure beside the impatient, irrepressible person of Mehmet, who seems to be omni-present in the siege.

My aim in retelling 'the tale of Constantinople' has been to construct out of these conflicts and difficulties a robust central version of events – as close to certainty as I can make it. I have picked my way through the sources, awkwardly at times, trying to square accounts and seeking the most likely explanations. Dates are notoriously uncertain, despite Barbaro's diary that does narrate the siege day by day. Every account chooses a different line in the detail of the sequencing and dating of events and many who have studied the subject will disagree with me on fine points. A forensic study of this book will reveal some small mysteries in the timing of events. I have let these stand as a record of what is unknowable and cannot be reconciled. I have decided in general to choose the chronology that seemed to me most likely and to limit, as far as possible, the dreaded words 'perhaps', 'possibly', 'might have' from my narrative. The alternative was to bog the general reader down in variant source versions, which would have added little to the overall dynamic of a story whose outlines are strong and brilliantly coloured. At the same time I have drawn straight lines to deductions that I feel are justifiable from the physical evidence of geography, landscape, weather and time.

My second aim for this book has been to capture the sound of human voices – to reproduce the words, prejudices, hopes and fears of the protagonists at first hand – and to tell something of 'the story of the story', the versions that they believed to be true as well as the verifiable facts. The sources are often personalities in their own right, almost as exotic and mysterious as the tale they tell; some, such as Barbaro, exist only in their telling and vanish back into silence. Others, such as Leonard of Chios and Isidore of Kiev, are more deeply embedded in the church history of the period. Among the most fascinating and problematic of the accounts is that of the Orthodox Russian Nestor-Iskander, who seems to have come to Constantinople as a conscript in the Ottoman army. By deduction it appears that he escaped into the city early in the siege, witnessed and participated in its events – he is particularly vivid on the subject of bombardment and events on the wall – and survived Ottoman retribution afterwards, possibly disguised as a monk in a monastery. His mystical and often fantastic mixture of legend, hearsay and first-hand observation is so confused about dates and sequence that many writers have been inclined to dismiss it altogether, but it contains a mass of convincing detail – he is uniquely concrete about the struggle for the wall and the process of disposing of the dead, a task in which he was probably involved. Almost alone amongst the sources, Nestor-Iskander also gives us reports of the Greeks actually fighting, for example in the incident that leads to the death of Rhangabes. The Venetians and Genoese would have us believe it was an almost exclusively Italian affair, with the Greek population at best passive and at worst, because of religious differences, obstructive, profiteering and cowardly.

Two other chronicles destined to a colourful afterlife are those of George Sphrantzes and Doukas respectively. Sphrantzes is famous for having written two versions of the story, known as the Lesser and the Greater chronicles. For a long time it was assumed that the Greater was just a later expansion of the Lesser, which says almost nothing about the siege – the most significant, if traumatic, event in Sphrantzes' long life. The Greater, which is vivid, detailed and highly plausible, was for a long time widely used as a major source of information about 1453. However, it has been conclusively shown to be an ingenious work of literary impersonation, written over a hundred years later by one Makarios Melissenos, taking on the first-person guise of Sphrantzes. His credentials do not inspire confidence: Melissenos was a priest known to have forged an imperial decree to win an ecclesiastical dispute. Consequently all the contents of the Greater chronicle have been thrown into doubt. Historians now tiptoe around the work in various ways – anyone who wants to write about the siege must decide how to tackle it. A case has been made, based on close textual analysis, for believing that it does rest on a longer version of Sphrantzes, now lost, and the sheer specificity of some of its content would argue for a historical novelist of a very high order if it were a complete invention. Melissenos is responsible for the incident in which Sphrantzes stands in the dark on the tower before the battle with Constantine; he is also the source for an iconic moment in Turkish history: the tale of Hasan of Ulubat, the giant Janissary who becomes the first to plant the Ottoman flag on the walls. The second at least seems to be too detailed to be invented.

Just as exotic is the chronicle of Doukas – a long-range history of the fall of Byzantium. Doukas witnessed many of the events surrounding the siege, if not the siege itself. He probably saw the test firing of Orban's great cannon at Edirne and the rotting bodies of the sailors impaled by Mehmet after their ship was sunk at the Throat Cutter. His vivid, intransigent account comes to a strange end: abruptly, in mid-sentence, during its description of the Ottoman siege of Lesbos in 1462, leaving the fate of its author, like so much in this story, hanging in the air. The vivid account of events on Lesbos gives a strong impression that the author was there, and prompts the speculation that he was stopped pen in hand by the final collapse of the Greek defence. Did he undergo the terrible fate of the defenders – sawn in two to fulfil a promise that their heads would not be cut off – or was he sold into slavery? He walks out of the room in mid-phrase.

Telling the story of Constantinople has an immensely rich history of its own. The present book rests on the shoulders of a long tradition of versions in English; there is a line of succession that runs through Edward Gibbon in the eighteenth century, via two English knights, Sir Edwin Pears in 1903, and the great Byzantine historian Sir Stephen Runciman in 1965, and a host of accounts in other languages. As to the difficulties of getting it right, Kritovoulos of Imbros, a man with a good line in historical awareness, spotted the problem five hundred years ago, and provided himself with a neat disclaimer in his dedication to Mehmet – a prudent measure when addressing the World Conqueror when you were not actually present yourself. Any subsequent version might wish to invoke his words: 'Therefore, O mighty Emperor, I have laboured hard, for I was not myself a witness of the events, to know the exact truth about these things. In writing the history I have at the same time inquired of those who knew, and have examined exactly how it all happened . . . And if my words seem inferior to your deeds . . . I myself . . . yield in the matter of historical record to others who in such things are far more competent than I.'

Source Notes

All references to authors relate to their books listed in the bibliography.

Epigraph

'Constantinople is a city . . .', quoted Stacton, p. 153
'I shall tell the story . . .', Melville Jones, p. 12

Prologue

page
4 'The horse faces East . . .', Procopius, p. 35
6 'The seat of the Roman . . .', Mansel, p. 1

1 The Burning Sea

9 'O Christ, ruler . . .', quoted Sherrard, p. 11
9 'In the name of Allah . . .', quoted Akbar, p. 45
10 'Tell him that . . .', quoted ibid., p. 44
11 'to wage the holy war by sea', Ibn Khaldun, vol. 2, p. 40
12 'like a flash . . .', Anna Comnena, p. 402
12 'burned the ships . . .', quoted Tsangadas, p. 112
12 'having lost many fighting . . .', quoted ibid., p. 112
12 'the Roman Empire was guarded by God', Theophanes Confessor, p. 676
14 'It is said that they even . . .', ibid., p. 546
14 'brought the sea water . . .', ibid., p. 550
14 'to announce God's mighty deeds', ibid., p. 550
14 'God and the all-holy Virgin . . .', ibid., p. 546
15 'In the jihad . . .', quoted Wintle, p. 245
16 'the place that's the vast . . .', Ovid, *Tristia*, 1.10
17 'more numerous than . . .', quoted Sherrard, p. 12
17 'the city of the world's desire', quoted Mansel, p. 3
17 'O what a splendid city . . .', quoted Sherrard, p. 12
18 'During this time . . .', quoted ibid., p. 51
18 'It seems not to rest . . .', quoted ibid., p. 27

18 'the golden stream . . . a drift of snow', quoted Norwich, vol. 1, p. 202
18 'We knew not whether . . .', quoted Clark, p. 17
19 'The city is full . . .', quoted ibid., p. 14
20 'They are introduced . . .', quoted Sherrard, p. 74
22 'will be the fourth kingdom . . .', quoted Wheatcroft, p. 54

2 Dreaming of Istanbul

23 'I have seen that God . . .', quoted Lewis, *Islam from the Prophet*, vol. 2, pp. 207–8
24 'Sedentary people . . .', Ibn Khaldun, vol. 2, pp. 257–8
24 'to revive the dying . . .', Ibn Khaldun, quoted Lewis, *The Legacy of Islam*, p. 197
24 'God be praised . . .', quoted Lewis, *Islam from the Prophet*, vol. 2, p. 208
26 'On account of its justice . . .', quoted Cahen, p. 213
26 'an accursed race . . . from our lands', quoted Armstrong, p. 2
26 'they are indomitable . . .', quoted Norwich, vol. 3, p. 102
27 'we must live in common . . .', quoted Mango, *The Oxford History of Byzantium*, p. 128
27 'Constantinople is arrogant . . .', quoted Kelly, p. 35
27 'since the beginning . . .', quoted Morris, p. 39
27 'so insolent in . . .', quoted Norwich, vol. 3, p. 130
28 'they brought horses . . .', quoted ibid., vol. 3, p. 179
28 'Oh city . . .', quoted Morris, p. 41
29 'situated at the junction . . .', quoted Kinross, p. 24
30 'It is said that he . . .', quoted Mackintosh-Smith, p. 290
31 'Sultan, son of . . .', quoted Wittek, p. 15
31 'The Gazi is . . .', quoted ibid., p. 14
31 'Why have the Gazis . . .', quoted ibid., p. 14
34 'in such a state . . .', Tafur, p. 146
35 'Turkish or heathen . . .', Mihailovich, pp. 191–2
35 'They are diligent . . .', Brocquière, pp. 362–5

3 Sultan and Emperor

37 'Mehmet Chelebi . . .', quoted Babinger, p. 59
38 'On his clothing . . .', quoted ibid., p. 418
38 'He never took anything . . .', Brocquière, p. 351
39 'If He has decreed . . .', quoted Inalcik, p. 59
40 'Your father has sent me . . .', quoted Babinger, p. 24
42 'my earnest desire . . .', Granville Brown, *A History of Ottoman Poetry*, vol. 2
43 'The Turks through such . . .', Mihailovich, p. 171
43 'The treaties that . . .', Doukas, *Fragmenta*, p. 228
43 'He left as a bequest . . .', Khoja Sa'd-ud-din, p. 41
44 'Why do my father's viziers . . .', Doukas, *Fragmenta*, p. 227
45 'a parrot's beak . . .', quoted Babinger, p. 424

45 'The sovereign, the Grand Turk . . .', quoted ibid., p. 112
47 'a large town . . . now at Venice', Brocquière, pp. 335–41
49 'a philanthropist and without malice', Nestor-Iskander, p. 67
51 'Whichever of my . . .', quoted Babinger, p. 47

4 Cutting the Throat

52 'The Bosphorus . . .', quoted Freely, p. 269
52 'a mob of venal . . .', quoted Babinger, p. 68
52 'Come, Mr Ambassador . . . since childhood', Sphrantzes, trans. Philippides, p. 59
53 'and by the angels . . .', Doukas, *Fragmenta*, p. 228
54 'Standing with their arms . . .', Tursun Beg, p. 33
54 'the Emperor of . . .', Doukas, *Fragmenta*, pp. 234–5
55 'You stupid Greeks . . .', quoted Nicol, *The Immortal Emperor*, p. 52
56 'path of the vessels . . .', Khoja Sa'd-ud-din, p. 11
56 'stone and timber . . .', Kritovoulos, *Critobuli*, p. 19
56 'for the construction . . .', Doukas, *Fragmenta*, pp. 237–8
57 'now you can see . . .', ibid., p. 238
57 'as a son would . . .', ibid., p. 239
57 'what the city contains . . .', ibid., p. 239
57 'Go away and tell . . .', ibid., p. 245
57 'well-prepared for . . .', Kritovoulos, *Critobuli*, p. 21
58 'masons, carpenters . . .', Mihailovich, p. 89
58 'the distance between . . .', Kritovoulos, *Critobuli*, p. 22
58 'twisting curves . . .', ibid., p. 22
59 'gave up all thoughts of relaxation', Tursun Beg, p. 34
59 'publicly offered . . .', Kritovoulos, *Critobuli*, p. 22
60 'since you have preferred . . .', Doukas, *Fragmenta*, p. 245
61 'not like a fortress . . .', Kritovoulos, *Critobuli*, p. 22
62 'like dragons with . . .', Pertusi, *La Caduta*, vol. 1, p. 311
62 'not even a bird . . .', ibid., p. 311
62 'In this manner . . .', Khoja Sa'd-ud-din, p. 12
64 'by a stake . . . I went there', Doukas, *Fragmenta*, p. 248

5 The Dark Church

65 'It is far better . . .', quoted Mijatovich, p. 17
65 'Flee from . . .', quoted in an article on the *Daily Telegraph* website, 4 May 2001
66 'Let God look and judge', quoted Ware, p. 43
66 'over all the earth . . .', quoted ibid., p. 53
67 'an example of perdition . . .', quoted Clark, p. 27
67 'a difference of dogma . . .', quoted Norwich, vol. 3, p. 184
67 'Whenever the Turks . . .', quoted Mijatovich, pp. 24–5
68 'the wolf, the destroyer', quoted Gill, p. 381

69 'If you, with your nobles . . .', quoted Runciman, *The Fall of Constantinople*, pp. 63–4
69 'Constantine Palaiologus . . .', quoted Nicol, *The Immortal Emperor*, p. 58
70 'apart from . . .', Pertusi, *La Caduta*, vol. 1, p. 125
70 'We don't want . . .', quoted Gill, p. 384
71 'with the greatest solemnity . . .', Pertusi, *La Caduta*, vol. 1, p.11
71 'the whole of the city . . .', ibid., p. 92
71 'nothing better than . . .', quoted Stacton, p. 165
72 'like the whole heaven . . .', quoted Sherrard, p. 34
72 'Wretched Romans . . .', Doukas, *Fragmenta*, p. 254
74 'has not stopped marching . . .', Kritovoulos, *Critobuli*, p. 30
74 'without it . . . on this very account', Kritovoulos, *History of Mehmet*, pp. 29–31
74 'We must spare nothing . . .', Kritovoulos, *Critobuli*, p. 32
75 'unusual and strange . . .', ibid., p. 37
75 'wheat, wine, olive oil . . .', Doukas, *Fragmenta*, p. 257
76 'And from this . . .', Barbaro, *Giornale*, p. 3
76 'as friends, greeting them . . .', ibid., p. 4
77 'firstly for the love of God . . .', ibid., p. 5
77 'With these ships . . .', ibid., p. 13
78 'with many excellent devices . . .', Doukas, *Fragmenta*, p. 265
78 'four hundred men . . .', Kritovoulos, *History of Mehmed*, p. 39
78 'We received as much . . .', Sphrantzes, trans. Philippides, p. 72

6 The Wall and the Gun

79 'From the flaming . . .', quoted Hogg, p. 16
79 'an expert in . . .', Kritovoulos, *Critobuli*, p. 40
79 'dredged the fosse . . .', Kritovoulos, *Critobuli*, p. 37
81 'a seven-year-old boy . . .', Gunther of Pairis, p. 99
82 'one of the wisest . . .', quoted Tsangadas, p. 9
82 'the scourge of God', quoted Van Millingen, *Byzantine Constantinople*, p. 49
82 'in less than two months . . .', quoted ibid., p. 47
84 'This God-protected gate . . .', quoted ibid., p.107
86 'a good and high wall', quoted Mijatovich, p. 50
87 'struck terror . . .', quoted Hogg, p. 16
87 'made such a noise . . .', quoted Cipolla, p. 36
87 'the devilish instrument of war', quoted DeVries, p. 125
90 'If you want . . .', Doukas, *Fragmenta*, pp. 247–8
91 'like a scabbard', Kritovoulos, *Critobuli*, p. 44
91 'iron and timbers . . .', ibid., p. 44
92 'so deep that . . .', ibid., p. 44
92 'On the day . . .', Chelebi, *In the Days*, p. 90
92 'the Vezirs . . .', ibid., p. 90
93 'The time limit having expired . . .', ibid., p. 91
93 'The bronze flowed out . . .', Kritovoulos, *Critobuli*, p. 44

93 'a horrifying and extraordinary monster', Doukas, *Fragmenta*, p. 248
94 'the explosion and . . .', ibid., p. 249
94 'so powerful is . . .', ibid., p. 249

7 Numerous as the Stars

95 'When it marched . . .', Pertusi, *La Caduta*, vol. 1, p. 315
95 'The Turkish Emperor storms . . .', Mihailovich, p.177
95 'heralds to all . . .', Doukas, *Fragmenta*, p. 262
96 'from among craftsmen and peasants', quoted Imber, *The Ottoman Empire*, p. 257
96 'When it comes . . .', ibid., p. 277
96 'When recruiting for the . . .', quoted Goodwin, *Lords of the Horizons*, p. 66
97 'Everyone who heard . . .', Doukas, *Fragmenta*, p. 262
97 'the promise of the Prophet . . .', Khoja Sa'd-ud-din, p.16
97 'from Tokat, Sivas . . .', Chelebi, *Le Siège*, p. 2
97 'cavalry and foot soldiers . . .', Kritovoulos, *Critobuli*, p. 38
98 'with all his army . . .', ibid., p. 39
98 'the ulema, the sheiks . . .', Khoja Sa'd-ud-din, p. 17
98 'begged God . . .', Doukas, *Fragmenta*, p. 262
99 'a river that transforms . . .', quoted Pertusi, *La Caduta*, vol. 1, p. xx
99 'According to custom . . .', Tursun Beg, p. 34
100 'his army seemed . . .', Sphrantzes trans. Carroll, p. 47
100 'There is no prince . . .', quoted Goodwin, p. 70
100 'as the halo . . .', Pertusi, *La Caduta*, vol. 1, p. 316
100 'the best of the . . .', Kritovoulos, *Critobuli*, p. 41
100 'A quarter of them . . .', Pertusi, *La Caduta*, vol. 1, p. 176
101 'although they were . . .', ibid., p. 5
101 'I can testify . . .', ibid., vol. 1, p. 130
101 'We had to ride . . .', Mihailovich, p. 91
102 'a river of steel', quoted Pertusi, *La Caduta*, vol. 1, p. xx
102 'as numerous as the stars', quoted ibid., p. xx
102 'Know therefore that . . .', Mihailovich, p. 175
102 'at the siege there were . . .', Pertusi, *La Caduta*, vol. 1, pp. 175–6
102 'tailors, pastry-cooks . . .', quoted Mijatovich, p. 137
102 'how many able-bodied men . . .', Sphrantzes, trans. Carroll, p. 49
102 'The Emperor summoned me . . . gloom', ibid., pp. 49–50
103 'In spite of the great size . . .', Sphrantzes, trans. Philippides, p. 69
103 'Genoese, Venetians . . . three thousand', Leonard, p. 38
103 'the greater part of the Greeks . . .', Pertusi, *La Caduta*, vol. 1, p. 146
103 'skilled in the use of . . .', Leonard, p. 38
103 'The true figure remained . . .', Sphrantzes, trans. Philippides, p. 70
104 'the principal persons . . .', Barbaro, *Giornale*, pp. 19
104 'an old but sturdy . . .', Pertusi, *La Caduta*, vol. 1, p. 148
104 'at their own . . .', ibid., p. 27

104 'John from Germany . . . able military engineer', Sphrantzes, trans. Philippides, p. 110
105 'the Greek Theophilus . . .' Pertusi, *La Caduta*, vol. 1, p. 148
105 'the most important . . .', Barbaro, *Giornale*, p. 19
106 'This was always . . .', Pertusi, *La Caduta*, vol. 1, pp. 152–4
106 'with their banners . . .', Barbaro, *Giornale*, pp. 19–20
106 'Nor do We punish . . .', *The Koran*, p. 198
107 'We accept neither . . .', Chelebi, *Le Siège*, p. 3
107 'encouraging the soldiers . . .', Doukas, trans. Magoulias, p. 217
107 'Icons sweated . . .', Kritovoulos, *Critobuli*, p. 37
109 'man experienced in war . . .', ibid., p. 40

8 The Awful Resurrection Blast

110 'Which tongue can . . .', Nestor-Iskander, p. 45
110 'killing some and wounding a few', Kritovoulos, *Critobuli*, p. 41
111 'bringing up stones . . .', ibid., p. 46
111 'burst out of the . . .', Doukas, *Fragmenta*, p. 266
111 'some firing . . .', ibid., p. 266
111 'When they could not . . .', Kritovoulos, *Critobuli*, p. 47
111 'thirty heavily-armed . . .', ibid., p. 48
112 'a terrible cannon', Pertusi, *La Caduta*, vol. 1, p. 130
112 'which was protected by neither . . .', Leonard, p. 18
112 'the weakest gate . . .', Barbaro, p. 30
112 'a shot that reached . . .', Nestor-Iskander, p. 43
112 'eleven of my . . .', Pertusi, *La Caduta*, vol. 1, p. 130
113 'stones balls for cannon . . .', Pertusi, *La Caduta*, vol. 1, p. 15
113 'whatever happened, it could not . . .', Kritovoulos, *Critobuli*, p. 45
113 'certain techniques . . . wide of the target', ibid., p. 45
114 'And when it had caught . . .', ibid., p. 45
114 'Sometimes it destroyed . . .', ibid., p. 45
114 'They pulverized the wall . . .', Pertusi, *La Caduta*, vol. 1. p. 130
115 'like the awful resurrection blast', Khoja Sa'd-ud-din, p. 21
115 'voicing petitions and prayers . . .', Nestor-Iskander, pp. 33–5
115 'all of the people . . .', ibid., p. 35
116 'shook the walls . . .', Melville Jones, p. 46
116 'but since there was . . .', ibid., p. 47
116 No ancient name . . .', Kritovoulos, *Critobuli*, p. 46
116 'The assault continued . . .', Sphrantzes, trans. Carroll, p. 48
117 'cracked as it was being fired . . .', ibid., pp. 48–9
118 'about thirty to . . . wall collapse', Doukas, *Fragmenta*, pp. 273–4
118 'the shot being carried . . .', Melville Jones, p. 45
118 'by experiencing the force . . .', Sphrantzes, trans. Philippides, p. 103
119 'buried in the soft . . .', Kritovoulos, *History of Mehmed*, p. 49
119 'The Turks fought bravely . . .', Leonard, p. 38
119 'immense power in . . .', Doukas, *Fragmenta*, p. 266

120 'And when one or two . . .', Barbaro, *Giornale*, p. 22
120 'the heavy infantry . . .', Kritovoulos, *History of Mehmed*, p. 49
120 'I cannot describe . . .', Pertusi, *La Caduta*, vol. 1, pp. 15–16
121 'the clatter of cannons . . .', Nestor-Iskander, p. 37
121 'slashed to pieces . . . completely broken corpses', ibid., p. 39
122 'the all-powerful God and . . .', ibid, p. 39

9 A Wind from God

123 'Battles on the sea . . .', quoted Guilmartin, p. 22
124 'thought that the fleet . . .', Kritovoulos, *Critobuli*, p. 38
125 'long ships . . .', ibid., p. 38
125 'skilled seamen . . .', ibid., p. 38
125 'a great man . . .', ibid., p. 43
125 'homeland of defenders of the faith', Pertusi, *La Caduta*, vol. 2, p. 256
126 'with cries and cheering . . .', Kritovoulos, *Critobuli*, p. 39
126 'the wind of divine . . .', Pertusi, *La Caduta*, vol. 2, p. 256
126 'we put ready for battle . . .', Barbaro, *Giornale*, p. 19
127 'in close array . . .', Barbaro, *Diary*, p. 29
127 'well armed . . .', Barbaro, *Giornale*, p. 20
128 'Seeing that we . . .', ibid., p. 20
128 'with determination', ibid., p. 21
128 'eager cries . . .', Pertusi, *La Caduta*, vol. 1, p. 15
128 'waiting hour after . . .', Barbaro, *Giornale*, p. 22
130 'wounding many . . .', Kritovoulos, *Critobuli*, p. 51
130 'and inflicted . . .', ibid., p. 51
131 'in the East . . .', Pertusi, *La Caduta*, vol. 1, p. lxxvi
132 'either to take . . .', Kritovoulos, *Critobuli*, p. 53
132 'many other weapons . . .', ibid., p. 53
133 'with ambition and . . .' ibid., p. 53
133 'with a great sounding . . .', Barbaro, *Giornale*, p. 23
133 'they fought from . . .', Kritovoulos, *Critobuli*, p. 53
134 'shouted in a commanding voice', ibid., p. 53
134 'like dry land', Doukas, *Fragmenta*, p. 269
134 'they threw missiles . . .', Leonard, p. 30
134 'that the oars . . .', Doukas, *Fragmenta*, p. 269
134 'There was great . . .', Kritovoulos, *Critobuli*, p. 54
136 'like demons', Melville Jones, p. 21
136 'defended itself brilliantly . . .', Pertusi, *La Caduta*, vol. 1, p. 140
136 'the water could hardly be seen', Barbaro, p. 33
136 'for they took it in turns . . .', Kritovoulos, *Critobuli*, p. 54
137 'and tore his garments . . .', Melville Jones, p. 22
137 'at least twenty galleys', Barbaro, *Giornale*, p. 24
137 'stunned. In silence . . .', Kritovoulos, *Critobuli*, p. 55

10 Spirals of Blood

138 'Warfare is deception', Lewis, *Islam from the Prophet*, vol.1, p. 212
138 'the ambitions of the Sultan . . .', Leonard, p. 18
139 'This unhoped-for result . . .', Kritovoulos, *Critobuli*, p. 55
139 'They prayed to their . . .', Barbaro, *Giornale*, pp. 23–4
139 'This event caused despair . . .', Tursun Bey, quoted Inalcik, *Speculum* 35, p. 411
140 'This event has caused us . . .', Pertusi, *La Caduta*, vol. 1, p. 301
140 'I have been accused . . .', ibid., pp. 301–2
140 'about ten thousand horse', Barbaro, *Diary*, p. 34
140 'groaned from the depths . . .', Sphrantzes, trans. Carroll, p. 56
140 'if you could not take them . . .', Barbaro, *Giornale*, p. 25
140 'You know, it was visible . . .', ibid., p. 25
141 'with a golden rod . . .', Doukas, *Fragmenta*, p. 214
142 'the one who was most . . .', Melville Jones, p. 4
142 'as the ripe fruit falls . . .', quoted Mijatovich, p. 161
143 'Lord Jesus Christ . . .', quoted Nicol, *The Immortal Emperor*, pp. 127–8
143 'This was the start . . .', Pertusi, *La Caduta*, vol. 1, p. 16
143 'For such a big stretch . . .', ibid., p. 16
143 'with only ten thousand men', Barbaro, *Diary*, p. 36
143 'These repairs were made . . .', ibid., p. 36
144 'their huge cannon . . .', Pertusi, *La Caduta*, vol. 1, p. 17
144 'could not be seen . . .', ibid., p. 17
144 'our merciful Lord . . .', ibid., p.16
145 'Be certain that if I knew . . .', Doukas, trans. Magoulias, p. 258
145 'by the recollections . . .', Leonard, p. 28
146 'The people of Galata . . .', Pertusi, *La Caduta*, vol. 1, pp. 134–6
147 'And having girdled them . . .', Kritovoulos, *Critobuli*, p. 56
148 'Some raised the sails . . .', ibid., p. 56
148 'It was an extraordinary sight . . .', ibid., p. 56
148 'of fifteen banks of oars . . .', Barbaro, *Giornale*, p. 28
149 'It was a marvellous achievement . . .', Sphrantzes, trans. Carroll, p. 56
150 'Now that the wall . . .', Kritovoulos, *Critobuli*, p. 57
150 'When those in our fleet . . .', Pertusi, *La Caduta*, vol. 1, p. 19
150 'to burn the enemy fleet . . .', Barbaro, *Giornale*, p. 29
150 'a man of action not words', Sphrantzes, trans. Philippides, p. 111
151 'From the twenty-fourth . . . perfidious Turks', Barbaro, *Giornale*, p. 30
152 'to win honour . . .', ibid., p. 31
152 'And this *fusta* could not have stayed . . .', ibid., p. 31
152 'There was so much smoke . . .', ibid., p. 32
153 'A terrible and ferocious . . .', ibid., p. 33
153 'Throughout the Turkish camp . . .', ibid., p. 33
153 'Giacomo Coco . . .', Barbaro, *Giornale*, pp 31–2
153 'The Grand Turk (makes) . . .', quoted Babinger, p. 429
154 'the stakes were planted . . .', Melville Jones, p. 5
154 'countless stakes planted . . .', Doukas, trans. Magoulias, p. 260

154 'the lamentation in the city . . .', Sphrantzes, trans. Carroll, p. 31
154 'Our men were enraged . . .', Pertusi, *La Caduta*, vol. 1, p. 144
154 'In this way . . .', ibid., p. 144

11 Terrible Engines

156 'There is a need . . .', *Siegecraft: Two Tenth-century Instructional Manuals by Heron of Byzantium*, ed. D. F. Sullivan, Washington DC, 2000, p. 29
156 'Alas, most blessed Father . . .', Leonard, p. 36
156 'This betrayal was committed . . .', Pertusi, *La Caduta*, vol. 1, p. 20
156 'so greedy for . . .', ibid., p. 142
156 'each side accusing . . .', ibid., p. 142
157 'put the rudders and sails . . . into your power', ibid., p. 23
157 'many of their men . . . half a mile', Barbaro, *Giornale*, p. 34
158 'that could fire the stone . . .', Kritovoulos, *Critobuli*, pp. 51–2
158 'came from the top . . .', Leonard, p. 32
158 'of three hundred botte . . .', Barbaro, *Giornale*, pp. 35–6
158 'some shots killing . . .', ibid., p. 36
158 'a woman of excellent reputation . . .', Leonard, p. 32
158 'whatever they were owed . . .', Doukas, *Fragmenta*, p. 279
158 'With this act of . . .', ibid., p. 278
159 'two hundred and twelve . . .', Barbaro, *Giornale*, p. 39
159 'because in that place . . .', Nestor-Iskander, p. 43
159 'clatter and flashing . . .', ibid., p. 45
159 'as if on the steppes . . . filled with blood', ibid., p. 45
160 'What is the defence . . .', Leonard, p. 44
160 'were full of hatred . . .', ibid., p. 46
160 'what certain people . . .', ibid., p. 44
160 'The Emperor lacked severity . . .', Pertusi, *La Caduta*, vol. 1, p. 152
160 'The forces defending . . .', Tursun Beg, p. 36
161 'fell silent for a long time . . .', Nestor-Iskander, p. 49
161 'he ordered all . . .', Nestor-Iskander, p. 53
162 'cries and the banging . . .', Barbaro, *Giornale*, p. 36
162 'bared his sword . . .', Nestor-Iskander, p. 55
162 'but they were unable . . .', ibid., p. 57
163 'there was great mourning . . .', ibid., p. 57
163 'On the eleventh . . . the unfortunate walls', Barbaro, *Giornale*, p. 39
163 'the blood remained . . .', Nestor-Iskander, p. 47
163 'Thus one could see . . .', ibid., p. 47
163 'In the jihad against . . .', quoted Wintle, p. 245
164 'let us see who . . .', Barbaro, *Giornale*, p. 37
165 'believed that night . . .', ibid., p. 39
165 'if it continues . . .', Nestor-Iskander, p. 57
165 'the Turks were already . . .', ibid., p. 59
165 'the Emperor arrived . . .', ibid., p. 61
165 'but the nobles of the imperial . . .', quoted Mijatovich, p. 181

166 'Day and night these cannon . . .', Barbaro, *Giornale*, p. 40
166 'good cannon and . . .', ibid., p. 40
166 'and we Christians . . .', ibid., p. 40
166 'they hurriedly started rowing . . .', ibid., p. 41
166 'more than seventy shots . . .', ibid., p. 41
166 'with a great sounding . . .', ibid., p. 44
166 'two hours after sunrise . . .', Barbaro, *Diary*, p. 55
167 'if the bridge . . .', Barbaro, *Giornale*, p. 43
167 'masters in the art . . .', Pertusi, *La Caduta*, vol. 2, p. 262
168 'John Grant, a German . . .', ibid., vol. 1, p. 134
169 'at the hour of Compline', Barbaro, *Diary*, p. 55
169 'the Christians dug counter-mines . . .', Melville Jones, p. 5
169 'overtopping the walls . . .', Barbaro, *Giornale*, p. 42
170 'so that shots from . . .', ibid., p. 43
170 'half a mile long . . .', ibid., p. 43
170 'such as the Romans . . .', Leonard, p. 22
170 'it seemed, from sheer high spirits', Barbaro, *Diary*, p. 53
170 'and when they saw it . . .', Barbaro, *Giornale*, p. 42
170 'suddenly the earth roared . . . from high', Nestor-Iskander, p. 51
171 'long battering rams . . .', Leonard, p. 22
171 'and when they had confessed . . .', Barbaro, *Giornale*, pp. 46–7
172 'a Christian land . . .', Pertusi, *La Caduta*, vol. 1, p. 26
172 'and so we want to return . . .', ibid., pp. 26–7
172 'began to weep . . . that they might guard it', Barbaro, *Giornale*, p. 35

12 Omens and Portents

173 'We see auguries . . .', quoted Sherrard, p. 167
173 'misfortune to you . . .', Yerasimos, *Les Traditions Apocalyptiques*, p. 59
174 'that universal ruin was approaching', Melville Jones, p. 129
174 'in time the squares . . .', Leonard, p. 14
174 'all of the people assembled . . .', Nestor-Iskander, p. 69
175 'life will be short, fortune unstable', quoted Yerasimos, *Les Traditions Apocalyptiques*, p. 70
175 'The air was clear and unclouded . . .', Barbaro, *Diary*, p. 56
175 'only three days old . . .', Pertusi, *La Caduta*, vol. 1, p. 26
175 'grew little by little . . .', ibid., p. 26
176 'the Emperor was greatly . . .', ibid., pp. 26–7
177 'Do thou save thy city . . .', quoted Tsangadas, p. 304
177 'without any reason . . .', Kritovoulos, *Critobuli*, p. 58
177 'were unable either to stand . . .', ibid., p. 58
177 'many following were in danger . . .', ibid., pp. 58–9
177 'certainly foretold the imminent . . .', ibid., p. 59
177 'departure of God . . .', ibid., p. 59
178 'great darkness began to gather over the city', Nestor-Iskander, p. 81
178 'at the top of . . .', ibid., p. 63

178 'This is a great sign . . .', ibid., p. 81
179 'Emperor: weigh all . . .', ibid., p. 63
179 'do not allow them . . .', ibid., p. 65
181 'many kings and sultans . . .', Pertusi, *La Caduta*, vol. 1, pp. 309–10
181 'the Turks began to shout . . .', Leonard, p. 50
182 'Men of Greece . . .', Melville Jones, pp. 47–8
182 'not of high rank', ibid., p. 48
182 'taking their possessions . . .', ibid., p. 48
182 'as a means of testing . . .', ibid., p. 48
183 'Impose as large a tribute . . .', Doukas, *Fragmenta*, p. 286
183 'Your power, which is already very . . .', Leonard, p. 50
184 'The Genoese are split . . .', ibid., p. 50
184 'the chance of making . . .', Melville Jones, p. 6
184 'Decide the day of battle . . .', Leonard, p. 50
184 'And all the tents . . .', Pertusi, *La Caduta*, vol. 1, p. 27
184 'This strange spectacle . . . like lightning', Doukas, *Fragmenta*, p. 281
184 'It seemed that the sea . . .', Pertusi, *La Caduta*, vol. 1, p. 181
185 '*Illala, Illala* . . .', Leonard, p. 54
185 'the sky itself would . . .', Barbaro, *Giornale*, p. 48
185 'they appeared to be half-dead . . .', Doukas, trans. Magoulias, p. 221
185 'Spare us, O Lord . . .', Doukas, *Fragmenta*, p. 281
185 'I cannot describe . . .', Pertusi, *La Caduta,* vol. 1, p. 27
186 'Misfortune to you . . .', quoted Yerasimos, *Les Traditions Apocalyptiques*, p. 157

13 'Remember the Date'

187 'These tribulations are . . .', quoted Inalcik, *The Ottoman Empire: The Classical Age*, p. 56
187 'a great rug to be . . .', Mihailovich, p. 145
188 'they did nothing apart from . . .', Barbaro, *Giornale*, p. 49
188 'the provincial governors and generals . . .', Kritovoulos, *Critobuli*, p. 59
188 'fashioned out of gold and silver . . .', ibid., p. 61
189 'once we have started . . .', ibid., p. 62
190 'to be silent . . .', ibid., p. 63
190 'You know how many . . .', Melville Jones, pp. 48–9
190 'But if I see . . .', ibid., p. 49
190 'by the four thousand . . .', Leonard, p. 54
191 'Once the city of . . .', quoted Babinger, p. 355
191 'O, if you had heard . . .', Pertusi, *La Caduta*, vol. 1, pp. 156–8
192 'and all us Christians . . .', Barbaro, *Giornale*, p. 49
193 'for the advantage of . . .', ibid., p. 21
193 'right away his resolution . . .', Nestor-Iskander, p. 75
193 'treated him all night . . .', ibid., p. 77
193 'it was a thing . . .', Barbaro, *Diary*, p. 60
194 'The Prophet said . . .', quoted Babinger, p. 85

195 'Gardens watered by . . .', *The Koran*, p. 44
195 'You well know . . .', Pertusi, *La Caduta*, vol. 1, p. 302
195 'God has promised you . . .', *The Koran*, p. 361
197 'that all who call themselves . . .', Barbaro, *Giornale*, p. 50
198 'evil Turks . . . for his horses', Leonard, p. 56
198 'You have decorated . . . immortal glory', ibid., p. 58
198 'with God's help . . .', Melville Jones, p. 35
198 'only two or three . . .', Kritovoulos, *Critobuli*, pp. 61–2
200 'fell to the ground . . . reached to heaven', Nestor-Iskander, p. 87
200 'Children of Muhammad . . .', Barbaro, *Giornale*, p. 49
201 'that to us it seemed . . .', Barbaro, *Diary*, p.56
201 'with all their weapons . . .', Barbaro, *Giornale*, p. 49
201 'and when each side . . .', Pertusi, *La Caduta*, vol. 1, p. 29
201 'from dusk till dawn . . .', Khoja Sa'd-ud-din, p. 27
201 'the Emperor mounted . . .', Sphrantzes, trans. Carroll, p. 74
202 'On the same night . . .', Sphrantzes, trans. Philippides, p. 61

14 The Locked Gates

203 'There is no certainty . . .', Ibn Khaldun, vol. 2, p. 67
203 'the moat has all been filled . . .', Kritovoulos, *History of Mehmed*, p. 62
204 'three thousand . . .', Doukas, *Fragmenta*, p. 283
205 'victory was assured', Pertusi, *La Caduta*, vol. 1, p. 42
206 'Christians, kept in his camp . . .', Pertusi, *La Caduta*, vol. 1, p. 30
206 'Greeks, Latins, Germans . . .', Leonard, p. 16
206 'with arrows from . . . blasphemies and curses', Kritovoulos, *Critobuli*, p. 66
206 'threw big stones down . . . dying on one side or the other', Barbaro, *Diary*, p. 62
207 'Advance, my friends . . .', Kritovoulos, *Critobuli*, p. 67
207 'with shouts and fearful yells', Kritovoulos, *History of Mehmed*, p. 67
207 'like lions unchained . . .', Barbaro, *Giornale*, p. 52
207 'When they heard . . .', Nestor-Iskander, p. 71
208 'killed an incredible number of Turks . . .', Barbaro, *Giornale*, p. 52
208 'We hurled deadly missiles . . .', Leonard, p. 60
208 'all brave men', Barbaro, *Giornale*, p. 52
208 'They continued to raise . . .', Leonard, p. 60
208 'Sometimes the heavy infantry . . .', Kritovoulos, *Critobuli*, p. 67
209 'that the very air . . .', Barbaro, *Giornale*, p. 53
210 'where the city's defences . . .', Leonard, p. 40
210 'they were frightened by nothing . . . terrible guns', ibid., p. 40
210 'men who were very . . .', Kritovoulos, *Critobuli*, p. 68
211 'neither hunger . . .', ibid., p. 68
211 'the blackness of night . . .', Pertusi, *La Caduta*, vol. 1, p. 158
211 'the bowmen, slingers and . . .', Kritovoulos, *Critobuli*, p. 68
211 'there were so many . . .', Melville Jones, p. 7
211 'the rain of arrows . . . war cry', Kritovoulos, *Critobuli*, p. 68

211 'not like Turks . . .', Barbaro, *Giornale*, p. 53
211 'With their great shouting . . .', ibid., p. 53
211 'eager and fresh . . .', ibid., p. 53
212 'like men intent . . .', ibid., p. 53
212 'all his nobles . . .', ibid., p. 53
212 'javelins, pikes . . .', Kritovoulos, *Critobuli*, p. 68
212 'fell, struck by . . .', Pertusi, *La Caduta*, vol. 1, p. 160
212 'taunts, those stabbing . . .', Kritovoulos, *Critobuli*, p. 69
212 'It seemed like something . . .', Barbaro, *Giornale*, p. 53
212 'We repelled them . . .', Pertusi, *La Caduta*, vol. 1, p. 161
212 'Brave soldiers . . .', Leonard, p. 44
213 'wicked and merciless fortune', Kritovoulos, *Critobuli*, p. 68
214 'Friends, we have the city . . .', ibid., p. 70
215 'such cries that it seemed . . .', Barbaro, *Giornale*, p. 54
215 'so that they made . . .', Melville Jones, p. 50
216 'Then all the rest of . . .', Kritovoulos, *Critobuli*, p. 70

15 A Handful of Dust

217 'Tell me please . . .', Sherrard, p. 102
217 'ordered his trumpeters . . .', Doukas, *Fragmenta*, p. 296
218 'attacked them . . .', Kritovoulos, *Critobuli*, p. 71
218 'to create universal terror . . .', ibid., p. 71
218 'everyone they found . . .', Barbaro, *Giornale*, p. 55
218 'threw bricks and . . .', Nestor-Iskander, p. 89
218 'The whole city was filled . . .', Melville Jones, p. 51
219 'their wives and children . . . friends and wives', Doukas, *Fragmenta*, p. 295
219 'beautifully embellished . . .', Doukas, trans. Magoulias, p. 228
219 'slaughter their aged . . .', Khoja Sa'd-ud-din, p. 29
219 'nations, customs and languages', Melville Jones, p. 123
219 'plundering, destroying . . .', Kritovoulos, *Critobuli*, p. 71
219 'terrible and pitiful . . . their bed chambers', ibid., pp. 71–2
220 'Slaughtered mercilessly . . . and the infirm', Leonard, p. 66
220 'The newborn babies . . .', Doukas, *Fragmenta*, p. 295
220 'dragging them out . . .', Kritovoulos, *Critobuli*, p. 72
220 'young and modest . . .', ibid., p. 72
220 'holy artifacts and . . .', ibid.,, p. 73
220 'walls of churches . . .', ibid., p. 73
220 'The consecrated images . . .', Melville Jones, p. 38
220 'led to the fleet . . .', Barbaro, *Diary*, p. 67
220 'hauled out of the . . . things were done', Kritovoulos, *Critobuli*, p. 73
221 'and from the West . . .', Doukas, *Fragmenta*, p. 292
222 'to search for gold . . .', Pertusi, *La Caduta*, vol. 1, p. 34
222 'and so they put . . .', Barbaro, *Diary*, p. 67
222 'churches, old vaults . . .', Kritovoulos, *Critobuli*, p. 74
223 'men, women, monks . . .', Doukas, *Fragmenta*, p. 296

223 'the fury of . . . help them', Pertusi, *La Caduta*, vol. 1, pp. 185–6
224 'not without great danger . . .', ibid., p. 44
224 'I always knew that . . .', ibid., p. 44
225 'We were in a terrible situation . . .', Pertusi, *La Caduta*, vol. 1, p. 36
225 'all of us would..', ibid., p. 37
225 'at midday with . . .', Barbaro, *Giornale*, p. 58
225 'like melons along a canal', Pertusi, *La Caduta*, vol. 1, p. 36
226 'some of whom had been drowned . . .', ibid., p. 36
227 'to the very heavens', Procopius, quoted Freely, p. 28
227 'suspended from heaven . . .', quoted Norwich, vol. 1, p. 203
228 'trapped as in a net', Kritovoulos, *Critobuli*, p. 74
228 'like sheep', Doukas, trans. Magoulias, p. 225
228 'a certain spot, and . . . extraordinary spectacle', Doukas, trans. Magoulias, p. 227
228 'in an instant . . .', Doukas, *Fragmenta*, p. 292
228 'ransacked and desolate', ibid., p. 227
229 'the blind-hearted emperor', Khoja Sa'd-ud-din, p. 30
230 'A desperate battle ensued . . .', Tursun Beg, p. 37
230 'the Emperor turned to . . .', Pertusi, *La Caduta*, vol. 1, p. 214
230 'The Emperor of Constantinople . . .', ibid., pp. 184–5
230 'Weep Christians . . .', Legrand, p. 74
231 'The ruler of Istanbul . . .', quoted Lewis, *The Muslim Discovery of Europe*, p. 30
231' seventy of eighty thousand . . .', quoted Freely, pp. 211–12
232 'like a fire or a whirlwind . . .', Kritovoulos, *Critobuli*, pp. 74–5
233 'mounting as (Jesus) . . . castle of Afrasiyab', quoted Lewis, *Istanbul*, p. 8
233 'dumbfounded by . . . a few pence', Pertusi, *La Caduta*, vol. 1, pp. 219–21
233 'gold and silver . . .', ibid., p. 327
234 'women and children . . .', Norwich, vol. 3, p. 143

16 The Present Terror of the World

235 'Whichever way I look . . .', Melville Jones, p. 135
235 'I ransomed . . . in pain and grief', Camariotes, p. 1070
236 'scattered across . . .', Pertusi, *La Caduta*, vol. 2, p. 416
236 'said that we did . . .', ibid., pp. 44–6
237 'full of wine . . . the bloodthirsty beast', Doukas, trans. Magoulias, pp. 234–5
237 'and the Islamic invocation . . .', quoted Lewis, *Istanbul*, p. 8
237 'the sweet five-times-repeated . . .', Khoja Sa'd-ud-din, p. 33
237 'What a city we have . . .', Kritovoulos, *Critobuli*, p. 76
238 'Nothing worse than this . . .', quoted Wheatcroft, *The Ottomans*, p. 23
238 'a great and excessive crying . . .', Pertusi, *La Caduta*, vol. 1, p. xxxviii
238 'the horrible and deplorable . . .', quoted Schwoebel, p. 8
239 'On the day when the Turks . . .', ibid., p. 4
239 'What is this execrable news . . .', quoted ibid., p. 9
239 'in this year was . . .', ibid., p. 4

239 'the cunning of the Pope . . .', Lewis, *The Muslim Discovery of Europe*, p. 32
239 'The Sultan and all the men . . .', Ibn Taghribirdi, pp. 38–9
240 'stuffed with straw . . . Turks', Doukas, *Fragmenta*, p. 300
240 'It is your responsibility . . .', Inalcik, *The Ottoman Empire*, p. 56
240 'There must be only . . .', quoted Schwoebel, p. 43
240 'Our Senators could not . . .', Barbaro, *Giornale*, p. 66
241 'I thank Muhammad . . .', quoted Schwoebel, p. 11
241 'The enemy is at . . .', quoted Babinger, p. 358
242 'We ourselves allowed . . .', quoted Babinger, pp. 170–71
245 'the general enemy Ottoman . . . malignant and turbaned Turk', *Othello*
245 'the first troop . . . their mother', quoted Matar, p. 158
245 'the churches which were within the city . . .', Khoja Sa'd-ud-din, p. 33
246 'Be Patriarch . . .', quoted Runciman, *The Fall of Constantinople*, p. 155
246 'Here in the land of . . .', quoted Mansel, p. 15
246 'by the counsel . . . Law of the Prophet', quoted Mansel, p. 32
246 'The Turks do not compel . . .', quoted Mansel, p. 47
246 'a second death for Homer and Plato', quoted Schwoebel, p. 9
246 'the garland of water', quoted Freely, p. 3
247 'made up of a horse and a man', quoted Matar, p. 159
247 'a reflection of the infinite . . .', quoted Levey, p. 15
250 'I beheld the prospect . . .', quoted *Istanbul: Everyman Guides*, p. 82
250 'What I have created . . .', quoted Levey, p. 18
250 'the sight whereof . . .', quoted Mansel, p. 57
251 'It seems to me . . .', quoted Freely, p. 14

Epilogue: Resting Places

253 'It was fortunate for . . .', quoted Babinger, p. 408
253 'a short, thick neck . . .', quoted ibid., p. 424
254 'men who have seen him . . .', quoted ibid., p. 424
254 'his father was domineering . . .', quoted ibid., p. 411
254 'There are no ties . . .', quoted ibid., p. 405
254 'The great eagle is dead', quoted Babinger, p. 408
256 'I am George Sphrantzes . . .', Sphrantzes, trans. Philippides, p. 21
256 'my beautiful daughter Thamar . . .', ibid., p. 75
256 'I confess with certainty . . .', ibid., p. 91
256 'either from his wound . . .', Pertusi, *La Caduta*, vol. 1, p. 162
256 'Here lies Giovanni Giustiniani . . .', quoted Setton, p. 429
259 'like a border of tulips', Chelebi, *Le Siège*, p. 2
260 'Among the fragments . . .', Gilles, p. 130

About the Sources

261 'There were so many . . .', Pertusi, *La Caduta*, vol. 2, p. 261
265 'Therefore, O mighty Emperor . . .', Kritovoulos, *History of Mehmet*, pp. 4–6

Bibliography

Collections of Sources

Jorga, N., *Notes et extraits pour servir à l'Histoire des Croisades au XVe siècle*, 6 vols, Paris and Bucharest, 1899–1916
Legrand, Emile, *Recueil de Chansons Populaires Grecques*, Paris, 1874
Lewis, Bernard, *Islam from the Prophet Muhammad to the Capture of Constantinople*, 2 vols, New York, 1974
Melville Jones, J. R., *The Siege of Constantinople 1453: Seven Contemporary Accounts*, Amsterdam, 1972
Pertusi, Agostino, *La Caduta di Costantinopoli*, 2 vols, Milan, 1976

Individual Sources

Barbaro, Nicolo, *Giornale dell' Assedio di Costantinopoli 1453*, ed. E. Cornet, Vienna, 1856; (in English) *Diary of the Siege of Constantinople 1453*, trans. J. R. Melville Jones, New York, 1969
Brocquière, Bertrandon de la, in *Early Travels in Palestine*, ed. T. Wright, London, 1848
Camariotes, Matthew, 'De Constantinopoli Capta Narratio Lamentabilis', in *Patrologiae Cursus Completus, Series Graeco-Latina*, vol. 160, ed. J. P. Migne, Paris, 1866
Chelebi, Evliya, *In the Days of the Janissaries*, ed. Alexander Pallis, London, 1951
Chelebi, Evliya, 'Le Siège de Constantinople d'après le Seyahatname d'Evliya Chelebi', trans. H. Turkova, *Byzantinoslavica*, vol. 14, 1953
Comnena, Anna, *The Alexiad of Anna Comnena*, trans. E. R. A. Sewter, London, 1969
Doukas, *Decline and Fall of Byzantium to the Ottoman Turks*, trans. Harry J. Magoulias, Detroit, 1975
Doukas, *Fragmenta Historicorum Graecorum*, vol. 5, Paris, 1870
Gilles, Pierre, *The Antiquities of Constantinople*, London, 1729
Gunther of Pairis, *The Capture of Constantinople: The Hystoria Constantinopolitana of Gunther of Pairis*, ed. and trans. Alfred J. Andrea, Philadelphia, 1997
Ibn Khaldun, *The Muqaddimah*, 3 vols, trans. Franz Rosenthal, London, 1958
Ibn Taghribirdi, Abu al-Mahasin Yusuf, *History of Egypt, Part 6, 1382–1469 A.D.*, trans, W. Popper, Berkeley, 1960

Khoja Sa'd-ud-din, *The Capture of Constantinople from the Taj-ut-Tevarikh*, trans. E. J. W. Gibb, Glasgow, 1879
Kritovoulos, *Critobuli Imbriotae Historiae*, ed. Diether Reinsch, Berlin, 1983; (in English) *History of Mehmed the Conqueror*, trans. Charles T. Riggs, Westport, 1970
Leonard of Chios, *De Capta a Mehemethe II Constantinopoli*, Paris, 1823
Mihailovich, Konstantin, *Memoirs of a Janissary*, trans. Benjamin Stolz, Ann Arbor, 1975
Nestor-Iskander, *The Tale of Constantinople*, trans. and ed. Walter K. Hanak and Marios Philippides, 1998
Ovid, *Tristia*, Cambridge, Massachusetts, 1989
Procopius, *Buildings*, London, 1971
Pusculus, Ubertino, *Constantinopoleos Libri IV*, in Ellissen, *Analekten der Mittel- und Neugriechischen Literatur III*, 1857
Spandounes, Theodore, *On the Origin of the Ottoman Emperors*, trans. and ed. Donald M. Nicol, Cambridge, 1997
Sphrantzes, George, *The Fall of the Byzantine Empire: A Chronicle by George Sphrantzes 1401–1477*, trans. Marios Philippides, Amherst, 1980
Sphrantzes, George, *A Contemporary Greek Source for the Siege of Constantinople 1453: The Sphrantzes Chronicle*, trans. Margaret Carroll, Amsterdam, 1985
Tafur, Pero, *Travels and Adventures, 1435–1439*, trans. Malcolm Letts, London, 1926
Theophanes Confessor, *The Chronicle of Theophanes Confessor*, trans. Cyril Mango and Roger Scott, Oxford, 1997
Tursun Beg, *The History of Mehmed the Conqueror*, trans. Halil Inalcik and Rhoads Murphey, Minneapolis and Chicago, 1978

Modern Works

Ak, Mahmut and Başar, Fahameddin, *Istanbul'un Fetih Günlüğü*, Istanbul, 2003
Akbar, M. J., *The Shade of Swords: Jihad and the Conflict between Islam and Christianity*, London, 2002
Armstrong, Karen, *Holy War: The Crusades and Their Impact on Today's World*, London, 1992
Atıl, Esin, *Levni and the Surname: The Story of an Eighteenth-century Ottoman Festival*, Istanbul, 1999
Ayalon, David, *Gunpowder and Firearms in the Mamluk Kingdom*, London, 1956
Aydın, Erdoğan, *Fatih ve Fetih: Mitler ve Gerçekler*, Istanbul, 2001
Babinger, Franz, *Mehmet the Conqueror and His Time*, Princeton, 1978
Bartusis, Mark C., *The Late Byzantine Army: Arms and Society, 1204–1453*, Philadelphia, 1992
Baynes, Norman H., *Byzantine Studies and Other Essays*, London, 1955
Bury, J. B., *A History of the Later Roman Empire from Arcadius to Irene, 395–800*, 2 vols, London, 1889
Cahen, Claude, *Pre-Ottoman Turkey*, trans. J. Jones-Williams, London, 1968

Carroll, Margaret, 'Notes on the authorship of the Siege Section of the Chronicon Maius', *Byzantion* 41, 1971
Chatzidakis, Manolis, *Mystras: The Medieval City and the Castle*, Athens, 2001
Cipolla, Carlo M., *European Culture and Overseas Expansion*, London, 1970
Clark, Victoria, *Why Angels Fall: A Journey through Orthodox Europe from Byzantium to Kosovo*, London, 2000
Coles, Paul, *The Ottoman Impact on Europe*, London, 1968
Corfis, Ivy A. and Wolfe, Michael (eds), *The Medieval City under Siege*, Woodbridge, 1995
DeVries, Kelly, *Guns and Men in Medieval Europe, 1200–1500*, Aldershot, 2002
Dirimtekin, Feridun, *Istanbul'un Fethi*, Istanbul, 2003
Emecen, Feridun M., *Istanbul'un Fethi Olayı ve Meseleleri*, Istanbul, 2003
Encyclopaedia of Islam, Leiden, 1960
Esin, Emel, *Ottoman Empire in Miniatures*, Istanbul, 1988
Freely, John, *The Companion Guide to Istanbul*, Woodbridge, 2000
Gill, Joseph, *The Council of Florence*, Cambridge, 1959
Goffman, Daniel, *The Ottoman Empire and Early Modern Europe*, Cambridge, 2002
Goodwin, Godfrey, *The Janissaries*, London, 1994
Goodwin, Jason, *Lords of the Horizons: A History of the Ottoman Empire*, London, 1999
Granville Browne, E. (ed.), *A History of Ottoman Poetry*, London, 1904
Guilmartin, John F., *Galleons and Galleys*, London, 2002
Haldon, J. and Byrne, M., 'A Possible Solution to the Problem of Greek Fire', *Byzantinische Zeitschrift* 70, pp. 91–99
Hall, Bert S., *Weapons and Warfare in Renaissance Europe: Gunpowder, Technology and Tactics*, Baltimore, 1997
Hattendorf, John B. and Unger, Richard W., *War at Sea in the Middle Ages and the Renaissance*, Woodbridge, 2003
Heywood, Colin, *Writing Ottoman History: Documents and Interpretations*, Aldershot 2002
Hogg, Ian V., *A History of Artillery*, London, 1974
Howard, Michael, *War in European History*, Oxford, 1976
Imber, Colin, 'The Legend of Osman Gazi', *The Ottoman Emirate 1300–1389*, Rethymnon, 1993
Imber, Colin, 'What Does Ghazi Actually Mean', *The Balance of Truth: Essays in Honour of Professor Geoffrey Lewis*, Istanbul, 2000
Imber, Colin, *The Ottoman Empire: 1300–1650*, Basingstoke, 2002
Inalcik, Halil, 'Mehmet the Conqueror and His Time', *Speculum* 35, pp. 408–427
Inalcik, Halil, *Fatih Devri üzerinde Tetkikler ve Vesikalar I*, Ankara, 1987
Inalcik, Halil, *The Ottoman Empire: Conquest, Organization and Economy*, London, 1978
Inalcik, Halil, *The Ottoman Empire: The Classical Age 1300–1600*, London, 1973
Istanbul: Everyman Guides, London, 1993
Kaegi, Walter Emil, *Byzantium and the Early Islamic Conquests*, Cambridge, 1992

Kazankaya, Hasan, *Fatih Sultan Mehmed'in Istanbul'un Fethi ve Fethin Karanlık Noktaları*, 2 vols, Istanbul, 1995
Keegan, John, *A History of Warfare*, London, 1994
Keen, Maurice (ed.), *Medieval Warfare: A History*, Oxford, 1999
Kelly, Laurence, *Istanbul: A Traveller's Companion*, London, 1987
Khadduri, Majid, *War and Peace in the Law of Islam*, Baltimore, 1955
Kinross, Lord, *The Ottoman Centuries*, London, 1977
Koran, The, trans. N. J. Dawood, London, 1956
Levey, Michael, *The World of Ottoman Art*, London, 1971
Lewis, Bernard, *Istanbul and the Civilization of the Ottoman Empire*, Norman, 1968
Lewis, Bernard, 'Politics and War' in J. Schacht and C. E. Bosworth (eds), *The Legacy of Islam*, Oxford, 1979
Lewis, Bernard, *Islam from the Prophet Muhammad to the Capture of Constantinople*, 2 vols, Oxford, 1987
Lewis, Bernard, *The Muslim Discovery of Europe*, London, 1982
Mackintosh-Smith, Tim, *Travels with a Tangerine*, London, 2001
Mango, Cyril, *Studies on Constantinople*, Aldershot, 1993
Mango, Cyril (ed.), *The Oxford History of Byzantium*, Oxford, 2002
Mansel, Philip, *Constantinople: City of the World's Desire, 1453–1924*, London, 1995
Massignon, Louis, 'Textes Prémonitoires et commentaires mystiques relatifs à la prise de Constantinople par les Turcs en 1453', Oriens 6, pp. 10–17
Matar, Nabil, *Islam in Britain 1558–1685*, Cambridge, 1998
Mathews, Thomas F., *The Art of Byzantium: Between Antiquity and the Renaissance*, London, 1998
McCarthy, Justin, *The Ottoman Turks: an Introductory History to 1923*, Harlow, 1997
McNeill, William H., *The Rise of the West: A History of the Human Community*, Chicago, 1990
Mijatovich, Chedomil, *Constantine Palaiologos: the Last Emperor of the Greeks, 1448–1453*, London, 1892
Morris, Jan, *The Venetian Empire: A Sea Voyage*, London, 1980
Murphey, Rhoads, *Ottoman Warfare 1500–1700*, London, 1999
Nicol, Donald M., *Byzantium and Venice*, Cambridge, 1988
Nicol, Donald M., *The Immortal Emperor: The Life and Legend of Constantine Palaiologos, Last Emperor of the Romans*, Cambridge, 1969
Nicol, Donald M., *The Last Centuries of Byzantium, 1261–1453*, London, 1972
Nicolle, David, *Armies of the Ottoman Turks 1300–1774*, London, 1983
Nicolle, David, *Constantinople 1453*, Oxford, 2000
Nicolle, David, *The Janissaries*, London, 1995
Norwich, John J., *A History of Byzantium*, 3 vols, London, 1995
Ostrogorsky, George, *History of the Byzantine State*, trans. Joan Hussey, Oxford, 1980
Parry, V. J., *Richard Knolles' 'History of the Turks'*, ed. Salih Özbaran, Istanbul, 2003

Parry, V. J. and Yapp, M. E. (eds), *War, Technology and Society in the Middle East*, London, 1975
Partington, J. R., *A History of Greek Fire and Gunpowder*, Cambridge, 1960
Pears, Edwin, *The Destruction of the Greek Empire and the Story of the Capture of Constantinople by the Turks*, London, 1903
Rose, Susan, *Medieval Naval Warfare, 1000–1500*, London, 2002
Runciman, Stephen, *The Eastern Schism: A Study of the Papacy and Eastern Churches during the 11th and 12th Centuries*, Oxford, 1955.
Runciman, Stephen, *The Fall of Constantinople*, Cambridge, 1965
Runciman, Stephen, *The Eastern Schism*, Oxford, 1955
Schwoebel, Robert, *The Shadow of the Crescent: The Renaissance Image of the Turk, 1453–1517*, Nieuwkoop, 1967
Setton, Kenneth M., *The Papacy and the Levant (1204–1571), vol. II: The Fifteenth Century*, Philadelphia, 1978
Shaw, Stanford, *History of the Ottoman Empire and Modern Turkey, vol. I: Empire of the Gazis*, Cambridge, 1976
Sherrard, Philip, *Constantinople: The Iconography of a Sacred City*, London, 1965
Simarski, Lynn Teo, 'Constantinople's Volcanic Twilight', *Saudi Aramco World*, Nov./Dec., 1996
Stacton, D., *The World on the Last Day*, London, 1965
Tsangadas, B. C. P., *The Fortifications and Defence of Constantinople*, New York, 1980
Vakalopoulos, Apostolos E., *The Origins of the Greek Nation: The Byzantine Period, 1204–1461*, New Brunswick, 1970
Van Millingen, Alexander, *Byzantine Churches in Constantinople*, London, 1912
Van Millingen, Alexander, *Byzantine Constantinople*, London, 1899
Vassilaki, Maria (ed.), *Mother of God: Representations of the Virgin in Byzantine Art*, Turin, 2000
Ware, Timothy, *The Orthodox Church*, London, 1993
Wheatcroft, Andrew, *Infidels: The Conflict between Christendom and Islam 638–2002*, London, 2003
Wheatcroft, Andrew, *The Ottomans: Dissolving Images*, London, 1995
Wintle, Justin, *The Rough Guide History of Islam*, London, 2003
Wittek, Paul, *The Rise of the Ottoman Empire*, London, 1963
Yerasimos, Stephane, *La Fondation de Constantinople et de Sainte-Sophie dans les Traditions Turques*, Paris, 1990
Yerasimos, Stephane, *Les Traditions Apocalyptiques au tournant de la Chute de Constantinople*, Paris, 1999

Acknowledgements

The idea for this book has been on the road for such a long time that the debts for its creation are many. The fact that it now exists is due most immediately to Andrew Lownie, my agent, Julian Loose at Faber and Bill Strachan at Hyperion for believing in the story, and then to the professional and enthusiastic teams at both publishers for making it happen.

For its deepest origins I am always grateful to Christopher Trillo, the champion of Istanbul, for persuading me to go there in 1973, and a small army of old friends who have advised along the way: Andrew Taylor, Elizabeth Manners and Stephen Scoffham for proposal and manuscript reading, Elizabeth Manners again for her cover photographs of the wall paintings from the monastery of Moldovita in Rumania, John Dyson for a huge amount of help in Istanbul sourcing books and for hospitality, Rita and Ron Morton for matching hospitality in Greece, Ron Morton and David Gordon-Macleod for taking me to Mount Athos to glimpse the living Byzantine tradition, Annamaria Ferro and Andy Kirby for translations, Oliver Poole for photographs, Athena Adams-Florou for scanning pictures, Dennis Naish for information on casting cannon, Martin Dow for advice on Arabic. To all these people I am very grateful. Last and always my deep thanks are to Jan, not only for proposal and manuscript reading, but also for surviving Turkish dog bites and the author year in, year out, with love.

I am also grateful to the following publishers for permission to reproduce substantial extracts included in this book. Material from *The Tale of Constantinople by Nestor-Iskander*, translated and annotated by Walter K. Hanak and Marios Philippides, courtesy Aristide D. Caratzas, Publisher (Melissa International Ltd); Material from

Babinger, Franz: *Mehmed the Conqueror and His Time* (1978 Princeton University Press, reprinted by permission of Princeton University Press.

Index